First World War
and Army of Occupation
War Diary
France, Belgium and Germany

47 DIVISION
Headquarters, Branches and Services
Royal Army Veterinary Corps
Deputy Assistant Director Veterinary Services
16 March 1915 - 31 March 1919

WO95/2716/2

The Naval & Military Press Ltd
www.nmarchive.com
Published in association with The National Archives

Published by

The Naval & Military Press Ltd

Unit 10 Ridgewood Industrial Park,

Uckfield, East Sussex,

TN22 5QE England

Tel: +44 (0) 1825 749494

www.naval-military-press.com

www.nmarchive.com

This diary has been reprinted in facsimile from the original. Any imperfections are inevitably reproduced and the quality may fall short of modern type and cartographic standards.

© Crown Copyright
Images reproduced by permission of The National Archives, London, England, 2015.

Contents

Document type	Place/Title	Date From	Date To
Heading	WO95/2716/2		
Heading	47th Division D.A. Dir. Veterinary Service Mar 1915-Mar 1919		
Heading	ADVS. 2nd London Division Vol I 16-31.8.15		
Heading	War Diary of Lieut.-Col. W.R. Walker A.D.V.S., 2nd London Divn., T.F. From 16th March, 1915 to 31st March, 1915		
War Diary		16/03/1915	18/03/1915
War Diary	Headquarters, 2nd Lond. Div	19/03/1915	19/03/1915
War Diary	Headqrs. 2nd Lond Divn. T.F.	20/03/1915	20/03/1915
War Diary	Headquarters, 2nd Lond. D. T.F.	21/03/1915	21/03/1915
War Diary	Divisional Headquarters	22/03/1915	22/03/1915
War Diary	Divisional Headquarters 4th Brigade Area	23/03/1915	23/03/1915
War Diary	Divisional Headquarters, 4th Brigade Area 5th Brigade Area.	24/03/1915	24/03/1915
War Diary	Divisional Headquarters.	25/03/1915	25/03/1915
War Diary	Headquarters Area	27/03/1915	28/03/1915
War Diary	Divisional Headquarters 6th Brigade Area	29/03/1915	29/03/1915
War Diary	Headquarters Area. 6th Brigade Area.	30/03/1915	30/03/1915
War Diary	Divisional Headquarters	31/03/1915	31/03/1915
Heading	A.D.V.S. 2nd London Division Vol II 1-30.4.15		
Heading	War Diary of Lieut. Col. W.R. Walker, From 1/4/15 to 30/4/1915		
War Diary	Headquarters, Lon. Div.	01/04/1915	01/04/1915
War Diary	Headqrs., London Divn.	02/04/1915	04/04/1915
War Diary	Headquarters, Lond. Divn.	05/04/1915	05/04/1915
War Diary	Headqrs., London Divn	06/04/1915	12/04/1915
War Diary	H.Q. 2nd Lon. Divn., T.F.	13/04/1915	18/04/1915
War Diary	Headqrs., London Division	19/04/1915	21/04/1915
War Diary	Hqrs., London Division	22/04/1915	24/04/1915
War Diary	Headqrs, London Divn.	25/04/1915	26/04/1915
War Diary	Headquarters, Lon. Div.	27/04/1915	27/04/1915
War Diary	Headqrs., London Div.	28/04/1915	30/04/1915
Heading	A.D.V.S. 47th (London) Division Vol III 1-30.5.15		
Heading	War Diary of Lieut.-Col. W.R. Walker 1/5/15-30/5/15		
War Diary	Headquarters, Lon. Div.	01/05/1915	11/05/1915
War Diary	Hqrs., 47th (London) Divn.	12/05/1915	14/05/1915
War Diary	Headqrs, 47th Div.	15/05/1915	15/05/1915
War Diary	Hqrs., 47th Div.	16/05/1915	18/05/1915
War Diary	Headquarters, 47th Div.	19/05/1915	20/05/1915
War Diary	Headqrs, 47th (Lon.) Div.	21/05/1915	22/05/1915
War Diary	Headqrs., 47th Division	23/05/1915	26/05/1915
War Diary	Headqrs., 47th (Lon) Divn.	27/05/1915	30/05/1915
Heading	47th Division War Diary A.D.V.S. 47th London Division Vol IV 3.1.5-30.6.15		
Heading	War Diary of Capt. Joseph Abson A.V.C. (T.F.) 31 May-30 June 1915		
War Diary	Headqrs., 47th (Lon.) Div. Bethune	31/05/1915	01/06/1915
War Diary	Headqrs., 47th (Lon.) Div. Bethune And Verquin	02/06/1915	02/06/1915
War Diary	Headqrs., 47th (Lon.) Divn Verquin	03/06/1915	04/06/1915

War Diary	Hqrs. 47th (Lon.) Divn. Verquin	05/06/1915	05/06/1915
War Diary	Hqrs., 47th Div Verquin	06/06/1915	10/06/1915
War Diary	Hqrs., 47th Lond. Divn, Verquin & Noeux-Les-Mines.	11/06/1915	11/06/1915
War Diary	Headqrs., 47th Lon. Divn. Noeux-Les-Mines	12/06/1915	12/06/1915
War Diary	Hqrs., 47th Lon Divn. Noeux-Les-Mines	13/06/1915	14/06/1915
War Diary	Hqrs., 47th Divn. Noeux-Les-Mines	15/06/1915	17/06/1915
War Diary	Headqrs., 47th Div Noeux-Les-Mines	18/06/1915	18/06/1915
War Diary	Headqrs, 47th (Lon.) Div. Noeux-Les-Mines	19/06/1915	19/06/1915
War Diary	Hqrs., 47th (Lon) Div. Noeux-Les-Mines	20/06/1915	21/06/1915
War Diary	Hqrs. 47th Div. Noeux-Les-Mines	22/06/1915	22/06/1915
War Diary	Headqrs., 47th Div. Noeux-Les-Mines	23/06/1915	25/06/1915
War Diary	Hqrs., 47th Lon. Divn Noeux-Les-Mines	26/06/1915	29/06/1915
War Diary	Hqrs, 47th Lon Div. Noeux-Les-Mines	29/06/1915	30/06/1915
Heading	47th Division A.D.V.S. 47th Division Vol V 1-31.4.15		
War Diary	Hqrs. 47th (Lon.) Divn., Noeux-Les-Mines.	01/07/1915	10/07/1915
War Diary	Headqrs., 47th (Lon) Divn, Noeux-Les-Mines	11/07/1915	13/07/1915
War Diary	Hqrs., 47th (Lon) Divn. Noeux-Les-Mines	14/07/1915	23/07/1915
War Diary	Hqrs., 47th Divn. Noeux-Les-Mines	24/07/1915	31/07/1915
Heading	47th Division ADVS 47th Division Vol VI From 1st to 31st August 1915		
War Diary	Hqrs. 47th (Lon) Divn Noeux-Les-Mines	01/08/1915	03/08/1915
War Diary	Hdqrs 47th (Lon) Divn	04/08/1915	04/08/1915
War Diary	Hdqrs 47th (Lon) Divn Gosnay	05/08/1915	31/08/1915
Heading	47th Division A.D.V.S. 47th Division Vol VII Sept. 15		
War Diary	Hdqrs 47th Lon Divn Gosnay	01/09/1915	02/09/1915
War Diary	Hdqrs 47th Lon Divn	03/09/1915	03/09/1915
War Diary	Hdqrs 47th Lon. Divn. Drouvin.	04/09/1915	23/09/1915
War Diary	Hdqrs 47th Lon. Divn. Drouvin. Chateau	24/09/1915	24/09/1915
War Diary	Hdqrs. 47th (Lon) Divn.	25/09/1915	25/09/1915
War Diary	Hdqrs. 47th (Lon) Divn. Noeux-Les-Mines	26/09/1915	30/09/1915
Heading	47th Division A.D.V.S. 47th Division Vol VIII Oct 15		
War Diary	Hdqrs. 47th Lon. Divn. Noeux-Les-Mines	01/10/1915	01/10/1915
War Diary	Hdqrs. 47th Lon. Divn. Gosnay	02/10/1915	06/10/1915
War Diary	Hdqrs. 47th Lon. Divn. Noeux-Les-Mines	07/10/1915	15/10/1915
War Diary	Hdqrs. 47th Lon. Divn. Mazingarbe	16/10/1915	31/10/1915
Heading	A.D.V.S. 47th Div. Nov. Vol IX		
War Diary	Hdqrs 47th Lon Divn Mazingarbe Map. France. 36 B Scale 140,000 L.23.c.	01/11/1915	01/11/1915
War Diary	Hdqrs 47th Lon Divn Mazingarbe	02/11/1915	15/11/1915
War Diary	Hdqrs 47th Lon Divn Marles-Les-Mines	16/11/1915	30/11/1915
Heading	A.D.V.S. 47 (London) Divn. Dec Vol. X		
War Diary	HQ. 47th Lon. Divn. Marles-Les-Mines.	01/12/1915	14/12/1915
War Diary	HQ. 47th Lon. Divn. Marles-Mines.	15/12/1915	15/12/1915
War Diary	HQ. 47th Lon. Divn. Vaudricourt. Sheet 26b. France. K.4.8	16/12/1915	16/12/1915
War Diary	HQ. 47th Lon. Divn. Vaudricourt.	17/12/1915	31/12/1915
Heading	A.D.V.S. 47th (London) Bn Jan Vol XI		
War Diary	Hdqrs., 47th (Lon) Divn. Vaudricourt	01/01/1916	06/01/1916
War Diary	HQ. 47th Lon. Divn. Noeux-Les-Mines	07/01/1916	15/02/1916
War Diary	HQ. 47th Lon. Divn. Lillers.	16/02/1916	29/02/1916
Heading	D.A.G., G.H.Q. 3rd Echelon. Vol XIII	01/04/1916	01/04/1916
War Diary	HQ. 47th Lon. Divn. Lillers	01/03/1916	08/03/1916
War Diary	HQ. 47th Lon. Divn. Bruay	09/03/1916	14/03/1916
War Diary	HQ. 47th Lon. Divn. Caucourt	15/03/1916	21/03/1916
War Diary	HQ. 47th Lon. Divn. Mesnil. Bouche W.10.A.	22/03/1916	22/03/1916
War Diary	HQ. 47th Lon. Divn Mesnil-Bouche	23/03/1916	31/03/1916

Heading	ADVS 47 Div Vol XIV		
War Diary	HQ. 47th Lon. Divn Mesnil-Bouche	01/04/1916	30/04/1916
Miscellaneous	D.A.G., G.H.Q., 3rd Echelon.	31/05/1918	31/05/1918
War Diary	HQ. 47th Lon Divn Maisnil-Bouche	01/05/1916	01/05/1916
War Diary		02/05/1916	31/05/1916
War Diary	HQ. 47th. Lon. Div. La Comtg	01/06/1916	01/06/1916
War Diary		02/06/1916	02/06/1916
War Diary	Chateau. Antigneul	03/06/1916	03/06/1916
War Diary		04/06/1916	13/06/1916
War Diary	Barlin	14/06/1916	14/06/1916
War Diary		15/06/1916	30/06/1916
Miscellaneous	Headquarters. 47th London Division.	02/08/1916	02/08/1916
War Diary	HQ. 47th Lon Divn Barlin	01/07/1916	01/07/1916
War Diary		02/07/1916	16/07/1916
War Diary	Camblain Labbe	17/07/1916	17/07/1916
War Diary		18/07/1916	27/07/1916
War Diary	La-Comte	29/07/1916	30/07/1916
War Diary	Flers	31/07/1916	31/07/1916
Miscellaneous	47th Division.	01/09/1916	01/09/1916
War Diary	Flers	01/08/1916	01/08/1916
War Diary	Frohen-Le-Grand	02/08/1916	02/08/1916
War Diary		03/08/1916	04/08/1916
War Diary	Yvrench	05/08/1916	05/08/1916
War Diary		06/08/1916	31/08/1916
Miscellaneous	Headquarters, 47th (London) Division.	01/10/1916	01/10/1916
War Diary	Baizieux	01/02/1916	01/02/1916
War Diary		02/09/1916	30/09/1916
Miscellaneous	47th Division 'Q'	02/11/1916	02/11/1916
War Diary	Albert E.9. Central	01/10/1916	01/10/1916
War Diary		02/10/1916	30/10/1916
Heading	Hq., 47th (London) Division.	01/01/1917	01/01/1917
War Diary		31/10/1916	31/10/1916
Miscellaneous	Hq., 47th (London) Division.	01/12/1916	01/12/1916
War Diary		01/11/1916	30/11/1916
War Diary		01/12/1916	31/12/1916
Miscellaneous	Hq., 47th Division.	01/02/1917	01/02/1917
War Diary		01/01/1917	31/01/1917
Heading	War Diary 1st-28 February 1917 of Major J. Hebbard A.V.G. A.D.V.J. 47th (London) Division		
War Diary		01/02/1917	28/02/1917
War Diary	G.14.c.1.4 Sheet 28	01/03/1917	01/03/1917
War Diary		02/03/1917	30/04/1917
War Diary	G.14.c.1.4 Sheet. 28	01/05/1917	01/05/1917
War Diary		02/05/1917	31/05/1917
War Diary	G.14.c.1.4 Sheet 28	01/06/1917	01/06/1917
War Diary		02/06/1917	31/07/1917
War Diary	Berthen R.22 Sheet 27	01/08/1917	01/08/1917
War Diary		02/08/1917	31/08/1917
War Diary	G.28.a7.4 Sheet 27	01/09/1917	01/09/1917
War Diary		02/09/1917	30/09/1917
War Diary	Victory Camp G.3.b.5.5 Sheet 51.	01/10/1917	01/10/1917
War Diary		02/10/1917	31/10/1917
War Diary	St. Catherine G.9 Central Sheet 51B	01/11/1917	01/11/1917
War Diary		02/11/1917	22/11/1917
War Diary	Hermaville	23/11/1917	23/11/1917
War Diary	Fosseux	24/11/1917	24/11/1917

War Diary	Achiet Le Petit	25/11/1917	25/11/1917
War Diary	Haplincourt	29/11/1917	29/11/1917
War Diary	Neville Bowjouval	30/11/1917	30/11/1917
War Diary	Neuville Bourjonval P.22 Central Sheet 51c	01/12/1917	01/12/1917
War Diary		02/12/1917	31/12/1917
War Diary	Heilly Sheet Amiens G.1.	01/01/1918	05/01/1918
War Diary	Etricourt Sheet 51 J.8.6.1.1	06/01/1918	31/01/1918
War Diary	Littlewood P.26 Central Sheet 51	01/02/1918	28/02/1918
War Diary	Ytres	21/03/1918	31/03/1918
War Diary	Rubempre Map ref E.6 Sheet Lens	01/04/1918	13/04/1918
War Diary	Canchy	14/04/1918	30/04/1918
War Diary	C.I.C. Central Sheet 61	01/05/1918	31/05/1918
War Diary		01/06/1918	20/06/1918
War Diary	Cavillon	21/06/1918	30/06/1918
War Diary	Cavillon B.I. Sheet Amiens	01/07/1918	31/07/1918
War Diary	Contay U27 Sheet 57d	01/08/1918	12/08/1918
War Diary	Heilly Sheet 62d	01/08/1918	31/08/1918
War Diary	A.5.c. Map Ref Sheet 62 C	01/09/1918	30/09/1918
War Diary	Lautecloque	01/10/1918	31/10/1918
War Diary	Willems M.5.D Sheet 37	01/11/1918	31/12/1918
War Diary		09/11/1918	30/11/1918
War Diary	Lozinghem C.11 Central Sheet 4.4b.	01/12/1918	24/12/1918
War Diary	Lozinghem C.18 Central Sheet. 44b	01/01/1919	28/02/1919
War Diary	Lazinghem	01/03/1919	31/03/1919

NO 05/2216/2

47TH DIVISION

D.A.DIR.VETERINARY SERVICE
MAR 1915-MAR 1919

A.D.V.S. 2nd London Division

Vol I 16 — 31.8.15

Confidential

War Diary
of
Lieut.-Col. W. R. Walker
A.D.V.S.,
2nd London Divn., T.F.

from 16th March, 1915

to 31st March, 1915.

Army Form C. 2118.

WAR DIARY
or
INTELLIGENCE SUMMARY
(Erase heading not required.)

A.D.V.S.
2nd London Division, T.F.

Instructions regarding War Diaries and Intelligence Summaries are contained in F. S. Regs., Part II. and the Staff Manual respectively. Title pages will be prepared in manuscript.

Hour, Date, Place	Summary of Events and Information	Remarks and references to Appendices
16th March, 1915. Tuesday.	Disembarked at Overseas Base. Proceeded overseas apart from units.	WMW
17th March, 1915 & 18th March, 1915. Wednesday & Thursday	Journey up country. Arrived (Thursday) at present location of Divisional Headquarters, & took up Offices assigned to A.D.V.S. Units still in process of arriving in Divisional area.	WMW
19th March, 1915. Friday. Headquarters, 2nd Lond. Dn.	Weather mild. Work at Office. Inspected the locality with a view to obtaining suitable accommodation for the Divisional Mobile Veterinary Section, which is at present en route. Selected field near Divisional Headquarters.	WMW
20th March, 1915. Saturday. Headqrs, 2nd Lond. Divn., T.F.	Inspected horses in Headquarters Area, including 2nd Headquarters Signal Company, A.S.C. &c. They were in very good condition, with few casualties sustained during transit. Received instructions from 1st Corps regarding rendering of returns of contagious diseases.	WMW

Army Form C. 2118.

WAR DIARY
or
INTELLIGENCE SUMMARY

(Erase heading not required.)

Instructions regarding War Diaries and Intelligence Summaries are contained in F. S. Regs., Part II. and the Staff Manual respectively. Title pages will be prepared in manuscript.

Hour, Date, Place	Summary of Events and Information	Remarks and references to Appendices
21st March, 1915. Sunday. Headquarters, 2nd Lond. D., T.F.	A.D.V.S., 1st Army, visited Divisional Headquarters. Received from him detailed instructions regarding Office work, duties of V.O's attached to Units, and functions of Mobile Veterinary Section. Units continue to arrive in Divisional Area.	W.
22nd March, 1915. Monday. Divisional Headquarters.	Divisional Mobile Veterinary Section arrived in Headqrs Area; installed in field near Hqr Offices. Visited Headquarters, 1st Army. Issued Routine instructions to all V.O's attached to Units, & allotted to each the units who were to receive veterinary assistance from him.	W.
23rd March, 1915. Tuesday. Divisional Headquarters. 4th Brigade Area.	Office work: a few horses left sick on Lines of Communication, to be collected, or collection arranged for. Inspected units in 4th London Infantry Brigade area, including No 2 Train Company, A.S.C. and 7th London Brigade, R.F.A. The horses seem in good condition and well looked after.	W.

1247 W 3299 200,000 (E) 8/14 J.B.C. & A.   Forms/C. 2118/1.

Army Form C. 2118.

WAR DIARY
or
INTELLIGENCE SUMMARY

(Erase heading not required.)

Instructions regarding War Diaries and Intelligence Summaries are contained in F. S. Regs., Part II. and the Staff Manual respectively. Title pages will be prepared in manuscript.

Hour, Date, Place	Summary of Events and Information	Remarks and references to Appendices
24th March, 1915. Wednesday. Divisional Headquarters, 4th Brigade Area, 5th Brigade Area.	D.D.V.S., 1st Army, visited Headquarters. Carried out an inspection, with D.D.V.S., 1st Army, of a number of units; viz:- 4th Lond. Fd. Brigade & Train Comps., 7th London Brigade, R.F.A.; 8th Lond. (How.) Bde. R.F.A., & 5th Lond. Brigade, R.F.A. Office work: issued detailed Routine instructions to O.C. Mobile Veterinary Section.	W^m
25th March, 1915. Thursday. Divisional Headquarters.	Office work. Saw transport of 7th & 8th (City of London) Battalions as the battalions marched past Divisional Headquarters. All the horses looked well.	W^m
26th March, 1915. Friday. Divisional Headquarters.	Office work. Received weekly reports (A.F. A 2000) of all unit Veterinary Officers; interviewed each personally with reference to their work. No mange or ringworm throughout the Division.	W^m
27th March, 1915. Saturday. Headquarters Area.	Inspected Divisional Ammunition Column, which arrived in Divisional Area yesterday. They have a V.O., Lieut. J.M. Stuart, A.V.C. (Temp.), who joined the unit on eve of departure from England. Rendered consolidated sick return to D.D.V.S., 1st Army. Casualties are chiefly Respiratory (a number of colds & 11 deaths from Pneumonia) & accidents, kicks &c. on voyage & journey.	W^m

Army Form C. 2118.

WAR DIARY
or
INTELLIGENCE SUMMARY

(Erase heading not required.)

Instructions regarding War Diaries and Intelligence Summaries are contained in F. S. Regs., Part II. and the Staff Manual respectively. Title pages will be prepared in manuscript.

Hour, Date, Place	Summary of Events and Information	Remarks and references to Appendices
28th March, 1915. Sunday. Headquarters Area.	Office work. Inspected A.S.C. horses, Headqrs & Headqrs Company and in the afternoon, horses of Divisional Ammunition Column.	WW
29th March, 1915. Monday. Divisional Headquarters 6th Brigade Area.	Rode out to 6th London Brigade, R.F.A., and inspected horses of 15th, 16th & 17th Batteries. No mange or skin trouble or infectious disease. Work at Office.	WW
30th March, 1915. Tuesday. Headquarters Area. 6th Brigade Area.	Inspected horses of A.S.C. Train Companies have now moved into Headquarters Area from Brigade Areas. The Heavy Draught horses are in good condition but must not be trotted. Routine Order published to this effect. Inspected also horses of Divisional Ammunition Column, & 6th London Brigade, R.F.A.	WW
31st March, 1915. Wednesday. Divisional Headquarters.	Work at Office & with Mobile Section. A number of horses are undergoing treatment there to be returned to units when cured; not vaccinated.	WW

[Stamp: A.D.V.S. 31 MAR. 1915 2ND LONDON DIVISION]

W.O.W.
Lieut Colonel

121/5166

A.D.V.S. 2nd London Division.

Vol II 1–30.4.15.

Confidential.

War Diary
of
Lieut.-Col. W. R. Walker,

from 1/4/1915 to 30/4/1915

Army Form C. 2118.

WAR DIARY
~or~
INTELLIGENCE SUMMARY.
(Erase heading not required.)

Instructions regarding War Diaries and Intelligence Summaries are contained in F.S. Regs., Part II. and the Staff Manual respectively. Title pages will be prepared in manuscript.

Hour, Date, Place	Summary of Events and Information	Remarks and references to Appendices
1st April, 1915. Thursday. Headquarters, Lon. Div.	Office work, & at Mobile Vety. Section. Inspected transport of Units of 4th London Infantry Brigade, who are now in advance of Division. Found horses in good condition.	MGW
2nd April, 1915. Friday. Headqrs. London Divn.	Office work. Received weekly reports, verbal & A 2000, from Unit V.O's. Inspected horses of A.S.C. Train Companies located in Headquarters Area; (also Signal Company & Mobile Veterinary Section).	MGW
3rd April, 1915. Saturday. Headqrs. London Divn.	Office work. A very wet day. D.D.V.S., 1st Army, visited these Headquarters. Weekly sick report rendered; shows large wastage due to Pneumonia outbreak.	MGW
4th April, 1915. Sunday. Headqrs. London Divn.	Office work. In afternoon, inspected Divisional Ammunition Column.	MGW

Army Form C. 2118.

WAR DIARY
INTELLIGENCE SUMMARY.
(Erase heading not required.)

Instructions regarding War Diaries and Intelligence Summaries are contained in F.S. Regs., Part II. and the Staff Manual respectively. Title pages will be prepared in manuscript.

Hour, Date, Place	Summary of Events and Information	Remarks and references to Appendices
5th April, 1915. Monday. Headquarters, Lond. Div.	Office work. Inspected transport horses of battalions of 5th London Infantry Brigade, and 5th Field Ambulance.	MEW
6th April, 1915 Tuesday. Headqrs., London Div.	Office work. Inspected horses of 4th Lond. Inf. Bde. & 4th Field Ambce. remainder in the latter remainder in good health. Inspected also horses of Divisional Ammunition Column: 4 deaths from Pneumonia & 4 serious cases remaining: 8 convalescent. Total of 14 deaths since arrival of unit in this country; outbreak proves to be exclusively among remounts received just prior to or just after embarkation.	MEW
7th April, 1915. Wednesday. Headqrs., London Div.	Office work. Mobile Veterinary Section. D.D.V.S. 1st Army, visited these Headquarters: afterwards inspected with him the sick horses of 2nd Ammunition Column.	MEW
8th April, 1915. Thursday. Headqrs., London Div.	Office work. Inspected a parade of cast horses of 5th London Brigade R.F.A. Mostly remount cases, D.R. present. Of veterinary cases ordered 2 to be destroyed, 4 to be cast & sent to Mobile Vety. Section 2, 6 to be retained.	MEW

Army Form C. 2118.

WAR DIARY
INTELLIGENCE SUMMARY.
(Erase heading not required.)

Instructions regarding War Diaries and Intelligence Summaries are contained in F.S. Regs., Part II. and the Staff Manual respectively. Title pages will be prepared in manuscript.

Hour, Date, Place	Summary of Events and Information	Remarks and references to Appendices
9 April, 1915. Friday. Headqrs., Lond. Divn.	Office work. Interviewed V.O's of units, bringing in weekly reports. A 2000. Afterwards inspected horses of 7th London Brigade, R.F.A., and Divisional Ammunition Column.	MWW
10 April, 1915. Saturday. Headqrs., Lond. Divn.	Office work. Inspected units of 1st London Infantry Brigade. Afterwards saw Mobile Veterinary Section, where a number of horses cast by D.D.S.R. await evacuation.	MWW
11 April, 1915. Sunday. Headqrs., Lond. Divn.	Office work. D.D.V.S., 1st Army, visited these Headquarters. Afterwards accompanied him on an inspection of horses of 7th London Bde., R.F.A., & Divisional Ammunition Column. 6.6. Mobile Vety. Section evacuated this day 32 horses for veterinary reasons, & 10 horses & mules cast for remount reasons.	MWW
12 April, 1915. Monday. Headqrs., Lond. Divn.	Office work. This day the 4th & 5th Lond. Field Ambulances paraded for inspection by G.O.C. the Division. Inspected transport horses at same time.	MWW

Army Form C. 2118.

WAR DIARY
or
INTELLIGENCE SUMMARY.
(Erase heading not required.)

Instructions regarding War Diaries and Intelligence Summaries are contained in F.S. Regs., Part II. and the Staff Manual respectively. Title pages will be prepared in manuscript.

Hour, Date, Place	Summary of Events and Information	Remarks and references to Appendices
13th April, 1915. Tuesday. H.Q., 2nd Lon. Divn., T.F.	Office work. Inspected transport of 6th London Infantry Brigade units, 6th Lond. Field Ambce.; 6th Dble Train Compy., & Military Mounted Police (Divl. Hqrs.).	MPW
14th April, 1915. Wednesday. H.Q., 2nd Lon. Divn., T.F.	Office work. Visited Headqrs. 2nd Division (1st Corps) & interviewed A.D.V.S. Inspected No. 3 Mobile Section: horses are all under cover.	MPW
15th April, 1915. Thursday. H.Q., 2nd Lon. Divn., T.F.	Office work. Rode over to Mobile Veterinary Section D.V.S. held an inspection of the Mobile Veterinary Section: accompanied by D.D.V.S., 1st Army. Afterwards visited Divl. Ammunition Column, & inspected heavy draught horses; several pneumonia cases among remounts.	MPW

Army Form C. 2118.

WAR DIARY
INTELLIGENCE SUMMARY.
(Erase heading not required.)

Instructions regarding War Diaries and Intelligence Summaries are contained in F.S. Regs., Part II. and the Staff Manual respectively. Title pages will be prepared in manuscript.

Hour, Date, Place	Summary of Events and Information	Remarks and references to Appendices
16 April, 1915 Friday. HQ., 2nd Ldn. Div., T.F.	Office work. Interviewed V.O's of Units, bringing in weekly return. Inspected Mobile Veterinary Section. The remaining pneumonia cases of 6.8. M.O.S., unable to move with unit, are in charge of Sergt Am Col; 4 deaths this morning. These will probably be the last; all the other cases have good chance of recovery.	
17 April, 1915. Saturday. HQ., 2nd Ldn. Div., T.F.	Change of Station of Divisional Headquarters. (morning) Office work - weekly return. Return still shows high wastage due to deaths in an outbreak of Pneumonia (chiefly in Sergt Am Col) among heavy draught remounts received just prior to embarkation. Of other casualties, large number "Cured"; no. "remaining" much smaller.	
18 April, 1915. Sunday. HQ., 2nd Ldn. Div. T.F.	Office work. D.D.V.S. 1st Army visited these Headquarters. Weekly telegram to 1st Corps shows no Mange, either confirmed or suspected; 6 cases of Ringworm remaining under treatment. A large proportion of units, especially artillery, are now in action, & are attached to other formations (1st & 2nd Divns.).	

Army Form C. 2118.

WAR DIARY
of
INTELLIGENCE SUMMARY.
(Erase heading not required.)

Instructions regarding War Diaries and Intelligence Summaries are contained in F. S. Regs., Part II. and the Staff Manual respectively. Title pages will be prepared in manuscript.

Hour, Date, Place	Summary of Events and Information	Remarks and references to Appendices
19 April, 1915. Headqrs, London Division. Monday.	Inspected horses of Hdqrs. & No. 1 Section, Signal Company; and also Div. Hdqrs. horses. All doing well. Office work. Weather bright & warmer.	
20 April, 1915. Tuesday. Headqrs, London Division.	Office work. Rode over to Div. Mobile Vety. Section. All the remaining pneumonia cases from Divisional Ammunition Column are doing well. 14 sick horses & 1 mule evacuated to Base Vety. Hpl. today: mainly debility cases & injuries.	
21st April, 1915. Wednesday. Headqrs, London Div.	Office work. Inspected two Train Companies, A.S.C., and all units at same station, i.e. 22nd & 23rd Battalions, 5th Field Amb., under veterinary charge of V.O. attached to A.S.C. All horses in good condition, looking & working well. Weather dull & inclined to rain.	

(9 29 6) W 4141—463 100,000 9/14 H W V Forms/C. 2118/10

Army Form C. 2118.

WAR DIARY
~~INTELLIGENCE~~ SUMMARY.
(Erase heading not required.)

Instructions regarding War Diaries and Intelligence Summaries are contained in F.S. Regs., Part II. and the Staff Manual respectively. Title pages will be prepared in manuscript.

Hour, Date, Place	Summary of Events and Information	Remarks and references to Appendices
22nd April, 1915. Thursday. Hqrs, London Division	Office work. Inspected detached Batteries of 5th Lond. Bde., R.F.A. (14th Battery) and 6th Lond. Bde., R.F.A. (15th Battery). Horses all cared for & free from disease or injuries. Weather fine & bright, but cold.	MGW
23rd April, 1915 Friday Hqrs, London Divn. &c	Office work. L.D.S. 1st Army, visited these H.Q. Accompanied him on an inspection of Divisional Ammunition Column; found considerably less sickness there, & H.D. horses in fairly good condition. Very cold, with high wind. Interviewed V.O.'s of units, bringing in sick returns.	MGW
24 April, 1915 Friday Hqrs, London Divn.	Office work. Change of station of Divisional Headquarters.	MGW

Army Form C. 2118.

WAR DIARY
INTELLIGENCE SUMMARY.
(Erase heading not required.)

Instructions regarding War Diaries and Intelligence Summaries are contained in F.S. Regs., Part II. and the Staff Manual respectively. Title pages will be prepared in manuscript.

Hour, Date, Place	Summary of Events and Information	Remarks and references to Appendices
25th April, 1915. Sunday Headqrs., London Divn.	Office work. Inspected all four Companies of Divisional Train, A.S.C. Weekly telegram re Infectious Diseases shows Mange nil. Ringworm 6 cured & 10 remaining. Weekly report shows slightly increased number of cases under treatment, but the total wastage is very much smaller than in the 3 preceding weeks.	
26th April, 1915. Monday Headqrs., London Divn.	Office work. D.D.V.S. "1st Army", visited these Headquarters. Inspected Divisional Ammunition Column: horses in good health : some defects in shoeing were pointed out. Inspected Transport of 6th Infantry Brigade; also of 6th Field Ambulance.	
27th April, 1915 Tuesday Headquarters, Lon. Div.	Office work. Visited No. 3 Mobile Veterinary Section (Second Division). Interviewed O.C. & also D.D.V.S. of 2nd Divn., with reference to movement of Section, & taking over of vacated premises for London Div. Mobile Vety. Section.	

Army Form C. 2118.

WAR DIARY
INTELLIGENCE SUMMARY.
(Erase heading not required.)

Instructions regarding War Diaries and Intelligence Summaries are contained in F.S. Regs., Part II. and the Staff Manual respectively. Title pages will be prepared in manuscript.

Hour, Date, Place	Summary of Events and Information	Remarks and references to Appendices
28th April, 1915. Wednesday. Headqrs., London Divn.	Office work. Inspected Transport of 5th London Field Ambulance.	
29th April, 1915. Thursday. Headqrs., London Divn.	Office work. Inspected Divisional Ammunition Column & Squadron King Edwards Horse (Divn. Mounted Troops). Arranged for V.O. to give assistance when necessary. Selected site for Mobile Vety. Section. Section moved in during the day. D.D.V.S. 1st Army visited these Headquarters.	
30th April, 1915. Friday. Headqrs., London Divn.	Office work. Interviewed Veterinary Officers, who came to render weekly sick reports. Inspected horses of 6th Lord. Bde, R.F.A. Ammunition Column, made post-mortem on horse suspected of Glanders: result, not glandered. Gave instructions for a number of horses to be malleined. Afternoon, inspected Divisional Ammunition Column & Squadron King Edwards Horse. Arranged for vetny. assistance for outlying batteries, 1st R.F.A.	

121/5445

A.D.V.S. 47 (London) Division

Vol III.   1 – 30. 5. 15

Confidential

War Diary
of
Lieut.-Col. W. R. Walker

[Stamp: A.D.V.S. 30 MAY 1915 4TH LONDON DIVISION]

1/5/15 — 30/5/15

Army Form C. 2118.

WAR DIARY
or
INTELLIGENCE SUMMARY.
(Erase heading not required.)

Hour, Date, Place	Summary of Events and Information	Remarks and references to Appendices
1st May, 1915. Saturday. Headquarters, Lon. Div.	Office work. Weekly state & return rendered. Weekly return records the end of the Pneumonia outbreak: the last 9 convalescent cases being evacuated on 30th ult. Visited & inspected Mobile Veterinary Section	MRW
2nd May, 1915. Sunday. Headquarters, Lon. Div.	Office work. Weekly Infectious Disease telegram shows 19 cases of Ringworm. No mange or suspected mange. Inspected batteries of 5th London Brigade, R.F.A. Horses in good condition; very little sickness.	MRW
3rd May, 1915. Monday. Headquarters, Lon. Div.	Office work. D.D.V.S., 1st Army, visited these Headquarters, and inspected Mobile Veterinary Section. Inspected draught horses of Companies of Divisional Train, A.S.C.	MRW

Army Form C. 2118.

WAR DIARY
INTELLIGENCE SUMMARY.
(Erase heading not required.)

Instructions regarding War Diaries and Intelligence Summaries are contained in F.S. Regs., Part II. and the Staff Manual respectively. Title pages will be prepared in manuscript.

Hour, Date, Place	Summary of Events and Information	Remarks and references to Appendices
4th May, 1915. Tuesday. Headquarters, Lon. Div.	Office work. Inspected transport horses of Battalions of 4th London Infantry Brigade. Mobile Veterinary Section.	MPW
5th May, 1915. Wednesday. Headquarters, Lon. Div.	Office work. Inspected horses of Divisional Ammunition Column, in good condition. Mobile Veterinary Section; 8 sick cases & 2 remount cases evacuated to Base Vety. Hospital.	MPW
6th May, 1915. Thursday. Headquarters, Lon. Div.	Office work. Inspected horses of Divisional Headquarters & Headquarter Units, R.A. & R.E.; also Signal Company. Mobile Veterinary Section.	MPW

Army Form C. 2118.

WAR DIARY
INTELLIGENCE SUMMARY.
(Erase heading not required.)

Instructions regarding War Diaries and Intelligence Summaries are contained in F.S. Regs., Part II. and the Staff Manual respectively. Title pages will be prepared in manuscript.

Hour, Date, Place	Summary of Events and Information	Remarks and references to Appendices
7th May 1915 Friday Headquarters, Lon. Div.	Office work. Interviewed Veterinary Officers of Units, who came to render weekly returns. Mobile Veterinary Section.	MRM
8th May 1915 Saturday Headquarters, Lon. Div.	Office work. Weekly return shows a marked decrease both in "wastage" & in number of horses remaining sick. 5 fatal cases of shell-wounds. Mobile Veterinary Section.	MRM
9th May 1915 Sunday Headquarters, Lon. Div.	Office work. D.D.V.S., 1st Army, visited their Headquarters. Mobile Veterinary Section.	MRM
10th May 1915 Monday Headquarters, Lon. Div.	Office work. Inspected horses of all four Companies of Divisional Train A.S.C. Horses in very good condition; very little sickness & very few kicks. Mobile Veterinary Section.	MRM

Army Form C. 2118.

WAR DIARY
or
INTELLIGENCE SUMMARY.
(Erase heading not required.)

Instructions regarding War Diaries and Intelligence Summaries are contained in F.S. Regs., Part II. and the Staff Manual respectively. Title pages will be prepared in manuscript.

Hour, Date, Place	Summary of Events and Information	Remarks and references to Appendices
11th May, 1915 Tuesday Headquarters, Lon. Div.	Office Work. Designation of Formation changed to "47th (London) Division: Infantry Brigades re-numbered (140th, 141st, 142nd). Mobile Veterinary Section.	
12th May, 1915. Wednesday Hqrs. 47th (London) Divn.	Office work. Inspected transport of 4th or 5th London Field Ambulances. Mobile Veterinary Section.	
13th May, 1915 Thursday Hqrs. 47th (London) Divn	Office work. Inspected wagon lines of 6th London Brigade, R.F.A. Mobile Veterinary Section. This day the Germans commenced shelling Bethune, after three months quiescence.	
14th May, 1915 Friday. Hqrs., 47th (London) Divn.	Office work. Interviewed Veterinary Officers, who came to render weekly returns. Mobile Veterinary Section.	

Army Form C. 2118.

WAR DIARY
or
INTELLIGENCE SUMMARY.
(Erase heading not required.)

Instructions regarding War Diaries and Intelligence Summaries are contained in F. S. Regs., Part II. and the Staff Manual respectively. Title pages will be prepared in manuscript.

Place	Date	Hour	Summary of Events and Information	Remarks and references to Appendices
Headqrs., 47th Div.	15th May, 1915. Saturday.		Office work. Weekly Return & Weekly State rendered. Weekly Return shows health of the horses of the Division to be remarkably good : less than ½ % sick. Mobile Veterinary Section.	WRN
Hqrs., 47th Div.	16th May, 1915 Sunday.		Office work. Inspected Transport horses of 6th London Field Ambulance. Mobile Veterinary Section; 8 sick horses evacuated; further bombardment of these Headquarters.	WRN
Hqrs., 47th Div.	17th May, 1915 Monday.		Office work. D.D.V.S., 1st Army, visited these Headquarters. Mobile Veterinary Section.	WRN
Hqrs., 47th Div.	18th May, 1915 Tuesday.		Office work. Inspected Mobile Veterinary Section. 8 sick horses evacuated to the Base.	WRN

Army Form C. 2118.

WAR DIARY
~~INTELLIGENCE SUMMARY.~~
(Erase heading not required.)

Instructions regarding War Diaries and Intelligence Summaries are contained in F.S. Regs., Part II. and the Staff Manual respectively. Title pages will be prepared in manuscript.

Hour, Date, Place	Summary of Events and Information	Remarks and references to Appendices
19th May, 1915. Wednesday. Headquarters, 47th Div.	Office work. Inspected horses of Divisional Headquarters, Sigrs. Sext. R.A. - R.E. Signal Co. (Agst. No 1 Section). Mobile Veterinary Section.	MRM
20th May, 1915. Thursday. Headquarters, 47th Div.	Office work. Inspected A.S.C., Hqrs. & the four companies of 47th Div'n. Inspected Sqnadron King Edwards Horse.	MRM
21st May, 1915. Friday. Headqrs. 47th (Lon.) Div.	Interviewed Veterinary Officers & received weekly reports. Office work. Mobile Veterinary Section.	MRM
22nd May, 1915. Saturday. Hqrs. 47th (Lon.) Div'n	Office work. D.D.V.S. 1st Army, visited these Headquarters Mobile Veterinary Section: 8 sick horses + 1 mare in foal evacuated to Base Vety. Hosp. Weekly Return: health of Division still good; 2 fatal cases of shell wounds	MRM

(73989) W4141—463. 400,000. 9/14. H.&J.Ltd. Forms/C. 2118/10.

Army Form C. 2118.

WAR DIARY
INTELLIGENCE SUMMARY.
(Erase heading not required.)

Instructions regarding War Diaries and Intelligence Summaries are contained in F.S. Regs., Part II. and the Staff Manual respectively. Title pages will be prepared in manuscript.

Hour, Date, Place	Summary of Events and Information	Remarks and references to Appendices
23rd May, 1915. Sunday Headqrs., 47th Division.	Office work. Divisional Headquarters moved to new station. Inspected horses of Hqr. Units (R.A., R.E. & Sigl. Sqn.) Mobile Veterinary Section.	
24th May, 1915. Monday Headqrs., 47th Division.	Office work. Inspected horses of 4th & 5th London Field Ambulance Mobile Veterinary Section.	
25th May, 1915. Tuesday Headqrs., 47th Division.	Office work. Visited wagon lines of 5th London Brigade, R.F.A. Four horses killed by 1 shell in Signal Company. Several horses suffering from shrapnel wounds belonging to formations other than 47th Division admitted to Mobile Vety. Section	
26th May, 1915 Wednesday Headqrs., 47th Division.	Office work. Saw transport horses of 6th London Field Ambulance. Siege & Garrison Artillery units attached to this Division viz. 1st & 4th Siege Batteries, 95th (Heavy) Battery, R.G.A. Mobile Veterinary Section.	

Army Form C. 2118.

WAR DIARY
or
INTELLIGENCE SUMMARY.
(Erase heading not required.)

Instructions regarding War Diaries and Intelligence Summaries are contained in F.S.Regs., Part II. and the Staff Manual respectively. Title pages will be prepared in manuscript.

Hour, Date, Place	Summary of Events and Information	Remarks and references to Appendices
27th May, 1915. Thursday. Headqrs. 47th (Lon.) Divn.	Office work. D.D.V.S. 1st Army visited these Headquarters. Mobile Veterinary Section: selected site for Section on removal from present quarters: application sent in to A.D.+Q.M.G. for permission to occupy new position.	WRM
28th May, 1915. Friday. Headqrs. 47th (Lon.) Divn.	Office work. Interviewed Vety. Officers, bringing weekly returns. 8 Sick horses + 1 mare in foal evacuated.	WRM
29th May, 1915. Saturday. Headqrs. 47th (Lon.) Divn.	Office work. Received application from Transport Officer of the Queen's Regt. for Veterinary assistance: Lieut. Southall detailed. Weekly Return: health of Division good: 5 horses died from shell-wounds. 8 sick horses (5 shrapnel wounds) + 1 mare with foal evacuated from Mobile Vety. Section.	WRM
30th May, 1915. Sunday. Headqrs. 47th (Lon.) Divn.	Office work. A.D.V.S. evacuated this day on account of injury to shoulder	WRM

[Stamp: A.D.V.S. 30 MAY 1915 LONDON]

121/5496

47th Division
War Diary.
A.D.V.S. 47th London Division
Vol: IX. 31.5. — 30.6./15.

Confidential

War Diary

of

Capt. Joseph Abson,
A.V.C. (T.F.)

—

31 May – 30 June
1915.

Army Form C. 2118.

WAR DIARY
or
INTELLIGENCE SUMMARY.
(Erase heading not required.)

Instructions regarding War Diaries and Intelligence Summaries are contained in F. S. Regs., Part II. and the Staff Manual respectively. Title pages will be prepared in manuscript.

Hour, Date, Place	Summary of Events and Information	Remarks and references to Appendices
31st May, 1915. Monday. Headqrs., 47th (Lon.) Div. BETHUNE.	Arrived at Headquarters, 47th (London) Division, BETHUNE, at 12.30 p.m. and reported myself for duty. Took up duty forthwith as A.D.V.S. and reported the fact to D.D.V.S., 1st Army.	JL
1st June, 1915. Tuesday. Headqrs., 47th (Lon.) Div. BETHUNE.	Routine office work; received calls from unit V.O's. Visited Mobile Veterinary Section; advised O.C. with regard to movement or otherwise of Section in view of probable forthcoming change of station of Divisional Headquarters; also with regard to treatment of certain cases. Routine office work. Visited ANNEZIN, to see horse of D.A.C. left behind unable to move; saw also two other injured horses of D.A.C. at FOUQUEREUIL. D.O. it A.S.C. & O.C. it D.A.C. report moves of their units.	JL JL
2nd June, 1915. Wednesday. Headqrs., 47th (Lon.) Div. BETHUNE and VERQUIN.	Routine office work. Visited Mobile Veterinary Section. Change of station of Divisional Headquarters. This Office transferred to VERQUIN.	JL

Army Form C. 2118.

WAR DIARY
INTELLIGENCE SUMMARY.
(Erase heading not required.)

Instructions regarding War Diaries and Intelligence Summaries are contained in F. S. Regs., Part II. and the Staff Manual respectively. Title pages will be prepared in manuscript.

Hour, Date, Place	Summary of Events and Information	Remarks and references to Appendices
3rd June, 1915. Headqrs. 47th (Lon.) Divn. VERQUIN. Thursday	Routine Office work. Inspected horses of Divisional Headquarters: in good condition, but farriery needs attention. One case of contused wound (kick). Inspected also horses of Headqrs. No. 1 Section, Signal Company. Found a mare in foal, and ordered her evacuation.	J.R.
4th June, 1915. Headqrs. 47th (Lon.) Divn. VERQUIN. Friday	Office work: dealt with correspondence. Visited horses of Divl. Headquarters & Signal Company. Unit Veterinary Officers rode in to these Headquarters, bringing their weekly reports.	J.R.
5th June, 1915. Saturday. Hqrs. 47th (Lon.) Divn. VERQUIN.	Office work: correspondence, &c. Inspected horses of Divl. Hqrs. and Signal Company. Weekly Report and Weekly State rendered to D.A.D.V.S., 1st Army. Report shows that the number of sick in the Division is decreasing. 3 died & 4 destroyed during the week. Visited Mobile Veterinary Section at HESDIGNEUL. Found everything satisfactory.	J.R.

Army Form C. 2118.

WAR DIARY
or
INTELLIGENCE SUMMARY.
(Erase heading not required.)

Instructions regarding War Diaries and Intelligence Summaries are contained in F.S. Regs., Part II. and the Staff Manual respectively. Title pages will be prepared in manuscript.

Hour, Date, Place	Summary of Events and Information	Remarks and references to Appendices
6th June, 1915. Sunday. Hqrs. 47th Div. VERQUIN	Inspected horses of Div: Headquarters. Visited Signal Company lines, and treated sick horses. Rode out to ESSARS, to see five sick horses left behind by the 6th London Brigade, R.F.A., after their last move. Found these cases, which were left at farms through the agency of the local Maire. One had died of Pneumonia. Routine Office work: dealt with correspondence.	J.I.
7th June, 1915. Monday. Hqrs. 47th Div. VERQUIN	Attended sick horses of Signal Company + Div. Hqrs. Rode to HESDIGNEUL to Mobile Vety. Section. Office work. Correspondence.	J.I.
8th June, 1915. Tuesday. Hqrs. 47th Div. VERQUIN	Routine Office Work. Inspected horses of Div: Headquarters + Signal Company. Rode to Mobile Veterinary Section, HESDIGNEUL. 8 Sick + injured horses evacuated today to Base Veterinary Hospl. from Mobile Section.	J.I.

Army Form C. 2118.

WAR DIARY
or
INTELLIGENCE SUMMARY.
(Erase heading not required.)

Instructions regarding War Diaries and Intelligence Summaries are contained in F.S. Regs., Part II. and the Staff Manual respectively. Title pages will be prepared in manuscript.

Hour, Date, Place	Summary of Events and Information	Remarks and references to Appendices
9th June, 1915. Wednesday. HqN 47th Div. VERQUIN.	Inspected horses of Divl Headqrs & Signal Company at VERQUIN. Rode to Mobile Vety. Section at HESDIGNEUL. Visited Divl Ammunition Column. Found 15 cases requiring attention; these included 8 cases of simple fever, & one or two strain cases. All necessary precautions taken. Rode to BEUVRY to see Vety. Offr. of 141st Infy. Bde. but failed to see him. Visited remaining sick horses of 6th Lond Bde. R.F.A. at ESSARS. Ordered pneumonia case (convalescent) to be walked in to Mobile Section. Rode to Headquarters 140th Infantry Brigade at MAZINGARBE.	JS.
10th June, 1915. Thursday. HqN 47th Div. VERQUIN.	Routine Office work; dealt with correspondence. Inspected horses of Divl Headquarters, & Signal Company, and gave attention to sick cases. Visited sick horses of details, Amm. Col.; all doing well except 1 bad laminitis case. Rode over to Mobile Vety. Section. The Section apparently occupy ground in the area of the 2nd Division, & have this day moved to another field, by permission of Headquarters 2nd Div., & Hqrs 47th Div.	JS.

Army Form C. 2118.

WAR DIARY
~~INTELLIGENCE SUMMARY.~~
(Erase heading not required.)

Instructions regarding War Diaries and Intelligence Summaries are contained in F.S. Regs., Part II. and the Staff Manual respectively. Title pages will be prepared in manuscript.

Hour, Date, Place	Summary of Events and Information	Remarks and references to Appendices
11th June, 1915. Friday. Hqrs. 47th Lond. Divn. VERQUIN & NOEUX-les-MINES.	Routine Office Work: dealt with correspondence. Saw horses of Headquarters, & also Signal Company. Rode out to DROUVIN to see sick horses of Divl. Ammun. Column; doing well. Change of Station of Divl. Headqrs., 3rd Echelon (including this Office) to NOEUX-les-MINES. D.D.V.S., 1st Army, visited these Headquarters. In the evening an urgent telegram from Div. Am. Col. requesting veterinary assistance for 3 sick horses. Rode over & found 12 bad cases several of simple fever, 1 meningitis, 1 congestion of the brain. Ordered removal to higher ground, & gave treatment.	A.
12th June, 1915. Saturday. Headqrs., 47th Lon. Divn. NOEUX-les-MINES.	Office Work: weekly report and sick state; dealt with correspondence. Rode over to HOUCHIN, 141st Infantry Brigade, to see V.O. (Lieut. Bryden). Gave him charge of horses of details, 47th Divn. Am. Col. at DROUVIN. Thence to HESDIGNEUL (Mobile Veterinary Section): everything satisfactory. Visited Headquarters, & Signal Company, & gave attention to sick horses. In evening, to DROUVIN, to see sick horses of details, Am. Col. Progressing satisfactorily.	A.

Forms/C. 2118/10

Army Form C. 2118.

WAR DIARY
~~INTELLIGENCE~~ SUMMARY
(Erase heading not required.)

Instructions regarding War Diaries and Intelligence Summaries are contained in F.S. Regs., Part II. and the Staff Manual respectively. Title pages will be prepared in manuscript.

Hour, Date, Place	Summary of Events and Information	Remarks and references to Appendices
13th June, 1915. Sunday. Hqrs. 47th Lon. Divn. NOEUX-LES-MINES	Office work: dealt with correspondence. Rode to HOUCHIN, DROUVIN & VERQUIN. HOUCHIN: Saw Lieut. Bryden & Craig (141st & 142nd Inf. Bdes.). Consultation with Lieut. Craig re Bay Draft Mare with open Maxillary joint. Allotted horses of 4th Lond. Ft. Amba to Lieut Craig for vety. assistance. DROUVIN: Saw sick horses of 47th D.A.C. (details) and 4th Lond. Field Amba - doing well. VERQUIN: Visited Headquarters, 47th Lond Divn, also Signal Company, & attended sick horses.	*[signature]*
14th June, 1915. Monday. Hqrs. 47th Lon Divn. NOEUX-LES-MINES	Routine Office work. To HOUCHIN to see Lieut. Bryden, and afterwards with that Officer to see the sick horses of the Ammunition Column at DROUVIN. Afterwards to Mobile Veterinary Section, HESDIGNEUL. Complaints having been received with regard to unsuitable shoes supplied, a visit to the Ordnance Refilling point at HESDIGNEUL made it appear that the fault lay in indenting. Rode on to A.S.C. & inspected with Lt. Henry some horses unsuitable for A.S.C. work. Recommended them to be cast, one as dangerous from vice, the other as a perfected gibbet. 8 sick horses, 2 mares in foal & 1 mare with foal at foot evacuated today from Mobile Vety. Section.	*[signature]*

Army Form C. 2118.

WAR DIARY
or
INTELLIGENCE SUMMARY.

(Erase heading not required.)

Instructions regarding War Diaries and Intelligence Summaries are contained in F.S. Regs., Part II. and the Staff Manual respectively. Title pages will be prepared in manuscript.

Hour, Date, Place	Summary of Events and Information	Remarks and references to Appendices
15th June, 1915. Tuesday. Hdqrs. 47th Div. NOEUX-les-MINES.	Office work: dealt with correspondence. Visited Divisional Headquarters, and saw A.A. & Q.M.G. Inspected horses of Hedqrs. & of Divl. Signal Company. Rode over to Divisional Ammunition Column (Bois des Dames): conference over watering arrangements. Returned through DROUVIN & HOUCHIN & saw horses of S.A.A. Section, Div. Am. Col., & 141st Inf. Bde., with Lieut. Boyden.	A.
16th June, 1915. Wednesday. Hdqrs. 47th Div. NOEUX-les-MINES.	Office work: dealt with correspondence. Rode to VERQUIN, & saw horses of Divl. Heodqrs. & of Signal Coy. On to HESDIGNEUL, to Mobile Veterinary Section: found everything satisfactory; very few cases in the lines. To LAPUGNOY & saw a horse of 6th London Brigade, R.F.A., with suspicious skin disease. Ordered it into Mobile Section for treatment.	A.
17th June, 1915. Thursday. Hdqrs. 47th Div. NOEUX-les-MINES.	Routine Office work. To VERQUIN, to inspect horses of Headqrs. of Division, & also of Sign. & No.1 Section, Signal Company, & to treat sick cases. Thence to DROUVIN to see sick horses of details, 47th Div. Am. Col., & of 4th Lond. Field Ambce.: all doing well. Afterwards to HOUCHIN, to see a number of vicious & unsuitable horses & mules of 141st Infantry Brigade. D.D.V.S., 1st Army, visited these Headquarters. Late in evening, rode to BÉTHUNE, re arrival of batch of remounts.	A.

Army Form C. 2118.

WAR DIARY
or
INTELLIGENCE SUMMARY.
(Erase heading not required.)

Instructions regarding War Diaries and Intelligence Summaries are contained in F.S. Regs., Part II. and the Staff Manual respectively. Title pages will be prepared in manuscript.

Hour, Date, Place	Summary of Events and Information	Remarks and references to Appendices
18th June, 1915: Friday Headqrs. 47th (Lon.) Div. NOEUX-les-MINES	Routine Office work. Veterinary Officers brought in their weekly returns, making verbal reports on the week's work. Rode over to HESDIGNEUL to examine the Remounts which arrived yesterday & were segregated in the Mobile Section. Rejected 9 as diseased, viz: 1 suspicious mange, 2 eye, 2 congestion of lungs, 4 lame. Full report sent to A.A. & Q.M.G. Afternoon rode to MAZINGARBE to see horses of 4th Field Coy. R.E. recommended by V.O. for evacuation. Received a complaint as to bad accommodation of 6th Field Ambulance stables. Investigated & reported to A.A. & Q.M.G., recommending movement of horses.	JA.
19th June, 1915: Saturday Headqrs. 47th (Lon.) Div. NOEUX-les-MINES	Office work: dealt with correspondence. Weekly sick state & sick report rendered. To VERQUIN to inspect horses of Divl. Headquarters & Signal Coy. & to treat sick cases. Rode over to MAZINGARBE, to see horses of 140th Infantry Bde. Headquarters; saw also 3rd & 4th Field Company R.E. horses in the Brewery there. Very crowded: impossible for horses to lie down. Report sent to A.A. & Q.M.G.	JA.

(73989) W4141—463. 400,000. 9/14. H.&J.Ltd. Forms/C. 2118/10.

Army Form C. 2118.

WAR DIARY
or
INTELLIGENCE SUMMARY.
(Erase heading not required.)

Instructions regarding War Diaries and Intelligence Summaries are contained in F.S. Regs., Part II and the Staff Manual respectively. Title pages will be prepared in manuscript.

Hour, Date, Place	Summary of Events and Information	Remarks and references to Appendices
20th June, 1915: Sunday. Hqrs., 47th (Lon.) Div. NOEUX-les-MINES	Routine Office work. Rode to HOUCHIN, to see horse of 23rd Battalion with Tetanus, which supervened on punctured foot. Lieut. Craig was trying to save the horse by injecting anti-tetanic serum. The horse made no progress & was shot later, having got down & unable to rise. Saw also horses of 19th Battalion. 2 mules & 1 horse examined for casting as useless. Rode on to HESDIGNEUL, Mobile Veterinary Section.	J.
21st June, 1915: Monday. Hqrs., 47th (Lon.) Div. NOEUX-les-MINES	Routine Office work. To DROUVIN, to see sick horses of 47th Div. Am. Col. & also 1st Field Ambulance. All making good progress. Afterwards to VERQUIN, to see horses of Div. Headquarters, & Div. Signal Company. 11 sick & 2 useless horses, & 1 mare with foal at foot were evacuated from Mobile Vety. Section today.	J.
22nd June, 1915: Tuesday. Hqrs. 47th Div. NOEUX-les-MINES	Office work: dealt with correspondence. Rode to VERQUIN, and visited horses of Headquarters, and also Signal Company. Afterwards to HESDIGNEUL, to Mobile Vety. Section: the sick Remounts are doing well, all except one with Congestion of the Lungs.	J.

Army Form C. 2118.

WAR DIARY
of
INTELLIGENCE SUMMARY.
(Erase heading not required.)

Instructions regarding War Diaries and Intelligence Summaries are contained in F.S. Regs., Part II. and the Staff Manual respectively. Title pages will be prepared in manuscript.

Hour, Date, Place	Summary of Events and Information	Remarks and references to Appendices
23rd June, 1915. Wednesday. Headqrs, 47th Div. NOEUX-les-MINES.	Routine Office work: dealt with correspondence. Visited 6th Lond. Field Ambce, & treated sick horses. Rode to VERQUIN, and inspected horses of Div. Headquarters and Signal Company. A number of reports received of cases of digestive trouble through injudicious feeding of green food: also of foot trouble through picked up nails from packing cases. Memo sent to A.A. & Q.M.G. on these subjects, resulting in insertion in Div. Routine Orders of notices regarding them.	J.T.
24th June, 1915. Thursday. Headqrs, 47th Div. NOEUX-les-MINES.	Office work: dealt with correspondence. Visited Div. Headquarters, VERQUIN, and conferred with A.A. & Q.M.G. Rode to HESDIGNEUL, Mobile Veterinary Section, & inspected sick horses: the 8 Remounts are progressing satisfactorily, except the bad pneumonia case, which will die. From thence to 'MONT EVENTÉ' Hqrs. Co. 47th Divn. to meet Lieuts Gosling, Thuilly, Stuart and Edwards. Saw Grey Mare of Hqrs. Coy. with suppurating feet & ordered her destruction. Saw also various cases in the different units, including 5th Lond. Bde. R.F.A. at ALOUAGNE & advised as to their treatment. On this day I continued to see every one of my Veterinary Officers.	J.T.

Army Form C. 2118.

WAR DIARY
or
INTELLIGENCE SUMMARY.
(Erase heading not required.)

Instructions regarding War Diaries and Intelligence Summaries are contained in F.S. Regs., Part II. and the Staff Manual respectively. Title pages will be prepared in manuscript.

Hour, Date, Place	Summary of Events and Information	Remarks and references to Appendices
25th June, 1915: Friday. Hdqrs., 47th Lon. Divn. NOEUX-les-MINES	Routine Office Work; dealt with correspondence. Dety. Officers called bringing weekly reports. Mobile Section evacuated 10 sick horses today. Visited 6th Lond. Field Ambulance at NOEUX-les-MINES; also horses of Divisional Headquarters and Signal Company. Rode to HOUCHIN & DROUVIN, Divn. Am. Col. & Infantry Brigades.	J.N.
26th June, 1915: Saturday. Hdqrs., 47th Lon. Divn. NOEUX-les-MINES	Office work; weekly states weekly report rendered. Rode to Divisional Headquarters Signal Company & all units in NOEUX-les-MINES or immediate vicinity. In afternoon, to Hdqrs., 141st Inf. Bde., at LES-BREBIS. While there, Event of Glanders outbreak among horses of neighbouring French Artillery Brigade. Telegraphic & telephonic messages from Divn. Hq. followed me here. Made preliminary enquiries & reported to AA&QMG.	J.N.
27th June, 1915: Sunday. Hdqrs., 47th Lond. Divn. NOEUX-les-MINES	Office work, correspondence &c. Rode again to LES BREBIS, with Lt. Bryden, re Glanders outbreak. Made fullest enquiries, especially of French V.O. &c., and rendered full reports to A.O. & Q.M.G. & A.D.V.S. 1st Army. Afternoon, to Mobile Vety Section HESDIGNEUL and to BOIS-des-DAMES, to various artillery units quartered there. Saw V.Os, & advised re treatment or evacuation of cases.	J.N.

Army Form C. 2118.

WAR DIARY
or
INTELLIGENCE SUMMARY.
(Erase heading not required.)

Instructions regarding War Diaries and Intelligence Summaries are contained in F.S. Regs., Part II. and the Staff Manual respectively. Title pages will be prepared in manuscript.

Hour, Date, Place	Summary of Events and Information	Remarks and references to Appendices
28th June, 1915. Monday. Hqrs., 47th Lond. Divn. NOEUX-les-MINES.	Routine Office Work; dealt with correspondence. Rode to VERQUIN, to see horses of Divisional Headquarters and Hqrs. of No.1 Section, Signal Company. Thence to HESDIGNEUL Mobile Vety. Section. Inspected all the horses of 21st & 22nd London (Howitzer) Batteries & 6th Lond.(How.) Bde. Am. Column in BOIS-des-DAMES, and advised re treatment of sick cases. Visited A.S.C. at GOSNAY at request of Lt. Thierry to see foot case. Looked up 2/3rd Lond. Fd. Co. R.E. at NOEUX, newly arrived. Saw horses of 6th London Field Ambulance.	J.A.
29th June, 1915. Tuesday. Hqrs. 47th Lond. Divn. NOEUX-les-MINES.	Office work; correspondence &c. Visited units at MAZINGARBE, viz. 2/3rd Lond. Fd. Co. R.E., and 6th Lond. Field Ambulance. Rode to HOUCHIN, DROUVIN & HESDIGNEUL, to see 141st & 142nd Inf. Bde. Transport horses, details of Divn. Am. Col. – Mobile Vety. Section.	J.A.
30th June, 1915. Wednesday. Hqrs. 47th Lond. Divn. NOEUX-les-MINES.	Office work; dealt with correspondence. Rode to VERQUIN, to see D.A.Q.M.G. and D.A.A. & Q.M.G. sd 1d horses of Divl. Headquarters and Signal Company. Afterwards to HESDIGNEUL Mobile Vety. Section; decided to take steps to move the Section back to its former site in HESDIGNEUL. Saw horses of 6th Lond. F. Amb. & 2/3rd Lond. Fd. Co. R.E. in NOEUX. Instructed Lt. Bryden to mallein certain horses of 1/1st Inf. Bde. Hqrs.	J.A.

121/6243

47th Division

ADVS 47th Division.

Vol IV

1-31-4-16

WAR DIARY of A.D.V.S. 47th (Lon) Divn. Army Form C. 2118.

INTELLIGENCE SUMMARY.
(Erase heading not required.)

Hour, Date, Place	Summary of Events and Information	Remarks and references to Appendices
1st July, 1915. Thursday. Hqrs. 47th (Lon.) Divn., NOEUX-LES-MINES.	Routine Office work: dealt with correspondence. Inspected horses of 6th London Field Ambulance and 2/3rd London Field Company, R.E., at NOEUX-LES-MINES. Saw also horses of the 25th (Hants) Fortress Coy. R.E. Rode up to Divl. Hqrs., & inspected horses there; also horses of 47th Divl. Signal Coy. (VERQUIN) Rode on to HOUCHIN & DROUVIN, and saw horses of Divl. Ammn. Column. Visited Mobile Veterinary Section at HESDIGNEUL. Evening, rode to LES BREBIS to ascertain condition of horses tested with Mallein.	[signature]
2nd July 1915. Friday. Hqrs. 47th (Lon.) Divn., NOEUX-LES-MINES.	Routine Office work: dealt with correspondence. Veterinary Officers from Units reported to this Office, bringing with them their weekly sick reports. Visited 25th (Hants) Fortress Coy. R.E. at NOEUX-LES-MINES. Saw also 2/3rd London Field Coy., R.E. Rode to Hqrs. 47th (Lon.) Divn., at VERQUIN, and inspected horses: also horses of 47th Signal Coy. Rode on to HESDIGNEUL to visit Mobile Vety. Section. Interviewed Lt. Bryden, and discussed with him the result of the Mallein testing at LES BREBIS: also visited LES BREBIS, to interview French Vety. Officer there in charge of the French horses, re outbreak of Glanders.	[signature]

WAR DIARY of A.D.V.S. 47th (1st Lon) Divn

Army Form C. 2118.

INTELLIGENCE SUMMARY.

(Erase heading not required.)

Instructions regarding War Diaries and Intelligence Summaries are contained in F.S. Regs., Part II. and the Staff Manual respectively. Title pages will be prepared in manuscript.

Hour, Date, Place	Summary of Events and Information	Remarks and references to Appendices
3rd July, 1915; Saturday. HdQrs. 47th (Lon.) Divn. NOEUX-les-MINES.	Routine work at Office. Visited sick horses of 6th Lond. Fd. Amb. & 2/3rd Lon. Fd. Coy. R.E. at NOEUX-les-MINES. Rode to LES BREBIS, to see sick horses of HqQrs., 141st Inf. Bde, after Mallein test. Afternoon, rode over to HESDIGNEUL, to see Mobile Vety. Section; inspected also 23 H.S. Remounts at GOSNAY.	[sig]
4th July, 1915; Sunday. HdQrs. 47th (Lon.) Divn. NOEUX-les-MINES.	Usual Office Routine. Weekly Report, A.F.A 2000, rendered to 1st Army. Visited 6th Lond. Fd. Ambulance lines, also 2/3rd Lond. Field Coy. R.E., at NOEUX-les-MINES. Rode to HdQrs. 47th Divn. at VERQUIN, and inspected Signal Company horses. Rode on to Mobile Vety. Section at HESDIGNEUL, and saw the A.S.C. horses at GOSNAY.	[sig]
5th July, 1915; Monday. HdQrs. 47th (Lon.) Divn. NOEUX-les-MINES.	Routine office work : dealt with correspondence. Visited 2/3rd Lond. Field Coy. R.E. at NOEUX-les-MINES. Rode down to LES BREBIS to see horses of HqQrs., 141st Infantry Brigade, especially those that had been malleined. On return, again visited 2/3rd Lond. Fd. Coy. R.E.	[sig]

WAR DIARY of A.D.V.S. 47th (Lon) Divn
or
INTELLIGENCE SUMMARY.

Army Form C. 2118.

(Erase heading not required.)

Hour, Date, Place	Summary of Events and Information	Remarks and references to Appendices
6th July, 1915. Tuesday. Hqrs. 47th (Lon.) Divn., NOEUX-les-MINES.	Routine Office Work: dealt with correspondence. Visited 2/3rd Lond. Field Coy. R.E., horse lines at NOEUX-les-MINES: also horses of 6th Lond. Field Ambulance. Rode over to Mobile Vety. Section at HESDIGNEUL, and inspected the horses: rode on to BETHUNE station, to examine batch of remounts (62) on arrival.	JN
7th July, 1915. Wednesday. Hqrs. 47th (Lon.) Divn. NOEUX-les-MINES.	Usual Office Routine. Visited horses of 2/3rd Lon. Fd. Coy. R.E. at NOEUX-les-MINES, and saw also transport horses of 7th & 8th (City of Lond.) Battalions. Visited 6th London Field Ambce.	JN
8th July, 1915. Thursday. Hqrs. 47th (Lon.) Divn., NOEUX-les-MINES.	Routine Office work: dealt with correspondence. Rode to VERQUIN, to see horses of Hqrs. 47th (Lon) Divn., and also of Hqrs. No. 1. Section, 47th Bn. Signal Coy. Rode on to HESDIGNEUL, and inspected 47th Divl. Mobile Vety. Section. Evening, visited horses of 2/3rd Lond. Field Coy. R.E. and 6th London Field Ambce, R.A.M.C.: also of 6th (City of Lond.) Battn. at NOEUX-les-MINES.	JN

Army Form C. 2118.

WAR DIARY of A.D.V.S.
47th (Lon.) Div.
INTELLIGENCE SUMMARY.
(Erase heading not required.)

Instructions regarding War Diaries and Intelligence Summaries are contained in F.S. Regs., Part II and the Staff Manual respectively. Title pages will be prepared in manuscript.

Hour, Date, Place	Summary of Events and Information	Remarks and references to Appendices
9th July, 1915. Friday. HQrs. 47th (Lon.) Div., NOEUX-les-MINES.	Routine Office Work: dealt with correspondence. Interviewed Unit V.O's, who came to bring in weekly returns. Visited 6th Lond. Field Ambulance horses, and 2/3rd London Field Company, R.E. at NOEUX-les-MINES. Rode over to MAZINGARBE, to interview C.R.E. re horses of 47th Divl. R.E., which are crowded in the brewery there.	[signature]
10th July, 1915. Saturday. HQrs. 47th (Lon.) Div., NOEUX-les-MINES.	Usual Office Routine. Inspected horses of 2/3rd London Field Coy. R.E. at NOEUX-les-MINES. Saw also sick horse of 47th Cyclist Company. Rode out to DROUVIN, & inspected heavy horses of Divl. Am. Col.(details). On to BOIS des DAMES, & saw 113th (Heavy) Battery, R.G.A. 2 D.V.S. visited their Headquarters. Saw draught horses of Divl. Train, A.S.C., on the race course at HESDIGNEUL: Some at GOSNAY. Inspected Mobile Veterinary Section, at HESDIGNEUL. In the evening, rode down to MAZINGARBE, to see 47th Div. R.E., and on to LES-BREBIS, horses of HQrs, 141st Infantry Brigade, subjected to Mallein test.	[signature]

Army Form C. 2118.

WAR DIARY of O.B.T.A.
4/1/4(Lon) Divn

INTELLIGENCE SUMMARY.
(Erase heading not required.)

Instructions regarding War Diaries and Intelligence
Summaries are contained in F.S. Regs., Part II.
and the Staff Manual respectively. Title pages
will be prepared in manuscript.

Hour, Date, Place	Summary of Events and Information	Remarks and references to Appendices
11th July, 1915: Sunday. Headqrs., 47th (Lon) Divn, NOEUX-les-MINES.	Routine Office work: weekly A.F. A 2000 rendered to 2 D.V.S., 1st Army. Visited 2/3rd London Field Coy, R.E., at NOEUX-les-MINES. Rode to VERQUIN, and saw horses of Sigs., 47th (Lon) Divn, and also of 47th Signal Company. Rode on to HESDIGNEUL, & inspected Mobile Vety. Section, also horses of Nos. 3 & 4 Train Companies, A.S.C. Rode to LAPUGNOY, and visited injured horses left behind by 17th London Battery, R.F.A. Inspected horses of 19th Battery.	J.R.
12th July, 1915: Monday. Headqrs., 47th (Lon) Divn, NOEUX-les-MINES.	Routine Office work: dealt with correspondence. Visited 2/3rd London Field Coy, R.E. at NOEUX-les-MINES. Saw also horses of 6th Lond. Fd. Ambce, R.A.M.C.	J.R.
13th July, 1915: Tuesday. Headqrs., 47th (Lon) Divn, NOEUX-les-MINES.	Usual Office work. Rode out in morning to meet Lieut. Craig at HOUCHIN. Inspected transport of all units of 142nd Infantry Brigade: saw also all units in DROUVIN WOOD, viz 4th London Field Ambulance, horses of details of 47th Divl. Am. Col., & S.A.A. sections of 5th, 6th & 7th Lond. Bde. Am. Cols. At NOEUX-les-MINES saw horses of 2/3rd Lond. Fd. Coy, R.E., & also 6th Lond. Fd. Ambce. Rode to VERQUIN, & saw sick & injured horses of 47th Divl. Hqrs.	J.R.

Army Form C. 2118.

WAR DIARY of O.T.N.L.
4/7th(Lond) Divn.

or

INTELLIGENCE SUMMARY.

(Erase heading not required.)

Instructions regarding War Diaries and Intelligence
Summaries are contained in F.S. Regs., Part II.
and the Staff Manual respectively. Title pages
will be prepared in manuscript.

Hour, Date, Place	Summary of Events and Information	Remarks and references to Appendices
14th July, 1915. Wednesday. Hqrs 47th (Lon.) Divn. NOEUX-LES-MINES.	Routine Office work. dealt with correspondence. Visited 2/3rd Lond. Field Coy. R.E. at NOEUX-LES-MINES. also 6th London Field Ambulance. Rode over to BOIS-DES-DAMES to inspect lines of Sec. Am. Column and to Haynecourt and Le Brebis to enquire where two Field bombadiers are. Evening rode over to Headquarters to bandage a suspected fracture.	Sd.
15th July, 1915. Thursday. (Hqrs. 47th(Lon) Divn. NOEUX-LES-MINES.	Usual Office routine. Rode over to inspect horses of Sec. Am. Column and from there to HOUCHIN to see brown mare with injured lock. also inspected 47th Divl. Mobile Vety Section.	Sd.
16th July 1915. Friday. Hqrs 47(Lon) Divn NOEUX-LES-MINES.	Routine Office work. dealt with correspondence. Rode over to HOUCHIN and gave a lecture to Farriers; also visited DROUVIN to inspect ground occupied by 6th Lon. Brigade. R.F.A. Forwarded V.O. of Units Brigades in weekly returns A.F. 2000	Sd.

(73989) W4141—463. 400,000. 9/14. H.&J.Ltd. Forms/C. 2118/10.

Army Form C. 2118.

WAR DIARY of A.D.V.S.
4/1st (Nov) Divn
INTELLIGENCE SUMMARY.
(Erase heading not required.)

Instructions regarding War Diaries and Intelligence Summaries are contained in F.S. Regs., Part II. and the Staff Manual respectively. Title pages will be prepared in manuscript.

Hour, Date, Place	Summary of Events and Information	Remarks and references to Appendices
17th July Saturday (Appx 4) 4th Lon Divn NOEUX-LES-MINES	Routine Office work: dealt with correspondence. Visited 6th London Field Ambulance, and 2/3rd. London Field Co. R.E., also inspected sick horses of 12th Lon. Battery R.F.A. and 7th London Am. Column. Rode on to the Mobile Vety Section at HESDIGNEUL and to 4th London Field Ambulance at DROUVIN.	G.
18th July Sunday. Appx 4/Lon Divn NOEUX-LES-MINES	Usual Office routine. Weekly Report A.F. 2000 rendered to 1st Army. Inspected horses of 6th London Field Ambulance and 2/3rd R.E.'s at NOEUX-LES-MINES.	G.
19th July 1915 Monday Appx 4/Lon Divn NOEUX-LES-MINES	Routine work of Office, dealt with correspondence. Gave a lecture and demonstration in farriery for one + half hours, and inspected shoes of each unit. Rode on to Sivil. Mobile Veterinary Section.	G.

Army Form C. 2118.

WAR DIARY of A.D.V.S. 47th London Div.
or
INTELLIGENCE SUMMARY.
(Erase heading not required.)

Instructions regarding War Diaries and Intelligence Summaries are contained in F.S. Regs., Part II. and the Staff Manual respectively. Title pages will be prepared in manuscript.

Hour, Date, Place	Summary of Events and Information	Remarks and references to Appendices
20th July 1915 Tuesday (Hqrs 47th Lon Div) NOEUX-LES-MINES.	Usual Office routine; dealt with correspondence. Visited lines of 2/3rd Field Co R.E. also 6th London Field Ambulance at NOEUX-LES-MINES. Rode on to inspect horses of Hqrs 47 London Divn and No.1 Section Signal Co, at VERQUIN.	[sig]
21st July 1915 Wednesday (Hqrs 47th Lon Div) NOEUX-LES-MINES.	Routine Office work. Inspected lines of 2/3rd Field Co R.E., 7th Bty of London Battn, and 6th Lon Field Ambulance at NOEUX-LES-MINES. Rode on to 14th and 15th London Batteries R.F.A./5 inspected horses, and visited Divn Mobile Vety Section at MESDIGNEUL.	[sig]
22nd July 1915 Thursday (Hqrs 47th Lon Div) NOEUX-LES-MINES.	Usual Office routine. Interviewed Lt Lodwig re Mallein testing. Horses inspected at Rafineur mills and also examined a batch of remounts at FOUQUEREIL. Visited Mobile Veterinary Section.	[sig]

Army Form C. 2118.

WAR DIARY of O.S.N.S. 47 H.(Lon) Divn

or

INTELLIGENCE SUMMARY.

(Erase heading not required.)

Instructions regarding War Diaries and Intelligence Summaries are contained in F.S. Regs., Part II. and the Staff Manual respectively. Title pages will be prepared in manuscript.

Hour, Date, Place	Summary of Events and Information	Remarks and references to Appendices
23rd July 1915. Friday. (HQrs 47th Lon Divn) NEUX les MINES.	Usual Office routine. Dealt with correspondence. Met Lieut. Snyder at VAUDRICOURT and inspected with him lines of transport and HQrs of 141st Infantry Brigade. Visited 25th (Batn) Godless Coy R.E. new lines with Shrapnel wound, also interviewed O.C. of Units bringing in weekly reports.	JR
24th July. Saturday. (HQrs 47th Div) NOEUX les MINES	Visited 2/3rd London Field Co. R.E. 6th Bn London Field Ambulance and 6th B'ty of London lines at NOEUX les MINES. Inspected Divl Mobile Tel Section at HESDIGNEUL.	JR
25th July. Sunday. (HQrs 47th Div) NOEUX les MINES	Office routine work. Rode over to VERGUIN to inspect lines of 47th Divl HQrs and No.1 Section Signal Company. Weekly Return A.F. 2000 rendered to 1st Army.	JR

(73989) W4141—463. 400,000. 9/14. H.&J.Ltd. Forms/C. 2118/10.

WAR DIARY of A.D.V.S. 47th (Lond) Divn

or

INTELLIGENCE SUMMARY.

(Erase heading not required.)

Army Form C. 2118.

Hour, Date, Place	Summary of Events and Information	Remarks and references to Appendices
26th July. Monday. (Hqrs 47th Divn) NOEUX-les-MINES	Office routine work. Dealt with correspondence. Visited 3rd Field Co. R.E. & inspected horses with fracture, also horses of 23rd Field Co. R.E. & 1/1 City of London Battn at NOEUX-les-MINES. Inspected horses of Divl Ammunition Column in DROUVIN wood, and gave a Lecture and Demonstration to Young Farriers.	J.R.
27th July. Tuesday. (Hqrs 47th Divn) NOEUX-les-MINES.	Usual office routine. Inspected horses of Divl Staffs, & No1 Section Signal Co, and visited Mobile Veterinary Section.	J.R.
28th July. Wednesday. (Hqrs 47th Divn) NOEUX-les-MINES.	Office routine work. Visited 2/3rd Field Co. R.E. at NOEUX-les-MINES. Rode over to DROUVIN wood and gave a Lecture in Farriery to Officers and men. Visited 5th Lond. Field Amb. at LABEUVRIERE. Inspected Unit generally and advised.	J.R.

Army Form C. 2118.

WAR DIARY
or
INTELLIGENCE SUMMARY.
(Erase heading not required.)

of A.D.V.S. 47th (London) Divn

Instructions regarding War Diaries and Intelligence Summaries are contained in F.S. Regs., Part II. and the Staff Manual respectively. Title pages will be prepared in manuscript.

Hour, Date, Place	Summary of Events and Information	Remarks and references to Appendices
29th July 1915, Thursday. Hqrs. 47th Divn. NOEUX-les-MINES	Usual office routine; dealt with correspondence. Visited MAZINGARBE to inspect R.A. and R.E. horses. Saw horses gravely injured from shell-fire and ordered three to be destroyed. Seen having already died. In afternoon rode over to Mobile Vety. Section at HESDIGNEUL.	JH
30th July 1915, Friday. (Hdqrs 47th Divn) NOEUX-les-MINES	Office routine work. Interviewed V.Os of Units, bringing in weekly reports. A.F. 2000.	JH
31st July 1915, Saturday. Hqrs 47th Divn NOEUX-les-MINES	Usual office routine. Inspected horses at 2/3rd Field Co. R. Engrs. & 1/4 London Field Amb. at NOEUX-les-MINES.	JH

Jack Moore
Capt A.V.C. (T)
A.D.V.S. 47th (London) Divn.

47th Division

121/6559

A.D.V.S. 47th Division

July

from 1st to 31st August 1915

Army Form C. 2118.

WAR DIARY
or
INTELLIGENCE SUMMARY. [No. 4 F.A.S.
(Erase heading not required.)   of these two.

Instructions regarding War Diaries and Intelligence Summaries are contained in F.S. Regs., Part II. and the Staff Manual respectively. Title pages will be prepared in manuscript.

Hour, Date, Place	Summary of Events and Information	Remarks and references to Appendices
1st August 1915 Sunday (Hqrs of 4 (Lon) Divn) NOEUX-les-MINES	Routine Office work dealt with correspondence. Rode out to MAZINGARBE reconnre. and arrange to arrange for evacuation to Mobile Fd. Section of a number of cases left behind by 4 Lon. Fd. Ambce to R.E. Interviewed several of my P.Ls. at Office & discussed generally.	[signature]
2nd August 1915 Monday (Hqrs of 4 (Lon) Divn) NOEUX-les-MINES	Usual Office routine. Inspected and attended Losses at 2nd Hdqrs. interviewed A. & Q.M.G. Inspected 6 Reg.t Lines at NOEUX-les-MINES, also Lines of N° 4 Cav. A.S.C. at FOUQUEREUIL with had been look pint and ordered removal.	[signature]
3rd August 1915 Tuesday (Hqrs of 4 (Lon) Divn) NOEUX-les-MINES	Office routine as usual. Visited G.R. & 1st Lord. & inspected several horses at Divl. Hqrs, and N°1 Signal Co. Rode on to Mobile Vet. Section, & advised upon all cases there, and then on to Aud. Am. column at BROWN WOOD re 3 cases for evacuation.	[signature]

Army Form C. 2118.

WAR DIARY
OF
INTELLIGENCE SUMMARY. of A.V.S. 47th (Lon) Div.

(Erase heading not required.)

Instructions regarding War Diaries and Intelligence Summaries are contained in F.S. Regs., Part II. and the Staff Manual respectively. Title pages will be prepared in manuscript.

Hour, Date, Place	Summary of Events and Information	Remarks and references to Appendices
4th August 1915 Wednesday (Hqrs 47th(Lon)Div)	5.15 a.m. rode to FOUQUEREUIL station to inspect batch of Remounts 30 in number. Moved with Headquarters to GOSNAY; visited Mobile section, also there, advising upon all cases. Halt with remounts arranged at place of leaving when everything was arranged in order of new quarters.	E.25.A. maps of Bethune embraces sheets 36.S.E. 36.S.W. 36.N.E. 36.N.W.
5th August 1915 Thursday (Hqrs 47th(Lon)Div) GOSNAY.	Usual Office routine dealt with correspondence. Visited Mobile Section. Rode over to No 1 Sub Sec. and 5th, 6th, & 7th London Brigades R.F.A., instructed and advised upon all matters conducive to the health of all horses concerned.	
6th August 1915 Friday (Hqrs 47th(Lon)Div) GOSNAY.	Office routine as usual. Rode over to 7th Bde R.F.A. & 47th Sub. Sec. and to Mobile Section. Interviewed my V.O. Officers, conversing with them the weekly reports, and discussed several questions.	

WAR DIARY
or
INTELLIGENCE SUMMARY
(Erase heading not required.)

Army Form C. 2118.

of H.D.V.S. 47th (Lon) Divn.

Hour, Date, Place	Summary of Events and Information	Remarks and references to Appendices
7th August 1915 Saturday Hdqrs 47th(Lon) Divn GOSNAY	General Office routine. Dealt with correspondence. Rode over to BOIS-DES-DAMES and lectured to twenty men and a similar number of Officers on shoeing and the care of the foot. 14 horses. 1 mule + 1 mule must evacuated to base. Interviewed D.D.V.S. here. Inspected several horses of squadron unit.	G.
8th August 1915 Sunday Hdqrs 47th(Lon) Divn GOSNAY	Office Routine as usual. Visited Mobile Section and horses of 2nd Kings + No. 1 Squad 60, also lines of King Edwards Horse. Interviewed several of my V.Os upon various subjects. Visited VAUDRICOURT to inspect sick case Offr attend by 6th London Battalion.	G.
9th August 1915 Monday Hdqrs 47th(Lon) Divn GOSNAY	Visited Mobile Section, toured upon all cases. Usual Office Routine, and engaged most of day in squaring office matters up generally.	G.

Army Form C. 2118.

WAR DIARY
or
INTELLIGENCE SUMMARY. 1. S. Y. L. 47th (Lon) Div.

(Erase heading not required.)

Instructions regarding War Diaries and Intelligence Summaries are contained in F.S. Regs., Part II. and the Staff Manual respectively. Title pages will be prepared in manuscript.

Hour, Date, Place	Summary of Events and Information	Remarks and references to Appendices
10th August 1915. Tuesday (Hdqrs 4th (Lon) Div) GOSNAY	Usual Office Routine, attended to correspondence. Delivered a lecture on Farriery at the Electric works GOSNAY, interviewed the D.D.V.S. Lent, and visited Mobile Section. Rode over to NOEUX-LES-MINES in evening to investigate death of horse at Hdqrs. C.R.E.	J.L.
11th August 1915. Wednesday (Hdqrs 47th (Lon) Div) GOSNAY	Office routine work as usual. Visited 6th London Bde. R.F.A. to inspect four Horses with a view to casting, also saw horses of 17th, 18th, 19th Batteries R.F.A. Mobile Vety Section.	J.L.
12th August 1915. Thursday (Hdqrs 47th (Lon) Div) GOSNAY	Usual Office Routine. Visited Mobile Section. Rode over to MARLES-LES-MINES and AUCHAGNE to inspect horses of Sup. Train and 6th Field Ambulance and to LAPUGNOY to see horses of 5th London Field Amb. also inspecting units of 140th Infantry Brigade at LABOURERE.	J.L.

Army Form C. 2118.

WAR DIARY
or
INTELLIGENCE SUMMARY. of A.D.S.S. 47 H(for) Divn.
(Erase heading not required.)

Instructions regarding War Diaries and Intelligence Summaries are contained in F.S. Regs., Part II. and the Staff Manual respectively. Title pages will be prepared in manuscript.

Hour, Date, Place	Summary of Events and Information	Remarks and references to Appendices
12th August 1915 continued	Interviewed several of my T.O.'s at Office with regard to numerous losses. Inspected Horses of Divl. Hdqrs & Signal Coy and Mobile Section. Rode over to NOEUX-LES-MINES in evening to see mess at 2/3rd Co. R. Engineers.	J.M.
13th August 1915 Friday Hdqrs 47th(London)Divn. GOSNAY	Usual Office Routine. Visited Mobile Section, 5th, 6th, 7th bdes R.F.A. & Howitzer bde R.G.A. & Divl. Train, & inspected all horses, & advised thereon. Interviewed my T.O's hanging in their weekly sick returns & discussing all matters connected therewith	J.M.
14th August Saturday Hdqrs 47th(London)Divn. GOSNAY	Office routine work dealt with correspondence. Mobile Section. In evening visited lines at Hdqrs and Signal Co. & lines of 6th bde R.F.A. to give opinion & advice upon all cases. Twenty-six sick horses evacuated to base.	J.M.

Army Form C. 2118.

WAR DIARY
or
INTELLIGENCE SUMMARY. of A.D.V.S. 47th (Lon) Divn.

(Erase heading not required.)

Instructions regarding War Diaries and Intelligence Summaries are contained in F. S. Regs., Part II. and the Staff Manual respectively. Title pages will be prepared in manuscript.

Hour, Date, Place	Summary of Events and Information	Remarks and references to Appendices
15th August 1915 Sunday. Hqrs 47th Lon Divn. GOSNAY.	Proceeded to England on leave for seven days, after dealing with correspondence and all business in hand. Duties carried out by LIEUT. J. SOUTHALL, Offr. commanding true Mobile Veterinary Section. Mule sent to D.D.V.S. 1st Army notifying departure.	W
16th August 1915 Monday. Hqrs 47th Lon Divn. GOSNAY	Usual Office Routine: attended to correspondence. Supervised and directed operations at Mobile Section incurred losses of Fin. Yeomany Squadron (Fife & Forfar Yeo.) advising upon all cases there, advised removal to Section of mule suffering from Skin Disease. Rode on to 2nd. Cyclist Bn. in BOIS DES DAMES & saw all horses there.	J.S.
17th August 1915 Tuesday. Hqrs 47th Lon Divn. GOSNAY	Office Routine work. Remainder of day spent at Mobile Section, many cases requiring attention there.	J.S.

WAR DIARY or INTELLIGENCE SUMMARY of 4 A.D.S. 47th (Lon) Divn.

Army Form C. 2118

Place	Date	Hour	Summary of Events and Information	Remarks and references to Appendices
GOSNAY	18th August 1915 Wednesday (Hdqrs 47th Lon Divn)		Routine Office work. Dealt with correspondence. Inspected horses of Divl Headquarters & Signal Co. + Divl Cyclist Co. Mobile Section. Rode over to 47th Divl Ammunition Column, made thorough inspection of all horses, & sent three to Mobile Section for next evacuation. In evening rode over to MARLES-LES-MINES to 6th Field Ambulance and on to LAPUGNOY. Saw all horses of Divl Train.	[signature]
GOSNAY	19th August 1915 Thursday (Hdqrs 47th Lon Divn)		Usual Office work. Spent morning at Mobile Section. Rode over to HOUCHIN and inspected horses of 6th & 7th London Battalions Transports.	[signature]
GOSNAY	20th August 1915 Friday (Hdqrs 47th Lon Divn)		Dealt with correspondence at Office. Received Weekly Reports, A.2000 from all Vety Officers, discussing all points regarding horses of Divn under their care. Wire received from D.D.V.S. 1st Army, stating would call next morning to interview Lee-Boyd, attached to Infantry Brigades. Lee-Boyd, summoned to His Office accordingly	[signature]

Army Form C. 2118

WAR DIARY
or
INTELLIGENCE SUMMARY
(Erase heading not required.)

J. A.D.V.S.
47th (Lon) Divn.

Instructions regarding War Diaries and Intelligence Summaries are contained in F.S. Regs., Part II. and the Staff Manual respectively. Title Pages will be prepared in manuscript.

Place	Date	Hour	Summary of Events and Information	Remarks and references to Appendices
(Hqrs 47th(Lon)Divn) GOSNAY	21st August 1915 Saturday		Routine Office work. D.D.V.S. interviewed Lce.Cpl. as arranged, with a view to promotion, not favourably impressed. Report received that Lieut. Thierry admitted sick to hospital: Lieut Dawson instructed to render every assistance to his Units. Weekly Sick Returns rendered to D.D.V.S. 1st Army.	
(Hqrs 47th(Lon)Divn) GOSNAY	22nd August 1915 Sunday		Dealt with correspondence at Office. Mobile Section. Inspected horses of Hdqrs & Signal Co, & King Edwards Horse(Divl Cav) Squadron) and all cases at 6th London Bde R.F.A.	
(Hqrs 47th(Lon)Divn) GOSNAY	23rd August 1915 Monday		Usual Office Routine. Instructions given for issuing of Smoke Helmets for Horses to all Units of Divn. Mobile Section. Wire received at 10.30 p.m. to receive batch of Remounts at FOUQUEREUIL Station at 5 a.m. Tuesday 24.8.15.	

Army Form C. 2118

WAR DIARY
or
INTELLIGENCE SUMMARY of A.D.V.S. of 47th (Lon) Div.

(Erase heading not required.)

Place	Date	Hour	Summary of Events and Information	Remarks and references to Appendices
GOSNAY	24th August—Tuesday (HQrs 47th Lon Div)		Inspected and allotted 32 Remounts at FOUQUEREUIL, all passed examination. Arrival of A.V.H.S. one day extension, owing to BOULOGNE Harbour being closed, and no leave boats or trains running. Attended to Office work, + dealt with all correspondence. Visited Mobile Section. Rode over to NOEUX-LES-MINES and LABOURSE, and inspected all horses of 3rd, 4th, + 2/3rd Field Co R.Es: and all Transport lines of their Infantry Brigade at HOUCHIN.	J.V.
GOSNAY	25th August—Wednesday (HQrs 47th Lon Div)		Office routine work. Visited + inspected all horses of Divl. Am. Col. at LAPUGNOY, + Divl. Train in BOIS-DES-DAMES, and 7th Bde. R.F.A. at LOZINGHAM generally advising upon all. Mobile Section. Wire from Major "V.V. of 47 Div. to be sent to 1st Divn. to temporarily take charge of Mobile Vet. Section	J.V.
GOSNAY	26th August—Thursday (HQrs 47th Lon Div)		Usual Office Routine. Interviewed Lt. EDWARDS, + instructed him to proceed to 1st Division. Rode over to HOUCHIN to inspect horses of 140th Inf. Bde. + to NOEUX-LES-MINES to enable me to report upon loss of 2/3rd R.Es. for casting. Interviewed Gen. BARTER at Divl. Headquarters.	J.V.

Army Form C. 2118

WAR DIARY
or
INTELLIGENCE SUMMARY

of A.D.V.S.
47th Lon. Divn.

(Erase heading not required.)

Instructions regarding War Diaries and Intelligence Summaries are contained in F.S. Regs., Part II. and the Staff Manual respectively. Title Pages will be prepared in manuscript.

Place	Date	Hour	Summary of Events and Information	Remarks and references to Appendices
GOSNAY (Hqrs 47th Lon Div)	27th August 1915 Friday		Routine Office work: dealt with correspondence. Visited Mobile Section & arranged for evacuation of 33 horses to base. Received weekly sick return from Vety. Officers, discussing all questions arising. Inspected sick horses of 7th Bde R.F.A. at MARLES-LES-MINES and 8th Howitzer Bde R.F.A. at MONTE-EVENTE and 4 companies of Divl. Train at LAPUGNOY, also some generally upon every call.	A.
GOSNAY (Hqrs 47th Lon Divn)	28th August 1915 Saturday		Usual Office Routine. Visited Mobile Section. Rode over to HOUCHIN and lectured to Farriers of 140th and 141st Inf. Bdes, at the same time holding a practical Demonstration. In evening examined all horses of Divl. Yeomanry Squadron (K.E.H.) and 6th Lond. Bde R.F.A.	A.
GOSNAY (Hqrs 47th Lon Div)	29th August 1915 Sunday		Routine office work, & Mobile Section. Tested 15th Battery R.F.A. locating several cases, & ordered evacuation of two to Mobile Section. Met O.C. Mobile Section at K.E.H. in BOIS·DES·DAMES & consulted him re a bowel case there. Inspected several horses of Divl. Am. Col. by request of D.A.Q.M.G. & reported thereon.	A.

Army Form C. 2118

WAR DIARY
or
INTELLIGENCE SUMMARY of A.D.M.S. 47th (Lon) Div.
(Erase heading not required.)

Instructions regarding War Diaries and Intelligence Summaries are contained in F. S. Regs., Part II. and the Staff Manual respectively. Title Pages will be prepared in manuscript.

Place	Date	Hour	Summary of Events and Information	Remarks and references to Appendices
GOSNAY	30th August 1915 Monday (1st 47th (Lon) Div.)		Routine Office work: dealt with correspondence. Visited Mobile Section, and Divl. Yeomany Squadron with LIEUT SOUTHALL A.V.C.(T) re a bowel case. Proceeded to lines of Divl. Am. Col. conferring with LIEUT. STUART. A.V.C.(T) upon several feet cases, & inspected horses for evacuation to Mobile Section. Visited 7th Bde R.F.A. & conferred with LT. GOSLING. A.V.C.(T) upon several bad feet cases in that Bde. Inspected all horses of 5th Bde R.F.A at MARLES-LES-MINES, 7th Howitzer Bde at MONTEVANTE, and 4th Bde 47th Divl Train at LAPUGNOY, arranging for evacuation of several horses, and advising upon all. A.D.V.S. 1st Army called this day, I was absent.	[signature]
GOSNAY	31st August 1915 Tuesday (1st 47th (Lon) Div.)		Usual routine Office work. Mobile Section. Inspected horses of Amm.Col. 6th Bde R.F.A and lines of Divl. Yeo.y Sq. (K.E.H.) in BOIS DES DAMES. Visited LABOUSIERE arranging for site for Mobile Vety. Section to occupy. Rode over to NOEUX-LES-MINES to advise upon several cases in lines of 2/3rd & 4th London Field Companies. R.E.	[signature]

[signature]
Capt. A.V.C. (T)

[Stamp: A.D.V.S. 31 AUG 1915 47 LONDON DIVISION]

121/6950

47th Division

A.D.V.S. 47th Division

Vol VII

Sept. 15

WAR DIARY or INTELLIGENCE SUMMARY

of A.D.V.S. 47th Lon. Division.

Army Form C. 2118

Place	Date	Hour	Summary of Events and Information	Remarks and references to Appendices
	1st September 1915 Wednesday		Routine Office work, dealt with correspondence. Visited 3 Batteries Ammn. Column of 6th London Bde. R.F.A.; Treated several cases, and arranged for horses unable to "rope" none with Bde.	
Hqrs. 47 Lon Divn. GOSNAY.			Visited Mobile Section prior to moving & inspected all horses prior to evacuation to Base. Mobile Section moved from "GOSNAY" to LABUISSIERE £.10 D.g.F. Made inspection of all horses of Headquarters and Signal Coy.	J.A.
	2nd September 1915 Thursday		Usual Office Routine. Inspected three horses left behind by 6th Bde. R.F.A. at GOSNAY, & horses left by 7th Houtber Bde. at MONTE-EVANTE, and two horses left at LOZINGHEM by 7th Lon.	
Hqrs 47(Lon) Divn. GOSNAY.			Bde. R.F.A, and made the necessary arrangements for removal of all. Ordered destruction of 1 Black gelding at D.J.L lines in BOIS-DES-DAMES. Visited all Transport Lines of 140th Inft. and two Company Dispodes at	J.A.
			Route on to Mobile Section at new Station.	
HOUCHIN				
	3rd September 1915 Friday		Attended to correspondence at Office. Arranged for 3 horses of 6th Lon. Bde. R.F.A, to be sent to Mobile Section.	
Hqrs. 47 Lon Divn.			Mobile Office with Headquarters to DROUVIN, and interviewed V.Os there bringing their weekly sick reports.	J.A.

Army Form C. 2118

WAR DIARY
or
INTELLIGENCE SUMMARY of A.D.V.S. 47th (Lond) Divn.
(Erase heading not required.)

Instructions regarding War Diaries and Intelligence Summaries are contained in F.S. Regs., Part II. and the Staff Manual respectively. Title Pages will be prepared in manuscript.

Place	Date	Hour	Summary of Events and Information	Remarks and references to Appendices
Hqrs. 47th Lon Divn. DROUVIN.	4th September 1915 Saturday		Usual Office Routine. Dealt with correspondence. Made inspection of all horses of 6th & 7th London Bdes. R.F.A. and advised upon all points as to the possible improvements in methods of feeding and to all matters conducive to the general efficiency of the animals. Attended conference of A.D.V.Ss at ESTAIRE by request of D.D.V.S. 1st Army.	J.R.
Hqrs. 47th Lon Divn. DROUVIN.	5th September 1915 Sunday		Office routine work. Rode over to HOUCHIN to see horses of 1st/1st and 1st/2nd Inf. Bdes, and advised re evacuation of these. Inspected horses of Divnl. Hdqrs & Signal Section, LABOUVRIERE.	J.R.
Hqrs. 47th Lon Divn. DROUVIN.	6th September 1915 Monday		Dealt with all business at Office. Conferred with A.D.M.S. at Divnl. Hdqrs. inspected Horses of Signal Coy. and sent two to Mobile Section for evacuation. Rode on to lines of 8th Howitzer Bde 5th & 6th Lccs R.F.A. and Divl. Ammn. Column all in and surrounding DROUVIN WOOD arranging many things in connection therewith. Called at Mobile Section.	J.R.

Army Form C. 2118.

WAR DIARY
or
INTELLIGENCE SUMMARY of A.D.V.S. 47th London Division

(Erase heading not required.)

Instructions regarding War Diaries and Intelligence Summaries are contained in F. S. Regs., Part II. and the Staff Manual respectively. Title pages will be prepared in manuscript.

Place	Date	Hour	Summary of Events and Information	Remarks and references to Appendices
	7th September 1915 Tuesday		Correspondence to deal with as usual. Held conference at office with all my V.Os. as to their duties during active operations in near future, discussing all questions arising as to the methods to be used to carry out everything as smoothly as possible and to the best advantage.	JM
Hdqrs. 47th London Divn. DROUVIN			Rode over to HOUCHIN to see horses of 140th + 141st Inf. Bde. Transport and advised upon many cases with V.Os. Inspected limbs of Divl. Ammn. Column, + arranged for removal of doubtful cases to Mobile Section.	
	8th September 1915 Wednesday		Routine Office work. Call from D.D.V.S. 1st Army, who accompanied him to fire V.O.s of units whom he interviewed. Inspected all horses at Mobile Section, + arranged for evacuation of several to Base. Visited Divl. Train and rendered advice upon several cases of foot lameness.	JM
Hdqrs. 47th Ldn. Divn. DROUVIN.				
	9th September 1915 Thursday		Usual Office Routine. Inspected all horses of Headquarters + Spinal Coo at DROUVIN CHATEAU. Rode on to Mobile Section, met the V.O. of 6th London Bde. F.A. & confer upon his cases, made thorough inspection of all horses of Divl. Ammn. Column and 5th Lon. R.A. R. in DROUVIN WOOD.	JM
Hdqrs. 47th Ldn. Divn. DROUVIN.				

2353 Wt. W2544/1454 700,000 5/15 D. D. & L. A.D.S.S./Forms/C. 2118.

Army Form C. 2118.

WAR DIARY
AT
INTELLIGENCE SUMMARY of A.D.V.S. 47th London Division

(Erase heading not required.)

Instructions regarding War Diaries and Intelligence Summaries are contained in F. S. Regs., Part II. and the Staff Manual respectively. Title pages will be prepared in manuscript.

Place	Date	Hour	Summary of Events and Information	Remarks and references to Appendices
Hdqrs. 47th Lon. Divn. DROUVIN.	10th September 1915 Friday		Usual Office work; dealt with correspondence. Call from D.D.V.S. 1st Army, informed upon several questions of importance relating to the courses to be taken during the anticipated active operations of the Division. Proceeded to Mobile Section with D.V.S. with a view to inter view with a view to filling vacancies for Sergeant and Infantry Supplies. In afternoon rode over to Canadian Heavy Battery, Engrd. Coys and Adors Royal Engineers, all in the vicinity of DROUVIN.	SA
Hdqrs. 47th Lon. Divn. DROUVIN	11th September 1915 Saturday		Routine work at Office. Made a general call upon 7th Bde. R.F.A, 2nd Lon. Column, 5th Bde. R.F.A. and interviewed Lt. MAC. BRIDE A.V.C. in charge of 7th Bde. R.F.A., attached to 47th Division. Instructed and advised upon all questions. Rode over to Mobile Section in evening, and arranged matters there. All weekly Returns and statements rendered to D.D.V.S. 1st Army.	for

Army Form C. 2118.

WAR DIARY
INTELLIGENCE SUMMARY of A.D.V.S. 47th (Lon.) Divn.

(Erase heading not required.)

Instructions regarding War Diaries and Intelligence Summaries are contained in F. S. Regs., Part II. and the Staff Manual respectively. Title pages will be prepared in manuscript.

Place	Date	Hour	Summary of Events and Information	Remarks and references to Appendices
Hqrs 47th (Lon) Divn DROUVIN	12th September 1915 Sunday		Usual Office Routine: dealt with correspondence. Visited Headquarters R.E's and Signal Co at DROUVIN CHATEAU. Rode over to MAZINGARBE and NOEUX-LES-MINES and made thorough inspection of all horses of 3rd & 4th Field Ambulances R.E's. Remainder of day spent at Office in clearing matters up.	JM
Hqrs 47th (Lon) Divn DROUVIN	13th September 1915 Monday		Work at Office. Inspected Horses of Pool Hqrs, Signal Coys & R.E., in grounds of DROUVIN CHATEAU, 4 & 8th Heavy Battery, 7th Bde Royal Horse Artillery, attached to 47th Division, Divl Am Column, & 5th Bde R.F.A. in DROUVIN WOOD.	JM
Hqrs 47th (Lon) Divn DROUVIN	14th September 1915 Tuesday		Usual Routine Office work. Kept appointment with V.Ds of 14th & 9 (4)15th Inf. Bdes at HOUCHIN to advise upon several horses. Afternoon rode over to Veterinaries at BETHUNE to enquire as to the best places obtainable for sick and shot horses.	JM

2353 Wt. W2544/1454 700,000 5/15 D. D. & L. A.D.S.S./Forms/C. 2118.

Army Form C. 2118.

WAR DIARY
or
INTELLIGENCE SUMMARY of A.V.S. 47th Division.
(Erase heading not required.)

Instructions regarding War Diaries and Intelligence Summaries are contained in F. S. Regs., Part II. and the Staff Manual respectively. Title pages will be prepared in manuscript.

Place	Date	Hour	Summary of Events and Information	Remarks and references to Appendices
Hqrs. 47th (1st.) Divn. DROUVIN.	15th September 1915. Wednesday.		Dealt with correspondence, & work at Office. Rode over to HOUCHIN to investigate suspected outbreak of ANTHRAX in cows, which died in a field near where our Troops are billeted. Necessary measures taken. Rode on to Mobile Section, visited & inspected horses of 7th Bde. R.F.A. Divl. Ammn. Col., 1st L.d. Squadron, Divl. Train, all these units being in the surrounding neighbourhood of of DROUVIN.	Sgd
Hqrs. 47th (2nd) Divn. DROUVIN.	16th September 1915 Thursday.		Office work. Interviewed R.A. at A.M.G. at Allouagne instructions to V.O. in event of action and other matters. Inspected horses at Allouagne — Signal Coy., Canadian Heavy Battery, and 1st Heavy Battery in DROUVIN WOOD. Rode on to HOUCHIN and saw horses of 8th Batty. of London Divl. Transport	Sgd

2353 Wt. W2544/1454 700,000 5/15 D. D. & L. A.D.S.S./Forms/C. 2118.

Army Form C. 2118

WAR DIARY
or
INTELLIGENCE SUMMARY. of A.D.V.S. 47th Division

(Erase heading not required.)

Instructions regarding War Diaries and Intelligence Summaries are contained in F. S. Regs., Part II. and the Staff Manual respectively. Title pages will be prepared in manuscript.

Place	Date	Hour	Summary of Events and Information	Remarks and references to Appendices
	17th September 1915 Morning.		Office routine work. Dealt with correspondence. Conferred with O.C. M.V.S. upon recommendations for reward for services rendered.	JN
DROUVIN.	Augs. 47th Div. Div.		Rode over to NOEUX-LES-MINES to report upon suitability of blacksmiths at LES-BREVIS to report Horses of Mountain Gun Section. In afternoon interviewed my V.Os. bringing in their weekly sick Returns.	
	18th September 1915 Saturday.		Office work to attend to. Visited all horses of Hdqrs, Signal Coy, Canadian + Heavy Batteries, and R.A.B, + A, B.+ C. of 4th Bde. R.F.A. making general survey of all noses, and the conditions, and feed of the animals, Mobile Section.	JN
DROUVIN.	Augs. 47th Div. Div.			
	19th September 1915 Sunday.		Dealt with work + correspondence at Office. Visited 5th Bde. R.F.A. + conferred with LIEUT. GOSLING A.V.C. upon cases of his and with LIEUT. EDWARDS at 8th Bde R.F.A. upon the horses under his charge. Arrived at FOUQUEREUIL at 4.30 p.m. with D.A.A.G. M.S. to inspect and indicate a batch of 52 Remounts, Examination showing all to be sound. In evening wrote on to Dral. Anim. Column, to give attention to Loose Hear.	JN
DROUVIN.	Augs. 47th Div. Div.			

2353 Wt. W2544/1454 700,000 5/15 D.D.&L. A.D.S.S./Forms/C. 2118.

WAR DIARY
INTELLIGENCE SUMMARY of A.D.M.S. of 7th Division

Army Form C. 2118

Place	Date	Hour	Summary of Events and Information	Remarks and references to Appendices
	20th September 1915 Monday		Attended to Office work and Correspondence. Rode over to HOUCHIN and inspected all Transport horses of 1400 & 1457 Indian Infantry Bdes. Rest of day with O.C. M.V.S.Coln. attending and arranging for the opening of an advanced Dressing & Collecting Station.	JR
Hqrs. 47th (London) Div. DROUVIN				
	21st September 1915 Tuesday		Routine Office work. Interviewed A.H. & G.M.L.O with reference to vacation in Genl. Routine Orders re legging of horses. Called upon 4th Heavy Battery. 9th Bde. R.F.A. S.A.A. supply Coln. etc. Dressing Station opened at NOEUX-LES-MINES, and attached to the O.C. the N.C.O. and 3 men. Rode over to 14th Field Ambulance at NOEUX-LES-MINES to enquire upon horse water by the Clapsham.	JR
Hqrs. 47th (London) Div. DROUVIN				
	22nd September 1915 Wednesday		Office work. Distributed position of Dressing Station to all P.M.O's of the Drouvin & funny outline of action to be taken. Visited Dressing Station and rode on to LES-BREVIS to select site of ground for a further advanced Dressing and Collecting Station. Saw all horses of 6th & 21st Battalions Transport at HOUCHIN.	JR
Hqrs. 47th (London) Div. DROUVIN				

Army Form C. 2118.

WAR DIARY
or
INTELLIGENCE SUMMARY of A.D.V.S. 47th (Lon) Division.
(Erase heading not required.)

Instructions regarding War Diaries and Intelligence Summaries are contained in F. S. Regs., Part II. and the Staff Manual respectively. Title pages will be prepared in manuscript.

Place	Date	Hour	Summary of Events and Information	Remarks and references to Appendices
	23rd September 1915		Routine Office work: dealt with correspondence.	
	Thursday		Visited Mobile Section at LABUSSIERE, 7th Bde. R.F.A. in DROUVIN WOOD	
Hqrs 47th (Lon) Divn.			Hqrs Signal Coy 47th Divn, inspecting all cases.	
DROUVIN			Met LIEUT. GOSLING, R.V.C. cart with him made inspection of whole of 1084 Bde. R.F.A. now attached to 47th Division, found horses in rather poor condition, sent several to Mobile Section for evacuation.	J.R.
	24th September 1915		Office work as usual.	
	Friday		Visited Advanced Collecting Station, 23rd & 4th Field A.R.E at NOEUX LES	
Hqrs 47th (Lon) Divn.			MINES. active operations having commenced, a great number of cases are being	
DROUVIN CHATEAU			received and evacuated.	
			Afternoon interviewed V.Os bringing in their weekly sick returns.	J.R.
	25th September 1915		Attended to correspondence at Office, & rode over to Advanced Dressing Station.	
	Saturday		Owing to rapid advance and success of Reinforcement orders received to move	
Hqrs 47th (Lon) Divn.			forward to NOEUX LES MINES, at once.	
			Instructions issued to O.C. MOBILE SECTION to open the further advanced Dressing Station at L.E.S. BREVIS on 11th nearly eleven.	J.R.

A.D.S.S./Forms/C. 2118.
2353 Wt. W5544/1454 700,000 5/15 D. D. & L.

WAR DIARY
or
INTELLIGENCE SUMMARY of A.D.M.S. 47 (Lon) Division

Army Form C. 2118

(Erase heading not required.)

Place	Date	Hour	Summary of Events and Information	Remarks and references to Appendices
	26th September 1915 Sunday. A.D.M.S. 47 (Lon) Div.		Correspondence at Office. Rode down to Advanced Dressing Station, and on to Mobile Section at LABUISSIERE, arranging for the opening of the further Advanced Dressing Station at LES BREBIS. Same duly opened in afternoon, and all concerned acquainted of position.	JR
NOEUX-LES-MINES				
	27th September 1915 Monday. A.D.M.S. 47 (Lon) Div.		Usual Office Routine. Mobile Section move to DROUVIN. Visited Dressing Stations at NOEUX-LES-MINES, and LES BREBIS, and inspected all Lorries & of Divl. Train and 6th Bde. R.F.A.	JR
NOEUX-LES-MINES				
	27th September 1915 Tuesday. A.D.M.S. 47 (Lon) Div.		Routine Office work. Rode down to Dressing Station, and on to Mobile Section at DROUVIN and 6th Bde. R.F.A at HALLICOURT, inspecting all horses, also of 4th Field Ambce. Superintended evacuation of Lorries. Mobile Section again move to NOEUX-LES-MINES, to same spot as Dressing Station.	JR
NOEUX-LES-MINES				

Army Form C. 2118.

WAR DIARY
or
INTELLIGENCE SUMMARY. of A.D.V.S. 47th (Lon) Division.
(Erase heading not required.)

Instructions regarding War Diaries and Intelligence Summaries are contained in F. S. Regs., Part II. and the Staff Manual respectively. Title pages will be prepared in manuscript.

Place	Date	Hour	Summary of Events and Information	Remarks and references to Appendices
	29th September 1915. Wednesday.		Office work, and correspondence attended to.	
Hdqrs. 47th (Lon) Divn.			Visited Mobile Section, and advanced Station at LES·BREVIS. Weather recently extremely wet and cold, which greatly increases the casualties amongst the animals owing to bad standings.	J.H.
NOEUX·LES·MINES			Rode over to FOUQUEREUIL to receive batch of remounts 70 in number as it was too late to allot them sent to Dud Train and D.A.C.	
	30th September 1915. Thursday.		Routine Office work.	
Hdqrs. 47th (Lon) Divn.			Visited Mobile Section, and Advanced Dressing Station at LES·BREVIS Division move back this Office to the CHATEAU·GOSNAY, and MOBILE SECTION	J.H.
			to HESDIGNEUL.	
NOEUX·LES·MINES.			Above Remounts examined, and allotted to Units.	

Joseph Hand
MAJOR. A.V.C.(T
A.D.V.S. 47th (London) Division.

2353 Wt. W2544/1454 700,000 5/15 D. D. & L. A.D.S.S./Forms/C. 2118.

121/7333

47th Division

ADVS. 47th Division
War Vet
Oct 15

Army Form C. 2118

WAR DIARY
or
INTELLIGENCE SUMMARY of A.D.V.S. 47th London Division.
(Erase heading not required.)

Instructions regarding War Diaries and Intelligence Summaries are contained in F.S. Regs., Part II. and the Staff Manual respectively. Title Pages will be prepared in manuscript.

Place	Date	Hour	Summary of Events and Information	Remarks and references to Appendices
Hqrs. 47th Lon Divn. NOEUX-LES-MINES.	1st October 1915. Friday		Office routine work: dealt with correspondence. Office moved from NOEUX LES MINES to the CHATEAU GOSNAY. Interviewed Veterinary Officers bringing in their weekly sick returns. In afternoon rode over to BETHUNE Station to receive batch of remounts. 79 arrived too late to distribute and were sent to lines of D.A.C. and Fuel Train.	JR
Hqrs. 47th Lon Dyn. GOSNAY	2nd October 1915. Saturday		Visited Mobile Section, and instructed O.C. to move from NOEUX LES MINES. Usual Office routine. Rode over to D.A.C. and Divisional Train, examined and allotted remounts to Units. Visited Mobile Section at HESDIGNEUL. Remainder of day spent in clearing up affairs at office.	JR
Hqrs. 47th Lon Dyn. GOSNAY	3rd October 1915. Sunday		Attended to correspondence at office. Rode over to HARICOURT to inspect horses of 5th and 6th London Brigades R.F.A. Visited Mobile Section, Lodgrs, and Signal Co.	JR

Army Form C. 2118

WAR DIARY
or
INTELLIGENCE SUMMARY
of A.D.V.S. 47" (London) Division

(Erase heading not required.)

Instructions regarding War Diaries and Intelligence Summaries are contained in F. S. Regs., Part II. and the Staff Manual respectively. Title pages will be prepared in manuscript.

Place	Date	Hour	Summary of Events and Information	Remarks and references to Appendices
Hospital 7th Mob. Div. GOSNAY	Oct. 4th 1915. Monday.		Office Routine work, dealt with correspondence. Rode over to LABOUVRIERE, and consulted with LT.EDWARDS, whom outbreak of disease amongst horses of 6th London Brigade R.F.A. resulting in death of two. Visited the wounded and visited again in evening. Progress towards recovery, satisfactory. Made inspection of all horses of 5th. 6th. and 7th. Bdes. Ammunition Columns, & advised generally upon all cases.	JL
Hospital 7th Mob. Div. GOSNAY	October 5th 1915. Tuesday.		Usual Office work. Again rode over to LABOUVRIERE to 6th Bde. R.F.A. poisoning cases now in convalescent stage. Went to BETHUNE afternoon to make post mortem upon horse died previous day, & on return visited Mobile Section, Hospl. and signed the losses.	JL
Hospital 7th Mob. Div. GOSNAY	October 6th 1915 Wednesday.		Dealt with office correspondence. Rode over to Divl. Ammn. Column at LABUISSIERE for inspection, and on the Mobile Section to interview O.C. with reference to suggested interchange of N.C.Os and men for same number from Veterinary Hospitals, names submitted to D.D.V.S. Moved over to NOEUX-LES-MINES, and Section to LABUISSIERE. Inspected all horses of 142nd Capt. Edn. at NOEUX-LES-MINES, with the	JL

V.O. LT. T & CRAIG.
2353 Wt. W2544/1454 700,000 5/15 D. D. & L. A.D.S.S./Forms/C. 2118.

Army Form C. 2118

WAR DIARY
of
INTELLIGENCE SUMMARY of A.D.V.S. 47th (London) Division

(Erase heading not required.)

Instructions regarding War Diaries and Intelligence Summaries are contained in F. S. Regs., Part II. and the Staff Manual respectively. Title pages will be prepared in manuscript.

Place	Date	Hour	Summary of Events and Information	Remarks and references to Appendices
	October 7th 1915 Thursday		Office routine work and correspondence.	
H.qrs. 47. Lon. Div.			Inspected horses of transport lines, & more on 16, 13th, 14th, 15th Batteries R.F.A at LABUISSIERE, sent Sergeant to Mobile Section for evacuation, also visited D.A.C. advising Lt. STUART upon matters to improve condition of animals. Mobile Section.	JM
NOEUX-LES-MINES				
	October 8th 1915 Friday		Routine Office work.	
H.qrs 47 (Lon) Div.			Met V.O. of 141st Infantry Brigade at DROUVIN, inspecting all horses, also Wagon and Signal Co. at DROUVIN CHATEAU.	
NOEUX-LES-MINES			Afternoon saw mule of 3rd Field to R.E at NOEUX-LES-MINES, and reported upon same to D.A.Q.M.G. for casting. Interviewed V.O's bringing in weekly sick reports, discussing several subjects with them.	JM
	October 9th 1915 Saturday		Usual office work.	
H.qrs 47 (Lon) Div.			Visited 4th Field Ambulance at LABUISSIERE, also D.A.C. 's report upon mare for casting, to D.A.Q.M.G., advising treatment of these animals whilst there.	
NOEUX-LES-MINES			Rendered weekly vet returns to D.D.V.S. 1st Army. Very little sickness in Division, and deaths and destruction few. Greater percentage of trouble due to fistula and upon galls through shortage of well seasoned	JM

#353 Wt. W2544/1454 700,000 5/15 D. D. & L. A.D.S.S./Forms/C. 2118.

Army Form C. 2118

WAR DIARY
or
INTELLIGENCE SUMMARY of A.D.M.S. 47th London Division

(Erase heading not required.)

Place	Date	Hour	Summary of Events and Information	Remarks and references to Appendices
Hqrs. 47th Lon Divn. NOEUX-LES-MINES	October 10th 19.15 Sunday		Usual Office Routine, attended to correspondence. Visited Lt. Smiljen Bde. R.F.A. having just assumed command of pack transport. Horses to Lieut. CRAIG. Called upon transport lines of 6th Field Ambulance and rode on to HOUCHIN to 141st Inf. Bde. Visit from D.D.M.S. conferred upon any further suggestions for position of Mobile Section and Advanced Dressing Station in event of Divison being engaged in combined attack. Previous arrangements have proved most satisfactory and adequate to cope with the situation. Also discussed the recent poisoning outbreak and all other questions concerned.	[sig]
Hqrs 47th Lon Divn NOEUX-LES-MINES	October 11th 19.15 Monday		Routine Office work. Rode over to MAZINGARBE to inspect horses of 140th Inf. Bde. and called upon A.D.V.S. of 1st Division, arranged for reception of sick and injured animals to respective Mobile Sections and Collecting Stations. Afternoon proceeded to Hqrs. and signals at DROUVIN, thence to 3rd and 2/3rd Field Co. R.E.	[sig]

Army Form C. 2118

WAR DIARY
or
INTELLIGENCE SUMMARY of A.D.V.S. 47th (London) Division.

(Erase heading not required.)

Instructions regarding War Diaries and Intelligence Summaries are contained in F.S. Regs., Part II. and the Staff Manual respectively. Title pages will be prepared in manuscript.

Place	Date	Hour	Summary of Events and Information	Remarks and references to Appendices
Hqrs. 47th Lon. Divn.	October 12th 1915. Tuesday		Routine work at Office & correspondence. Visited Hqrs. and Signals at DROUVIN and all horses of Transport Bets at HOUCHIN, and of No. 16 MOBILE SECTION.	JR.
NOEUX-LES-MINES			Afternoon with Lt. SOUTHALL to select site for Advanced Dressing Station: decided upon piece of ground between NOEUX and MAZINGARBE. Received Remounts at NOEUX-LES-MINES & sent them to lines of Divl. Train and Ammunition Column.	
Hqrs. 47th Lon. Divn.	October 13th 1915. Wednesday		Office routine as usual. Rode to Divl. Train and Am. Column to make examination of allot Remounts.	JR.
NOEUX-LES-MINES			Afternoon to MARLES-LES-MINES to report upon nine horse at 6th and 7th Bdes R.F.A. for casting. To D.H.Q.M.S. Advanced Dressing and Collecting Station opened.	
Hqrs. 47th Lon. Divn.	October 14th 1915. Thursday		Office work. Rode over to the INDIAN Mountain Gun Section at MAZINGARBE. Horses and mules found to be in excellent condition. Inspected horses of Divl. Train and 6th Field Ambulance at NOEUX, and Hqrs. to practically no sick has been experienced. Instructions sent to D.C. Mobile Section to move to NOEUX-LES-MINES early following morning.	JR.
NOEUX-LES-MINES				

Army Form C. 2118

WAR DIARY
or
INTELLIGENCE SUMMARY of A.D.V.S. 47th Division.
(Erase heading not required.)

Instructions regarding War Diaries and Intelligence Summaries are contained in F. S. Regs., Part II. and the Staff Manual respectively. Title pages will be prepared in manuscript.

Place	Date	Hour	Summary of Events and Information	Remarks and references to Appendices
	October 15th 1915 Friday		Routine Office work. Dealt with correspondence.	
Hdqrs. 47th Lon. Divn.			This office transferred to VILLA ARNAULD, MAZINGARBE.	
NOEUX LES MINES			Interviewed Veterinary Officers bringing in their weekly sick reports, conferring with them upon their various charges. Visited Hdqrs. and Signals, now here to Mobile Section.	JA
	October 16th 1915 Saturday		Usual Office work. Morning spent at Mobile Section NOEUX, inspecting upon cases here, and informing the Driving operations.	
Hdqrs. 47th Lon. Divn.				
MAZINGARBE			Rode over to MARKLES MINES in afternoon to inspect horse left behind by 6th Corps R.F.A. Found same in a very exhausted condition with open sore, point and destroyed it. Returns rendered to D.D.V.S.	JA
	October 17th 1915 Sunday		Work at office. Visited horses of Hqrs. and Signals at MAZINGARBE, also Canadian Heavy Battery.	
Hdqrs. 47th Lon. Divn.				
MAZINGARBE			Was called to see horse of 2/3rd Coys. R.E., found same to be suffering from sublined stomach, and over dosing afterwards.	JA

Army Form C. 2118

WAR DIARY
~~INTELLIGENCE~~ SUMMARY of A.D.V.S. 47th (London) Division.
(Erase heading not required.)

Instructions regarding War Diaries and Intelligence Summaries are contained in F. S. Regs., Part II and the Staff Manual respectively. Title pages will be prepared in manuscript.

Place	Date	Hour	Summary of Events and Information	Remarks and references to Appendices
Hqrs. 47th Lon. Divn. MAZINGARBE	October 18th 1915 Monday		Correspondence and Routine Office work dealt with. Made general visiting round of 5th, 6th Northern Bde. R.F.A., 5th Bde. R.F.A., and 4th, 5th, 6th Field Ambulances, the object being to inspect the shoeing and amount of care being exercised with regard to the feet, also why repeated Demonstrations and lectures upon this all important subject.	J.R.
Hqrs. 47 Lon. Divn. MAZINGARBE	October 19th 1915 Tuesday		Routine office work. Interviewed D.A.Q.M.G. about headquarters upon sending number of men for course of instruction in farriery, to BEBEVILLE submitted names to D.D.V.S. 1st Army for instructions. Inspected 140th, 141st and 142nd Infantry Brigades Transport, all in vicinity of MAZINGARBE, found harness clean, and vans great improvement, and number of post-nasal residues to a minimum.	J.R.
Hqrs. 47 (Lon) Divn. MAZINGARBE	October 20th 1915 Wednesday		Usual Office routine. Visited Hqrs. Signals, and 5th Lon. Bde. R.F.A. to investigate a further outbreak of TOXIC poisoning, probably caused by eating a certain Bark. Rode over to BETHUNE in afternoon to trace a post-mortem upon Grey Laurel died but no trace of cart found.	J.R.

Army Form C. 21

WAR DIARY
INTELLIGENCE SUMMARY of A.D.M.S. 47th (London) Division
(Erase heading not required.)

Instructions regarding War Diaries and Intelligence Summaries are contained in F. S. Regs., Part II. and the Staff Manual respectively. Title pages will be prepared in manuscript.

Place	Date	Hour	Summary of Events and Information	Remarks and references to Appendices
Hqrs. 47th (Lon) Divn. MAZINGARBE	October 21st, 1915 Thursday		Office routine work; dealt with correspondence. Visited Mobile Section, and King Edward Horse at NOEUX-LES-MINES to report upon suitability of building to supply horses for other purposes. Met D.D.R. by appointment and attended with him upon 5th, 7th Bdes. R.F.A. and 7th. Lond (Gen) dealing with several Removals proposed for railway.	J.H.
Hqrs. 47th (Lon) Divn. MAZINGARBE	October 22nd, 1915 Friday		Usual Office work. Rode over to Mobile Section to arrange affairs with Lt. SOUTHALL before he proceeded on leave. Inspected horses of Divisional Train, 6th Gen. R.F.A, and 4th Field Ambulance. Interviewed V.O. bringing in fair weekly reports.	J.H.
Hqrs. 47th (Lon) Divn. MAZINGARBE	October 23rd, 1915 Saturday		Routine Office work. Visited Mobile Section and Divnl Transport Horse to Divl Ammn. Column at LABUISSIERE to see horses for evacuation. Week by week reports rendered to D.D.V.S.	J.H.

Army Form C. 21

WAR DIARY
INTELLIGENCE SUMMARY of A.D.M.S. 47th Division
(Erase heading not required.)

Instructions regarding War Diaries and Intelligence Summaries are contained in F. S. Regs., Part II. and the Staff Manual respectively. Title pages will be prepared in manuscript.

Place	Date	Hour	Summary of Events and Information	Remarks and references to Appendices
Hqrs. 47th Div. MAZINGARBE.	October 24th 1915 Sunday		Routine Office work, correspondence, returns etc. Rode over to Mobile Section at NOEUX-LES-MINES, arranged evacuation to take place on Tuesday 26th inst. Treated numerous cases there. Called at Hqrs. upon return, and 2/5th Field Co. R.E. to see horse suddenly taken ill.	JR
Hqrs. 47th (Lon) Div. MAZINGARBE.	October 25th 1915 Monday		Morning spent at Office, in dealing with matters and all correspondence here. Incessant rain the whole night and day and severely cold change of weather, rendering all doings for horses extremely unfavourable. Interviewed D.A.Q.M.G. at Headquarters.	JR
Hqrs. 47th (Lon) Div. MAZINGARBE.	October 26th 1915 Tuesday		Usual Office routine. Visited Mobile Section at NOEUX-LES-MINES also 4th (Lon) Field Ambulance, saw horses of Signal Co., and M.M. Police upon return.	JR

2353 Wt. W2544/1454 700,000 5/15 D.D.&L. A.D.S.S./Forms/C 2118.

Army Form C. 2118

WAR DIARY
of
INTELLIGENCE SUMMARY of A.D.N.S. 47th (Lon) Division
(Erase heading not required.)

Place	Date	Hour	Summary of Events and Information	Remarks and references to Appendices
	October 27th 1915 Wednesday		Usual Office routine: dealt with correspondence. Met D.D.R. and inspected loads of 6th Bn R.E.R. Signal Company	
Hqrs 47th (Lon) Divn MAZINGARBE			M.A. Police for cabling and concealing. Examined and allotted batch of remounts (56) at NOEUX LES MINES. Return from there to Mobile Section and Divl Train to inspect horse suffering from applicamia, ordered Destruction. Visited horse at Hqrs upon return.	JR
	October 28th 1915 Thursday		Office routine and correspondence. Visited Hqrs Signal to trace locus - radical case of bowel trouble ordered the ailment.	
Hqrs 47th (Lon) Divn MAZINGARBE			Interviewed CAPT. FERGUSSON R.A.M.C. & inspected his charges - hams. Visited Mobile Section, and Signal Co again upon return.	JR

WAR DIARY
or
INTELLIGENCE SUMMARY of A.D.T.S. 47 (Lon) Division

Army Form C. 2118

Instructions regarding War Diaries and Intelligence Summaries are contained in F.S. Regs., Part II. and the Staff Manual respectively. Title pages will be prepared in manuscript.

(Erase heading not required.)

Place	Date	Hour	Summary of Events and Information	Remarks and references to Appendices
MAZINGARBE	October 29th 1915 Friday Hagrs. 47th (Lon) Divn		Usual Office work; dealt with correspondence. Visited Signal Co. at Lagry, thence to Mobile Section. Received and allotted 186 Remounts at NOEUX-LES-MINES drawn in afternoon in Omnibus. 7etc. Officers bringing in their weekly returns.	JA
MAZINGARBE	October 30th 1915 Saturday Hagrs 47th Lon Divn		Office routine. With D.A.Q.M.G. rode to NOEUX-LES-MINES which full descriptions of above remounts. Visited Mobile Section. In afternoon attended a conference of A.D.T.S. at LOZON of S.D.T.S. on enemy again resisted loss of signal to S.D.T.S. M(ostly?) A.2000 & return rendered to D.A.T.S.	JA
MAZINGARBE	October 31st 1915 Sunday Hagrs 47th Lon Divn		Office work and correspondence. Inspected horses of 140th Infantry Bde, with Lt. CRAIG, and of 141st Mobile Section. Visited horses of Signal Coy, now progressing favourably. Inspected all horses of King Edwards Horse.	JA

Joseph Aham
Major A.V.S.(?)
A.D.T.S.
47th (Lon) Division

A.D.V.S. 47th Div.

No. 9

June IX

12/7/71

Army Form C. 2118

WAR DIARY
INTELLIGENCE SUMMARY of A.D.V.S. 47th (London) Division
(Erase heading not required.)

Place	Date	Hour	Summary of Events and Information	Remarks and references to Appendices
	1st November 1915 Monday		Went at Office: dealt with correspondence. Inspected horses of Headquarters and signals 47th Divn, healed several cases there.	J.S.
Hqrs 47th Lon Divn MAZINGARBE			Visited Divl. Royal Engineers Hqrs and all horses of 16th, 17th, 18th and 19th Batteries. R.F.A and conferred with MAJOR LONGDEN 2nd L.R.F.A. upon condition of his horses, and suggested certain alterations in feeding of same.	J.S.
MAP. FRANCE. 36 B SCALE 1/40,000 6.13 Z				
	2nd November 1915 Tuesday		Went at Office routine. Visited horses of signals and Hqrs. and Hqrs. 1 2nd & 3rd London Field Cos. R.E.s all in neighbourhood of MAZINGARBE.	N.S.
Hqrs 47th Lon Divn MAZINGARBE			General inspection of all horses of 19th London Battery, R.F.A. and sent several poor cases to Mobile Section for evacuation.	
	3rd November 1915 Wednesday		Office work as usual. Inspected all horses of signals and Transport of 140th Inf. Bde and Royal Engineers advising upon all cases; hence to 19th Battery R.F.A. found same in somewhat neglected condition.	N.S.
Hdqrs 47th Lon Divn MAZINGARBE			Rode on to Mobile Section at NOEUX-LES-MINES in afternoon to arrange matters there.	

Army Form C. 2118

WAR DIARY
or
INTELLIGENCE SUMMARY. of A.D.V.S. 47th (London) Division
(Erase heading not required.)

Instructions regarding War Diaries and Intelligence Summaries are contained in F.S. Regs., Part II. and the Staff Manual respectively. Title pages will be prepared in manuscript.

Place	Date	Hour	Summary of Events and Information	Remarks and references to Appendices
H.K.	November 4th 1915 Thursday		Work at Office and correspondence. Inspection horses of 4th Divl. and Signals & 19th London Battery.	[sig]
Hqrs 47th Lon. Divn.			Rode over to Mobile Section, from there to NOEUX LES MINES & Labour.	
MAZINGARBE			received for Remounts; examined and allotted same, en R.Q.M.L.	
			Interviewed Town-Major NOEUX with reference to a permanent site there for Mobile Section.	
5th November 1915 Friday			Routine office work. Attended Divl Amunn. Column at LABOURSIERE; met D.D.V.S. and	[sig]
Hqrs. 47th Lon. Divn.			selected pieces at horses beginning next from wind; proceeded to 7th and 8th London Coys., arranging for any inspection, and notification to D.D.V.S. of	
MAZINGARBE			horses 1st London Coy, that would be condemned. Visits forward or branch Mobile Section to advise in cases for evacuation.	
			Interviewed Vety. Officers, bringing up their weekly sick returns.	
6th November 1915 Saturday			Work and correspondence at office. Visited horses of Signal Signals, and Divl. M.M.P., very small percentage	[sig]
Hqrs 47th Lon. Divn.			of sick men. Remainder of day spent at office.	
MAZINGARBE			Weekly reports rendered to D.D.V.S. 1st Army	

Army Form C. 2118

WAR DIARY
or
INTELLIGENCE SUMMARY of A.D.V.C. 47th Division
(Erase heading not required.)

Instructions regarding War Diaries and Intelligence Summaries are contained in F. S. Regs., Part II. and the Staff Manual respectively. Title pages will be prepared in manuscript.

Place	Date	Hour	Summary of Events and Information	Remarks and references to Appendices
Hqrs 47th Lon Divn MAZINGARBE	Nov 7th 1915 Sunday		Office routine work and correspondence. Hours of Signals and Headquarters. Rode over to Middle section at NOEUX-LES-MINES to superintend operations and dressing treatment of all cases.	J.S.
Hqrs 47th Lon Divn MAZINGARBE	November 8th 1915 Monday		Usual office work. Headquarters to interview D.A. + D.M.S. upon various subjects. Mobile Section. General inspection of all horses of 7th Bde. R.F.A. at NOEUX-LES-MINES.	J.S.
Hqrs 47th Lon Divn MAZINGARBE	November 9th 1915 Tuesday		Attended to correspondence and work at office. Visited horses of Divnl. Signals, Divnl. Cyclist Co. and 19th and 20th Batteries R.F.A. Met LIEUT CRAIG R.V.C. at lines of 4th Battn. Royal Welch Fusiliers to inspect horses recommended for examination. Mobile section.	J.S.
Hqrs 47 Lon Divn MAZINGARBE	November 10th 1915 Wednesday		Office work. Made general inspection all horses of 17th 18th and 19th Batteries R.F.A. with Vety Officer 1/c, suggesting many improvements conducive to better condition of animals.	J.S.

2353 Wt. W2544/1454 700,000 5/15 D. D. & L. A.D.S.S./Forms/C. 2118.

Army Form C. 211

WAR DIARY
or
INTELLIGENCE SUMMARY of A.D.V.S. 47th London Division
(Erase heading not required.)

Instructions regarding War Diaries and Intelligence Summaries are contained in F. S. Regs., Part II. and the Staff Manual respectively. Title pages will be prepared in manuscript.

Place	Date	Hour	Summary of Events and Information	Remarks and references to Appendices
Hqrs. 47th Lon. Divn. MAZINGARBE	November 11th 1915 Thursday		Routine Office work and correspondence. Last consignment post D.D.V.S. 1st Army at Mobile Section's work upon question of permanent site for Section at NOEUX LES MINES pit. Concluded accommodation for sick horses. Inspected horses of 1/5th Bn. London Regt. and 19th Battery R.F.A. at MAZINGARBE. Interviewed D.A.D.M.S. at headquarters.	J.S.
Hqrs. 47th Lon. Divn. MAZINGARBE	November 12th 15 Friday		Went at Office. Horses of 2/2nd Field Coy. R.E. and 4th Battn. Royal Welsh Fusiliers. Received weekly reports from Vety. Officers and held conference upon all matters concerning the health and efficiency of animals of the Division, the great importance of this aim to be always kept in view. Visited Mobile Section.	J.S.
Hqrs. 47th Lon. Divn. MAZINGARBE	November 13th 15 Saturday		Office routine. Field Days & Signal Co. horses. Trip towards FOSSE. Made visiting round of 17th, 18th, 19th Batteries R.F.A. sending several sick horses to Mobile Section to be evacuated for rest. Weekly sick returns rendered to D.D.M.S. 1st Army. Very little sickness and a few deaths, trouble mostly attributable to sore and galls.	J.S.

WAR DIARY
or
INTELLIGENCE SUMMARY of A.D.V.S. 47th Division

Army Form C. 2118.

(Erase heading not required.)

Place	Date	Hour	Summary of Events and Information	Remarks and references to Appendices
Hqrs. 47th Lon. Div. MAZINGARBE	November 14th 1915 Sunday		Work at office; attended to correspondence. Applied notes of Headquarters Divn. Met Lt.Col. E.G. Martin, new B.D.V.S. 1st Army in close touch up duties elsewhere. Inspected Lines of 5th Lon. Fd. Amb. R.F.A. and also Lt.Col. Newsom, D.D.V.S. also Lt.Col. Newsom, D.D.V.S. 1st Army Inspected Lines of 5th Lon. Fd. Amb. R.F.A. and Col. 7th Lon. R.F.A. at MAZINGARBE NOEUX-LES-MINES, and upon return horses of 5th London Battalion at MAZINGARBE	J.S.
Hqrs. 47th Lon. Divn. MAZINGARBE	November 15th 1915 Monday		Usual Office routine. Two Office moves to MARLES-LES-MINES (map reference FRANCE sheet 36.2. scale 1:40,000 — C.30.B) and Mobile Section from NOEUX-LES-MINES to MENSE t.Q. Visited Lone Left horses at MAZINGARBE by 6th London Battalion, opened sole, inflamed farrier, and left in charge of Gloucesters. Inspected charges at stages 5th Bde. R.F.A. sent horses to Mobile for evacuation.	J.S.
Hqrs. 47th Lon. Divn. MARLES-LES-MINES	November 16th 1915 Tuesday		Office work: dealt with correspondence. Kept in all day on account of lame foot.	J.S.

Army Form C. 2118

WAR DIARY
or
INTELLIGENCE SUMMARY. of A.D.V.S. 47th Division
(Erase heading not required.)

Instructions regarding War Diaries and Intelligence Summaries are contained in F. S. Regs., Part II. and the Staff Manual respectively. Title pages will be prepared in manuscript.

Place	Date	Hour	Summary of Events and Information	Remarks and references to Appendices
Hqrs.47th Lon.Divn. MARLES-LES-MINES	November 17th 15 Wednesday		Work at office & correspondence. Visited Headquarters and Signals troops rode over to Mobile Section at M.N.S.E.C.Q. Great difficulty in getting about, owing to foot problems, no spare remainder of day in getting latters up to date.	J.S.
Hqrs.47th Lon.Divn. MARLES-LES-MINES	November 18th 15 Thursday		Inspected horses of Divl. H.Q. Signal Coy. and M.M. Police, all in MARLES. Rode over to 5th Lon. Field Ambulance at AUCHEL to see transport horses. to Mobile Section to make arrangements with O.C. for provision of short standings and coverings for sick horses, as a permanent site for Mobile Section.	J.S.
Hqrs.47th Lon.Divn. MARLES-LES-MINES	November 19th 15 Friday		Routine office work. Inspected horses of 6th Bde. R.F.A. at AUCHEL with Lt. STUART R.V.C. advising treatment, and evacuating a few Debility cases. Received sick reports from 7/D/s. Officers and re-allotted vet.reports units made necessary by move of entire Division.	J.S.
Hqrs.47th Lon.Divn. MARLES-LES-MINES	November 20th 15 Saturday		Dealt with correspondence at office. Inspected horses of 1/4th Inf. Bde. at RAIMBERT and BURBURE. Proceeded to LABUSSIERE to investigate suspected outbreak of York and Discards, and reported to D.D.V.S. that same did not exist, it had been North A.F.M.4.K. Forms, 1,000,000 5/15 D.D.&L. A.D.S.S./Forms/C. 2118.	J.S.

Army Form C. 2118

WAR DIARY
or
INTELLIGENCE SUMMARY of A.D.V.S. 47th London Division.
(Erase heading not required.)

Instructions regarding War Diaries and Intelligence Summaries are contained in F. S. Regs., Part II. and the Staff Manual respectively. Title pages will be prepared in manuscript.

Place	Date	Hour	Summary of Events and Information	Remarks and references to Appendices
Hqrs 47th Lon Div MARLES-LES-MINES	November 21st 1915 Sunday		Went at Office dealt with correspondence. Rode over to FERFAY and AUCHEL, examined and allotted 110 Remounts to various units. Inspected horses of 1st Br Battery R.F.A at CAUCHY-A-LA-TOUR, sent 11/6 Mobile Section for evacuation. Visited Divisional Train and Mobile Section.	J.S.
Hqrs 47th Lon Divn MARLES-LES-MINES	November 22nd 1915 Monday		Routine Office work. Inspected horses of Divl. Hqrs and signals at MARLES Mobile Section to arrange everything before my departure on leave.	J.S.
Hqrs 47th Lon Divn MARLES-LES-MINES	November 23rd 15 Tuesday		Dealt with correspondence at Office. Proceeded to England on leave for 10 days, duties carried out by Lt. J. SOUTHALL. D.I.C. Mobile Section. 59 horses evacuated to base.	J.S.
Hqrs 47th Lon Divn MARLES-LES-MINES	November 24th 15 Wednesday		Attended to duties at Mobile Section at MENSER? To de over to the Office + dealt with correspondence Inspected horses of 140th Inf. Bde at LILLERS upon return, also A.R. Seron Lallerin Transport horses at LILLERS.	J.S.

Army Form C. 2118.

WAR DIARY
of
INTELLIGENCE SUMMARY of A.D.V.S. 47th London Division

(Erase heading not required.)

Place	Date	Hour	Summary of Events and Information	Remarks and references to Appendices
Hdqrs. 47th Lon. Divn. MARLES-LES-MINES	November 25th 15 Thursday	D.A.D.M.S.	Routine office work and correspondence. Inspected two lines of 6th Lon. Field Ambulance for readiness and reported to D.A.D.M.S. Visited King Edwards Horse at HURIONVILLE, and dealt remainder of day at Mobile Section.	J.S.
Hdqrs. 47th Lon. Divn. MARLES-LES-MINES	November 26th 15 Friday		Dealt with correspondence at Office. Received weekly sick return from Dly. Officer. Visited F.A. S to report upon removal to D.A.D.M.S. Evacuated 26 Horses to Base.	J.S.
Hdqrs. 47th Lon. Divn. MARLES-LES-MINES	November 27th 15 Saturday		Received 140 Remounts at LILLERS Station, examined and allotted same with D.A.D.M.G. Mostly sick return rendered to D.D.V.S. 1st Army, and correspondence dealt with.	J.S.
Hdqrs. 47th Lon. Divn. MARLES-LES-MINES	November 28th 15 Sunday		Attended to cases at Mobile Section. Routine Office work. Inspected horses of 4th Lon. Field Ambulance at LILLERS.	J.S.

Army Form C. 2118.

WAR DIARY
or
INTELLIGENCE SUMMARY. of A.D.V.S. 47th London Division
(Erase heading not required.)

Place	Date	Hour	Summary of Events and Information	Remarks and references to Appendices
Lagn: 47th Lon Divn. Marles Les Mines	November 29th 1915 Monday		Office work on & correspondence. Instructions received for Divisional Route March from 38M/1.S. No. 2.12.15, and preparations made accordingly. 19 horses evacuated to base.	J.
Lagn: 47th Lon Divn. Marles Les Mines	November 30th 1915 Tuesday		Above march now cancelled by one day. Routine Office work. Inspected horses of Signal Coy. reported upon one for casting to D.A.D.R.V. Made final arrangements for Route March.	J.

Fouchan Lieut AVC(T)
(for) Major. A.V.C.T.S
A.D.V.S.
47th London Division.

A.V.S. 47/demands.

Sec.

Vol. X.

bebl
75
12,1

Army Form C. 2118.

WAR DIARY
or
INTELLIGENCE SUMMARY.
(Erase heading not required.)

Instructions regarding War Diaries and Intelligence Summaries are contained in F. S. Regs., Part II. and the Staff Manual respectively. Title pages will be prepared in manuscript.

Place	Date	Hour	Summary of Events and Information	Remarks and references to Appendices
Hq.47th Lon.Divn. MARLES-les-MINES.	1st December 1915. Wednesday,		Left at 6.30 a.m. for Divisional Route March.	J.R.
Hq.47th Lon.Divn. MARLES-les-MINES.	2nd December 1915. Thursday,		Returned from Divisional Route March during afternoon.	J.R.
Hq.47th Lon.Divn. MARLES-les-MINES.	3rd December 1915. Friday,		Routine office work and correspondence. Interviewed Coy. Officers, bringing in Weekly work reports. Motor Section.	J.R.
Hq.47th Lon.Divn. MARLES-les-MINES.	4th December 1915. Saturday,		Returned from absence of leave, and reported fact to Headquarters. Day spent at office in clearing matters no generally, and dealing with correspondence	J.R.

Army Form C. 2118.

WAR DIARY
or
INTELLIGENCE SUMMARY.
(Erase heading not required.)

Instructions regarding War Diaries and Intelligence Summaries are contained in F. S. Regs., Part II. and the Staff Manual respectively. Title pages will be prepared in manuscript.

Place	Date	Hour	Summary of Events and Information	Remarks and references to Appendices
Hq.47th Lon.Divn. MARLES-les-MINES.	5th December 1915. Sunday.		Routine office work. Rode over to AUCHEL and inspected all Loads of Transport there. R.F.A. sending several pairs away to Mobile Section for examination. Afternoon rode over to Mobile Section at MENSEIL showing harness of cases there. Visited Lories of Signal Coy, and Divl. Headquarters on return.	JM
Hq.47th Lon.Divn. MARLES-les-MINES.	6th December 1915. Monday.		Office work & usual: dealt with correspondence. Enabled a horse for rushing at 7th Coy R.F.A. and reported to D.D.A.M.S. Visited Mobile Section, thence to 140th Infantry Brigade at LILLERS inspecting all transport Lories there. Located and harness upon a few poor cases.	JM
Hq.47th Lon.Divn. MARLES-les-MINES.	7th December 1915. Tuesday.		Office routine work. Met LT.COL.FOOT, A.D. & D.M.G. at 9.15 a.m. with him proceeded to AUCHEL to inspect whole of horses of Divl. Ammn Column. In afternoon rode over to AUCHEL and CAUCHY-LES-TOURS and examined 120 Remounts at 5A, 6th & 7th Brigades R.F.A respectively. Visited Headquarters and interviewed A.D. & D.M.B.	JM

2353 Wt. W2544/1454 700,000 5/15 D. D. & L. A.D.S.S./Forms/C. 2118.

WAR DIARY
or
INTELLIGENCE SUMMARY.
(Erase heading not required.)

Army Form C. 2118.

Place	Date	Hour	Summary of Events and Information	Remarks and references to Appendices
Hq. 47th Lon. Divn. MARLES-les-MINES.	8th December 1915. Wednesday.		Office work and correspondence. Visited Mobile Section and instructed O.C. with regard to provision of stabling and coverings for horses. Made general inspection of horses of 5th Bde. R.F.A at BUCHEL. Received instructions from D.D.V.S. 1st Army to prepare to hand all horses of Division listed for Blanders by the India-dermal palpebral method of Mallenation.	J.M.
Hq. 47th Lon. Divn. MARLES-les-MINES.	9th December 1915. Thursday.		Usual Office routine. Interviewed at SOUTHWELL A.V.T. O.C. Mobile Section at office upon various subjects including the new Descriptive Roll to accompany horses evacuated explaining its many details. Visited by D.D.V.S. 1st Army, and conferred upon the question of Mallening Lists for Mobile Sections and standings for horses.	J.M.
Hq. 47th Lon. Divn. MARLES-les-MINES.	10th December 1915. Friday.		Office work. Made inspection of all horses of 4th Bde R.F.A at BUCHEL. Interviewed Vety Officers brought in weekly with returns, and instructed them to meet me at Mobile Section following afternoon. Sent return rendered to D.D.V.S. 1st Army; images shown known non particular four.	J.M.

Army Form C. 2118.

WAR DIARY
or
INTELLIGENCE SUMMARY of A.D.V.S. 47th London Division
(Erase heading not required.)

Instructions regarding War Diaries and Intelligence
Summaries are contained in F. S. Regs., Part II.
and the Staff Manual respectively. Title pages
will be prepared in manuscript.

Place	Date	Hour	Summary of Events and Information	Remarks and references to Appendices
Hq.47th Lon.Divn. MARLES-les-MINES.	11th December 1915. Saturday.		Office routine and correspondence. Inspected whole of horses of Bde. R.F.A. at RUCHELY ending few bad cases to Mobile Section for evacuation. Inspected and allotted batch of Remounts at FERFAY, and proceeded to Mobile Section at MENSEES and subsequently upon the Mother Section for my most Veterinary Officers.	
Hq.47th Lon.Divn. MARLES-les-MINES.	12th December 1915. Sunday.		10 a.m. at Office. Rode over to FERFAY and made inspection of horses of the London Bde R.F.A. Mobile Section. Inspected horses of Lieut. Hoggard and Signal Coy. horses at NOEULES.	
Hq.47th Lon.Divn. MARLES-les-MINES.	13th December 1915. Monday.		Office routine and correspondence. Met Lieuts. EDWARDS and GOSLING at 5th Brigade R.F.A. and assigned plan to inspect the horses of 3 batteries of that Brigade which engaged the remainder of the day.	

Army Form C. 2118.

WAR DIARY
or
INTELLIGENCE SUMMARY. of A.D.S. 47th London Division

(Erase heading not required.)

Instructions regarding War Diaries and Intelligence Summaries are contained in F.S. Regs., Part II. and the Staff Manual respectively. Title pages will be prepared in manuscript.

Place	Date	Hour	Summary of Events and Information	Remarks and references to Appendices
Hq. 47th Lon. Divn. MARLES-les-MINES.	14th December 1915. Tuesday.		Office routine. Dealt with correspondence. Again rode on to RUITEL to examine the horses for vacancies respect vacancies and assisted in the Mastering of the remainder of 5th Brigade R.F.A. In the afternoon visited horses at Dvnl Headquarters and Signal Coy at MARLES. Mobile Section.	G.A.
Hq. 47th Lon. Divn. MARLES MINES.	15th December 1915. Wednesday.		Office work as usual. Inspected horses visited during day to vaccinations. Two Office transport 16 VAUDRICOURT, and Mobile Section 16 DROUVIN. Visited Headquarters for the purpose of having a more provider for an office, the one I intended to use having already been taken by another unit, nothing available in the following morning.	G.A.
Hq. 47th Lon. Divn. VAUDRICOURT. Sheet 36b.FRANCE. K.4.a.	16th December 1915. Thursday.		Moved in to new quarters. Attended to up to routine and correspondence. Inspected lines of several units taken over at LABOURSE, SAILLY-LABOURSE and VERQUIGNEUL, and found condition very indifferent condition owing to incessant rains and continual use of same ground. Visited horses of Signal Coy. at VAUDRICOURT.	G.A.

Army Form C. 2118.

WAR DIARY
or
INTELLIGENCE SUMMARY of A.D.V.S. 47th (London) Division

(Erase heading not required.)

Place	Date	Hour	Summary of Events and Information	Remarks and references to Appendices
Hq.47th Lon.Divn. VAUDRICOURT.	17th December 1915. Friday.		Office routine: dealt with correspondence. Met D.D.V.S. 1st Army at 10 a.m. with him made general inspection of all horses of Divisional Artillery, excluding all Demobilier animals for rest, engaged until 3pm. Interviewed Vety. Officer at Office bringing in their monthly sick returns.	GH
Hq.47th Lon.Divn. VAUDRICOURT.	18th December 1915. Saturday.		Office work. Leaving for Flanders took over of 7th Bde. R.F.A. at VERQUIN with the Brigade V.O. Officer. Visited Lorries at Headquarters and signed copy at VAUDRICOURT. Weekly sick returns rendered to D.D.V.S. 1st Army.	GH
Hq.47th Lon.Divn. VAUDRICOURT.	19th December 1915. Sunday.		Usual routine at Office. Inspected mares obtained previous day from no. 1 Corps — No. 1 Mobile Section at DROUVIN. Re-distributed units to Vety. Officers forwarding back one bat of charges.	GH

Army Form C. 2118.

WAR DIARY
or
INTELLIGENCE SUMMARY. of A.D.V.S. 47th (London) Division
(Erase heading not required.)

Instructions regarding War Diaries and Intelligence Summaries are contained in F. S. Regs., Part II. and the Staff Manual respectively. Title pages will be prepared in manuscript.

Place	Date	Hour	Summary of Events and Information	Remarks and references to Appendices
Hq.47th Lon.Divn. VAUDRICOURT.	20th December 1915. Monday.		Office routine and correspondence. Completed listing of loads of the two F.A. Reserves to LABOURSE and NOYELLES, and inspected transport lines of 142nd Bde & de. Saw two poor cases left behind by 15th Division, ordered destruction of one with sunstruck flesh below jawbone and issued orders notifying A.D.V.S. of fact. Visited Mobile Section	G.
Hq.47th Lon.Divn. VAUDRICOURT.	21st December 1915. Tuesday.		Work at Office Visited Bde. Headquarters, Signals and Mobile Section. Inspected Mobilised horses for re. actions. Attended to many cases for 706 Officers, they being engaged in testing for glanders horses of 6th Lac F.F.B.	G.
Hq.47th Lon.Divn. VAUDRICOURT.	22nd December 1915. Wednesday.		Usual office routine. Inspected horses for re. actions, which engaged greater part of day. Mobile Section installed arrival of Remounts at NOEUX les MINES Station. Examined A.R.& M.L. unit with regard to complaints of exhaustion of horses and needed a report upon its relations. Many being issued for horses and needed a report upon its relations. qualities at present time of year.	G.

Army Form C. 2118.

WAR DIARY
or
INTELLIGENCE SUMMARY
(Erase heading not required.)

of A.D.V.S. 47th London Division

Place	Date	Hour	Summary of Events and Information	Remarks and references to Appendices
Hq.47th Lon.Divn. VAUDRICOURT.	23rd December 1915. Thursday,		Office work and correspondence. Inspected Mobilized horses for M.Anderson. Wrote Letters and Xmas Card. Rode over to HESDIGNEUL to inspect 130 remount Mules, and 32 Army Draught at. in good condition, belonging to Divl. Train Column. 28 occupied by the Unit for time is most deplorable state, wanting in some of construction on adjoining ground. 5 commenced Lt. WILLIAMS R.V.C. of 15th Divn. came on reference to casual visit of Vet. attached to the 47th Division.	A.
Hq.47th Lon.Divn. VAUDRICOURT.	24th December 1915. Friday,		Work at Office. Letter continuance of officers with 47th Divn. Officers allotting additional attached units to them for attendance and answering the Mentions of Units at Divl. Headquarters.	A.
Hq.47th Lon.Divn. VAUDRICOURT.	25th December 1915. Saturday,		Office routine as usual. Lent over to LABOURSE and SAILLY LABOURSE and inspected mounted various units with Lt. CRAIG R.V.C. also horses listed for destruction. Lt. returned rendered to D.D.V.S. 1st Army, what was and remained owing to indefectible owing to indefectible number of Purchases.	A.

Army Form C. 2118.

WAR DIARY
or
INTELLIGENCE SUMMARY. of A.D.M.S. 47th (London) Division

(Erase heading not required.)

Instructions regarding War Diaries and Intelligence Summaries are contained in F. S. Regs., Part II. and the Staff Manual respectively. Title pages will be prepared in manuscript.

Place	Date	Hour	Summary of Events and Information	Remarks and references to Appendices
Hq. 47th Lon. Divn. VAUDRICOURT.	29th December 1915. Wednesday.		Office routine and correspondence. Visited units at VERQUIN, LABOURSE and VERQUIGNEUL. Infantry transports and R.E. Companies, at the same time inspecting lines for re-distribution obtained Decem. day. Divl. Headquarters Signal Co, and Mobile Section.	JA
Hq. 47th Lon. Divn. VAUDRICOURT.	30th December 1915. Thursday.		Routine office work. Inspected lines of 5th Field Ambulance, 19th Battalion, 23rd and 4th Field Companies R.E. at NOEUX-les-MINES, and LABOURSE. Transport losses of 7th Battalion at VERQUIN, and Machine Gun School of 140th Infantry Bde, Headquarters and Signal Co, at VAUDRICOURT.	JA
Hq. 47th Lon. Divn. VAUDRICOURT.	31st December 1915. Friday.		Office work and correspondence. Inspected hut of 4th Field Ambulance and 19th Battalion for re-action. Also Officers of Column 7th Divl. R.F.A. Interviewed July Officers at Offices twice weekly, sick Reports conferring with them upon the Medicines and other subjects of topical interest. Mobile Section at Divl. Headquarters.	JA

Joseph Adam
Major R.A.M.C. (T)
A.D.M.S. 47th London Division.

31 DEC. 1915
A.D.M.S. 47 LONDON DIVISION

2353 Wt. W2544/1454 700,000 5/15 D.D. & L. A.D.S.S./Forms/C. 2118.

A.D.v.S. 47ig (den Som)the / Som / Vol XI

Army Form C. 2118.

WAR DIARY
of
INTELLIGENCE SUMMARY.
(Erase heading not required.)

Instructions regarding War Diaries and Intelligence Summaries are contained in F.S. Regs., Part II. and the Staff Manual respectively. Title pages will be prepared in manuscript.

Place	Date	Hour	Summary of Events and Information	Remarks and references to Appendices
1st January 1916. Saturday. Hdqrs.,47th (Lon) Divn. VAUDRICOURT.			Office routine; dealt with correspondence. Visited Mobile Section, attended to, and advised upon all cases under treatment there. Visited horses of Lagga and Signal Coy. at VAUDRICOURT and inspected horses of 5th Lon. Field Ambulance, ordering a previous days' cactions oil. Weekly return rendered to D.D.M.S. 1st Army.	J.A.
2nd January 1916. Sunday. Hq.47th Lon.Divn. VAUDRICOURT.			Usual Office routine. Made general inspection of all horses of Divl. Ammn Column at HESDIGNEUL sending a few debilitated cases to Mobile Section for evacuation to Base. In afternoon inspected transport horses of 140th Infantry Brigade at HOUCHIN and conferenced G.O.C. with regard to listing over horses refused by French horses at LES-BREBIS. Saw serious foot case of 20th London battery at NOEUX-LES-MINES and ordered destruction. No flexor acis linicum being punctured.	J.A.
3rd January 1916. Monday. Hq.47th Lon.Divn. VAUDRICOURT.			Office work and correspondence. Rode out to LES-BREBIS, interviewed the Vety. Officer in charge of French horse there, and conferenced with him upon the recent occupation of sheds and coverings by our horses and the possibility of any contagion or infection. Rendered full report of this interview to Divl. Headquarters and D.D.V.S. 1st Army.	J.A.

Army Form C. 2118.

WAR DIARY
of
INTELLIGENCE SUMMARY.
(Erase heading not required.)

Instructions regarding War Diaries and Intelligence Summaries are contained in F. S. Regs., Part II. and the Staff Manual respectively. Title pages will be prepared in manuscript.

Place	Date	Hour	Summary of Events and Information	Remarks and references to Appendices
Hq.47th Lon.Divn. VAUDRICOURT.	4th January.1916. Tuesday.		Routine Office work and rounds as usual. 7.15 a.m. Lieut of Divl. Signal Coy. in VAUDRICOURT. Went to 6th London F.A. column at VERQUIN. Inspected horses — labelled previous days. One inspected nearly sent forward to Mobile Section isolated, and D.D.V.S. 1st Army notified. Rode over to LEOURSE and JOUY-SERVICRE to 4th & 5th Lond. Ambulances, and several units in the neighbourhood. In afternoon interviewed D.D.V.S. at Office with regard to the case of suspected Glanders.	G.
Hq.47th Lon.Divn. VAUDRICOURT.	5th January.1916. Wednesday.		Usual Office work. Mobile Section. Called upon 5th & 6th Lond. Ambulances, 2nd Field C.R.E. inspecting all horses and treating several cases. Later Tely. Operations engaged with Mallemy ... Signal Coy. went on to 47th Divl. Amm. Column DESIGNED to arrange for general inspection of all horses on following morning.	G.
Hq.47th Lon.Divn. VAUDRICOURT.	6th January.1916. Thursday.		Office routine. Proceeded to D.A.C. 25 animals in very bad condition sent to Mobile Section to be evacuated to base for rest & recovery. Rode over to NOEUX-les-MINES and LES BREBIS saw horses of 7th London Bde. R.F.A. and 14th Infantry Bde. Mobile Section. DROUVIN.	G.

WAR DIARY
of
INTELLIGENCE SUMMARY.
(Erase heading not required.)

Army Form C. 2118.

Place	Date	Hour	Summary of Events and Information	Remarks and references to Appendices
7th January 1916. Friday. Hq.47th Lon.Divn. NOEUX-les-MINES.			Office routine and correspondence. Office moved to 16 NOEUX-les-MINES in Mine Buildings. Interviewed Veterinary Officer at Office brought in their Weekly Sick returns. Matters of local interest explained and discussed. Visited Horses of Divl. Hqrs. and Signal Coy. Mobile Section.	
8th January 1916. Saturday. Hq.47th Lon.Divn. NOEUX-les-MINES.			Routine Office work. Inspected Horses of 7th C.A.C. 2/3rd Field Co.R.E. 5th & 6th Field Ambulances at vicinity of NOEUX-les-MINES. Reports rendered to D.D.V.S. rate of sickness slow comparatively low; only serious trouble being heel cases, owing to number of pickets-up-rails. Rode over to Mobile Section and King Edwards Horse at DROUVIN.	
9th January 1916. Sunday. Hq.47th Lon.Divn. NOEUX-les-MINES.			Office work and correspondence. Rode over to Divisional train at HALLICOURT, inspected a horse alleged, for leading- results negative- and conferred with V.O.i/c upon treatment of these cases. Interviewed LT.TOWNSEND-AMC at Mobile Section, and inspected him horse of recruit 2nd London Bde. attached to 47th Division	

Army Form C. 2118.

WAR DIARY
or
INTELLIGENCE SUMMARY.
(Erase heading not required.)

Instructions regarding War Diaries and Intelligence Summaries are contained in F. S. Regs., Part II. and the Staff Manual respectively. Title pages will be prepared in manuscript.

Place	Date	Hour	Summary of Events and Information	Remarks and references to Appendices
Hq.47th Lon.Divn. NOEUX-les-MINES.	10th January 1916. Monday.		Office Routine, dealt with correspondence. Rode over to Mobile Section: O.C. absent on sick leave, therefore carry out his duties. Inspected horses of King Edwards Horse at DROUVIN, hence to Divl. Ammn. Column at HESDIGNEUL. Made general visiting round of all units in neighbourhood of NOEUX-les-MINES.	
Hq.47th Lon.Divn. NOEUX-les-MINES.	11th January 1916. Tuesday.		Rendered full report to D.D.V.S. about number of Depôts in case of removal of late in area of IVth Corps. - Lastly due to having no depôt Legrist zone. Visit Office Routine. Inspected horses of 6th Bde.R.F.A. 7th Arnmn.Col. and 5th Field Ambulance in NOEUX-les-MINES. Rode over to Mobile Section, supervised Dressing operations and described horses for evacuation. Inspected 10th Divl. Ammn. Column returned to 47th D.A.C. the unit having suffered specially previous to forming 47th Divn. from skin Disease, signs of which are still shown.	
Hq.47th Lon.Divn. NOEUX-les-MINES.	12th January 1916. Wednesday.		Office Routine. Mobile Section. Received, examined and allotted 169 Remounts at NOEUX-les-MINES Station; all healthy sound and fit. Visited 7th Bde. Ammn.Col. Divl. Supp. Coln. Signal Coy.	

WAR DIARY of INTELLIGENCE SUMMARY

Army Form C. 2118.

Place	Date	Hour	Summary of Events and Information	Remarks and references to Appendices
Hq.47th Lon.Divn. NOEUX-les-MINES.	13th January 1916. Thursday.		Routine Office work and correspondence. Visited 7th Bn.attchd. Col. 5th London Ambulances Hence 1/3/ Lon an Bde F.A. at LES-BREBIS. Rode over to Mobile Section and King Edwards Horse at DROUVIN. Divl. Headquarters and Signal Coy.	JR
Hq.47th Lon.Divn. NOEUX-les-MINES.	14th January 1916. Friday.		Office Routine Mobile Section: Special attention being given to feet cases on inspection. Horses of 1/1st London Bde. attached to the Division all looking well in every good condition. Interviewed Holy Officers at Office, bringing with them their weekly sick reports: death rate considerable, higher this week owing to number killed by shell fire.	JR
Hq.47th Lon.Divn. NOEUX-les-MINES.	15th January 1916. Saturday.		Work at Office. Mobile Section moving great bone in dealing with all cases. Reports received 1st D.D.M.S. 1st Army. Visited 5th Field Ambulance and 2/3rd Field Co.R.E., Divl. Headquarters and Signal Coy.	JR

WAR DIARY of INTELLIGENCE SUMMARY.

Army Form C. 2118.

Place	Date	Hour	Summary of Events and Information	Remarks and references to Appendices
Hq.47th Lon.Divn. NOEUX-les-MINES.	16th January 1916. Sunday.		Office work and correspondence. Visited Divl. Headquarters & Signal Coy and 7th Coe Mobile Column at NOEUX-les-MINES. Rode over to Mobile Section at DROUIN and 1/2nd London Brigade R.F.A. at VERQUIN. Remainder of day spent in clearing up matters at Office.	J.A.
Hq.47th Lon.Divn. NOEUX-les-MINES.	17th January 1916. Monday.		Office Routine. Visited 5th Field Ambulance and 7th Coe. Mobile Column at NOEUX-les-MINES. Mobile Section. Inspected 47th and 10th Division Columns at HESDIGNEUL, seeing the booked cases to Mobile for evacuation. Rebored A.D.M.S. upon the Officers in the Division progressing very slowly, suggesting that steps be taken to urge the matter.	J.A.
Hq.47th Lon.Divn. NOEUX-les-MINES.	18th January 1916. Tuesday.		Work at Office. Rode over to 1st London Fd. R.F.A. and 23rd London battalion at LES BREBIS, inspecting all horses. Lines and Sig. pl. Coy. Mobile Section.	J.A.

Army Form C. 2118.

WAR DIARY
of
INTELLIGENCE SUMMARY.
(Erase heading not required.)

Instructions regarding War Diaries and Intelligence Summaries are contained in F. S. Regs., Part II. and the Staff Manual respectively. Title pages will be prepared in manuscript.

Place	Date	Hour	Summary of Events and Information	Remarks and references to Appendices
Hq. 47th Lon. Divn. NOEUX-les-MINES.	19th January 1918. Wednesday.		Routine Office Work. Visit with correspondence. Visited lines of D.w.C. Headquarters Signal Coy. and 7th Bde Amm. Column in NOEUX-les-MINES. Proceeded to Mobile Section, included a report the present treatment and evacuation of animals. Hence to London Fusiliers in VAUDRICOURT. Afternoon inspected transport lines of 140th Infantry Bde. with LIEUT. CRAIG, AVC. in charge.	Gt.
Hq. 47th Lon. Divn. NOEUX-les-MINES.	20th January 1918. Thursday.		Office work. Visited 5th and 7th Bde Amm. Columns, - 13th M.M. Battery in NOEUX. Mobile Section and 2nd London Fusiliers at VAUDRICOURT. 47th D.A.C. HESDIGNEUL. Afternoon call from D.D.V.S. 1st Army with him several hours for reading.	Gt.
Hq. 47th Lon. Divn. NOEUX-les-MINES.	21st January 1918. Friday.		Routine Office work. Mobile Section and Maj Edwards horse at DROUVIN Afternoon met Veterinary Officers at Office with Recn N°s. (i) discussing the Walloping (Clipping) Lamps, and	Gt.

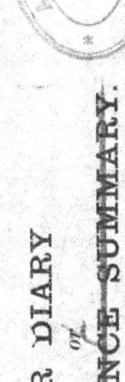

Army Form C. 2118.

WAR DIARY
or
INTELLIGENCE SUMMARY.
(Erase heading not required.)

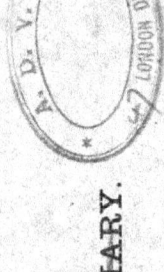

Place	Date	Hour	Summary of Events and Information	Remarks and references to Appendices
Hq.47th Lon.Divn. NOEUX-les-MINES.	22nd January 1916. Saturday.		Office work, correspondence etc. Called upon D.H.Q. Signal Coy, 4th and 6th Field Ambulance Mobile Section. Inspected horses 47th Divl. Ammn. Column RESIGNED also 10th D.A.C. on an 3 rotary A.T.C. Proceeded to RESBEDIE in afternoon & horse hors of 1st London Bde R.F.A. purely injured by shellfire two having to be destroyed.	A.
Hq.47th Lon.Divn. NOEUX-les-MINES.	23rd January 1916. Sunday.		Routine Office work. Visited stables 6th Field Ambulance and several Artillery units in the notion at NOEUX Les MINES. Went through all horses of Divisional Train at HALLICOURT with the D.D.V. Mobile Section.	A.
Hq.47th Lon.Divn. NOEUX-les-MINES.	24th January 1916. Monday.		Office work. Inspected horses of 8th Sanitary brigade R.F.A. at HOUCHIN. 4th & 6th Field Ambulance Mobile Section. Destroyed the Enteric Glanders case Horse, made post mortem examination, and reported fully to D.D.V.S. 1st Army Re about.	A.

Army Form C. 2118.

WAR DIARY
of
INTELLIGENCE SUMMARY.
(Erase heading not required.)

Instructions regarding War Diaries and Intelligence Summaries are contained in F. S. Regs., Part II. and the Staff Manual respectively. Title pages will be prepared in manuscript.

Place	Date	Hour	Summary of Events and Information	Remarks and references to Appendices
Hq. 47th Lon.Divn. NOEUX-les-MINES.	25th January 1916. Tuesday.		Routine work at Office and corroborating. Called upon Lords of Headquarters and Signal Cop. 6 in Field Ambce. & para field to R.E. Mobile Section. Made roughs on section of 10th Dent Ammon Column as DESBIGNEVS, having several cases of than cases and ordered immediate dressing of mangeness, section fully to D.D.V.S.-1st Army.	J.A.
Hq. 47th Lon.Divn. NOEUX-les-MINES.	26th January 1916. Wednesday.		Office work. Headquarters Signals. Mobile Section. Received and allotted 2 Remounts in afternoon. Informed A.D.V.S. of 16th Division to Office also sent some R.V.C. arranging veterinary admission for attached units.	J.A.
Hq. 47th Lon.Divn. NOEUX-les-MINES.	27th January 1916. Thursday.		Usual Office work. Visited Lords of Dent Rys. at Engineers, 5th & 8th Bris. R.F.A. making thorough inspection, eliminating all cases requiring evacuating. Mobile Section.	J.A.

WAR DIARY
INTELLIGENCE SUMMARY.
(Erase heading not required.)

Army Form C. 2118.

Place	Date	Hour	Summary of Events and Information	Remarks and references to Appendices
Hq. 47th Lon. Divn. NOEUX-les-MINES.	28th January 1916. Friday.		Office routine. Replied to D.D.V.S. 1st Army report shewing number of punctured feet, suggesting that as a preventive measure leather belts with nail plates during the periods of my own employment in this matter. Visited 2nd London Base R.F.A. & 6th Lond. R.F.A. Horse on 1st of London Horse Mobile Section - Interviewed Veterinary Officers and Office.	A.1
Hq. 47th Lon. Divn. NOEUX-les-MINES.	29th January 1916. Saturday.		 Usual Office routine and correspondence. Called upon A.D.V.S., Reg. Sub. Corp. 7th Div. R.F.A. on field duties at NOEUX, reported to 5th & 6th Dies. Ambce. Columns at LOURAIN and Mobile Section BROUAIN. Afternoon inspected 47th Divl. Ammn. Column and 10th D.A.C. for any sick reaction to Mallien test. Weekly sick reports rendered to D.D.V.S. 1st Army.	A.1
Hq. 47th Lon. Divn. NOEUX-les-MINES.	30th January 1916. Sunday.		Routine Office work and correspondence. Visited Signal Corp, wits and inspected with A.E.S.R.Y. D.T.C. all animals of 2nd Echelon base R.F.A. attached to this Division. Rode on to Mobile Section, treated cases on hand and detailed men for evacuation on following day. Remainder of day spent in Office.	A.1
Hq. 47th Lon. Divn. NOEUX-les-MINES.	31st January 1916. Monday.		Office routine. Inaugurating Agrical div. 20th London Battery. Rode on to Mobile Section, inspected Lieut Edmund there BROWN and 10th and 47th D.Am. Column HESDIGNEUL. Received a call from several Vet. Officers on duty.	A.1

Joseph Ahern
Capt. A.D.V.S. 47th Lon. Division.

Army Form C. 2118.

WAR DIARY
or
INTELLIGENCE SUMMARY.
(Erase heading not required.)

Instructions regarding War Diaries and Intelligence Summaries are contained in F. S. Regs., Part II. and the Staff Manual respectively. Title pages will be prepared in manuscript.

Place	Date	Hour	Summary of Events and Information	Remarks and references to Appendices
Hq.47th Lon.Divn. NOEUX-les-MINES.	1st February 1918. Tuesday		Officer routine and correspondence. Visited lines of Divl. Headquarters Signal Coy and whole of 3rd and 6th London brigades R.F.A. in neighbourhood of NOEUX, talking and advising upon all rates. Afternoon, rode over to Mobile Section instructing upon treatment of sick Horses. Hence to 3rd London both Divisions.	
Hq.47th Lon.Divn. NOEUX-les-MINES.	2nd February 1918 Wednesday		Usual office routine morning and evening. Inspected lines of Divl. Ammn. Column at HERDIN-ZUL, several horses requiring rest sent to Mobile Section for examination. Saw also horses of Divnl. Train. Found all in good condition and no actual Mobile Section. London Battery R.F.A. and 6th Lon. Field Ambulance.	
Hq.47th Lon.Divn. NOEUX-les-MINES.	3rd February 1918 Thursday		Office routine morning and evening. Made inspection of lines of 1/2nd London Brigade R.F.A. at HERDUIN, with A.D.V.S. Gave advice upon cases of lame examinations of horses. Proceeded to Mobile Section, arranged for evacuation of sick. Afternoon, rode over to LES-BREDIS, to See Transport animals of 140th Inf. Brigade. Inspected Divl. Dragon Hydrate Horse upon return.	

Army Form C. 2118.

WAR DIARY
of
INTELLIGENCE SUMMARY.
(Erase heading not required.)

Instructions regarding War Diaries and Intelligence Summaries are contained in F. S. Regs., Part II. and the Staff Manual respectively. Title pages will be prepared in manuscript.

Place	Date	Hour	Summary of Events and Information	Remarks and references to Appendices
Hq.47th Lon.Divn. NOEUX-les-MINES.	4th February 1916. Friday.		Office routine morning and evening. Quarparters visit signal Coy. & tank 6.h Con. Field Ambulance NOEUX. Rode over to Zing Mr. Force and Mobile Section at DROUVIN. In afternoon held conference at office with Div. officers on the prevention and treatment of skin diseases and prevention in addition to other matters of a monentous character here discussed. Received a weekly act. returns. casualties comm. at. & carry. evag. to unusual number of shell fire cases, and losses & men's attacks for & Ordinary administration.	J.1
Hq.47th Lon.Divn. NOEUX-les-MINES.	5th February 1916. Saturday.		Usual Office routine. Visited lines of D.H.S. Signal Coy. and 3rd London Field Coy. R.E. Made general inspection of Divl. Train. Inspection of animals very satisfactory. Mobile Section. 1/2 – 1/3th Battalions R.F.A. NOEUX les MINES.	J.1
Hq.47th Lon.Divn. NOEUX-les-MINES.	6th February 1916. Sunday.		Office routine. Visited Signal Coy. & 6th Field Ambulance. Again called at Divl. Train. owing to a case of obstruction of bowels. Men under special treatment. Mobile Section.	J.1

Army Form C. 2118.

WAR DIARY
of
INTELLIGENCE SUMMARY.
(Erase heading not required.)

Place	Date	Hour	Summary of Events and Information	Remarks and references to Appendices
Hq.47th Lon.Divn. NOEUX-les-MINES.	7th February 1918. Monday		Daily Office Routine morning and evening. Called at the hours of Lynel Coy from whom proceeded to Divl. Train Mobile Section. Afternoon inspected various Artillery units in turn at NOEUX-LINGNES Medical Arrangements, supervised the shoeing, and demonstrated to the farriers upon the care of the foot and the avoidance of loss of shoeing in this respect.	J.B.
Hq.47th Lon.Divn. NOEUX-les-MINES.	8th February 1918. Tuesday		Usual Office Routine. Visited Divl. Train and 5/4th Field Ambulance. Divl. Train Lines are now almost recovered. Inspected horses of 5th and 6th London Brigades from. Letters and compared with the T.O. upon improvement in feeding conditions. Mobile Section and King Edwards Horse.	J.B.
Hq.47th Lon.Divn. NOEUX-les-MINES.	9th February 1918. Wednesday		Daily Office routine morning & evening. Interviewed A.D.V.S. 4r Division with regard to taking over office arrangements on move of Division. Mobilised Artillery units in turns NOEUX-LINGNES. Have reports for Mobile Section.	J.B.

Army Form C. 2118.

WAR DIARY
or
INTELLIGENCE SUMMARY.
(Erase heading not required.)

Instructions regarding War Diaries and Intelligence Summaries are contained in F. S. Regs., Part II. and the Staff Manual respectively. Title pages will be prepared in manuscript.

Place	Date	Hour	Summary of Events and Information	Remarks and references to Appendices
Hq.47th Lon.Divn. NOEUX-les-MINES.	10th February 1916. Thursday		Usual Office Routine morning and evening. Rode over to TILLERS to arrange for Officers and ORs fit for Mobile Section. Sent up horses at Mobile Section DROUVIN on their journey. Filimen inspected horses of 5th Lon Amm Col HOUCHIN. Interviewed D.B.D.D.S. & gave opinion upon a new improved nosebag. Received, examined and allotted batch of Remounts at NOEUX MINES. Watered all passed as a pair sample. 	J.M.
Hq.47th Lon.Divn. NOEUX-les-MINES.	11th February 1916. Friday		Daily office routine. Inspected Dinethages, signed los hores, 6th Lond Ambulance & 2nd Field Co R.E. NOEUX. Remainder of morning spent at Mobile Section. Conferred with T. Officers at Office in afternoon upon completion of Matters relating to horses of Division. Received from them weekly sick returns.	J.M.
Hq.47th Lon.Divn. NOEUX-les-MINES.	12th February 1916. Saturday		Usual Office Routine. Inspected Transport horses of 141st Infantry Brigade at LES-BREBIS. and one battalion of 142nd Inf Bde. Mobile Section & King Amm Horse. Sick report rendered to D.D.V.S 1st Army.	J.M.

WAR DIARY
of
INTELLIGENCE SUMMARY.
(Erase heading not required.)

Army Form C. 2118.

Instructions regarding War Diaries and Intelligence Summaries are contained in F. S. Regs., Part II. and the Staff Manual respectively. Title pages will be prepared in manuscript.

Place	Date	Hour	Summary of Events and Information	Remarks and references to Appendices
Hq. 47th Lon.Divn. NOEUX-les-MINES.	13th February 1918. Sunday		Office routine morning and evening. Visited hosts of Signal Coy. & 2nd Field Ambulance at NOEUX. Thence to Hrs. of 7th Brigade R.F.A at unit - a few foot cases, a skin trouble at present under treatment. Various units of Division caused by the scattering of nails on Roads. Saw cases at Divl. Train HALLICOURT, and inspected horse of 5th Bde Ammn Column at DOUCHIN. Mobile Section.	
Hq. 47th Lon.Divn. NOEUX-les-MINES.	14th February 1918. Monday		Usual Office routine. Inspected horses of 142nd London Bde. R.F.A. at VERDRIN: a suspicious case to Matters Clot: isolated at Mobile Section and reported fully to D.D.V.S. Several sore cases sent from this Bde for examination. Afternoon inspected horses of 10th Divl Ammn Column at VERDIGNEUL. Many activated cases here also cleaned out. Mobile Section.	
Hq. 47th Lon.Divn. NOEUX-les-MINES.	15th February 1918. Tuesday		Office routine morning and evening. Visited Divl. Hqrs. Signal & 6/5 Losses, & 2/1st Field Ambulance at work in Rheumatic practically nil. Inspected 5th horses 6.w. R.F.A. & coy. at NOEUX-les-MINES. Mobile Section.	

Army Form C. 2118.

WAR DIARY
of
INTELLIGENCE SUMMARY.
(Erase heading not required.)

Instructions regarding War Diaries and Intelligence Summaries are contained in F. S. Regs., Part II. and the Staff Manual respectively. Title pages will be prepared in manuscript.

Place	Date	Hour	Summary of Events and Information	Remarks and references to Appendices
Hq. 47th Lon.Divn. LILLERS.	16th February 1916. Wednesday		Office transferred to LILLERS, also Mobile Section. Visited Mobile Section. Afternoon spent at office in dealing with correspondence and routine work generally.	JR
Hq. 47th Lon.Divn. LILLERS.	17th February 1916. Thursday		Usual Office Routine. Inspected horses of 140th Infantry Bde LILLERS, arranged for erection of shelters where not provided. Did Linga. Lines and Signal Coy. Mobile Section. Visited Artillery units at BUSNES.	JR
Hq. 47th Lon.Divn. LILLERS.	18th February 1916. Friday		Office routine morning & evening. Visited No. Lon. Field Ambulance - 6th London Battalion LILLERS. Mobile Section. Examined 30/y Officers at Office & discussed all subjects of topical interest.	JR

2353 Wt. W2544/1454 700,000 5/15 D. D. & L. A.D.S.S./Forms/C. 2118.

Army Form C. 2118.

WAR DIARY
of
INTELLIGENCE SUMMARY.
(Erase heading not required.)

Place	Date	Hour	Summary of Events and Information	Remarks and references to Appendices
19th February 1916. Saturday Hq. 47th Lon.Divn. LILLERS.			Office routine morning and evening. Mobile Section. Visited Divl. Stage Signal Coy. who proceeded to APPUGNY on its general inspection of Engineer Companies & Divisional Signal Annex. Column BUCKEL. Went by car. Returns rendered to D.D.V.S. 1st Army	JA
20th February 1916. Sunday Hq. 47th Lon.Divn. LILLERS.			Usual Routine. 1/5 Infantry Brigade Field Ambulance. Genl. Artillery less mm Col. Loan area for manoeuvres. Inspected Transport Horses of 142nd Infantry Bde at ALLOUAGNE and district. Mobile Section.	JA
21st February 1916. Monday Hq. 47th Lon.Divn. LILLERS.			Early office routine Mobile Section Visited 7th Nown Curtr. LIKEPS, and Divl. Supply & Signal Coy at MENZEB. Instructions to proceed in advance to ABBEVILLE received to attend conference there.	JA

WAR DIARY or INTELLIGENCE SUMMARY

Army Form C. 2118.

Place	Date	Hour	Summary of Events and Information	Remarks and references to Appendices
Hq.47th Lon.Divn. LILLERS.	22nd February 1918. Tuesday		Attended to usual office routine. Record of Mullen transferred to D.D.V.S. Proceded to ABBEVILLE, conference at Headquarters V.V.C. re on Veterinary Personnel.	
Hq.47th Lon.Divn. LILLERS.	23rd February 1918. Wednesday		Returned from ABBEVILLE in evening.	
Hq.47th Lon.Divn. LILLERS.	24th February 1918. Thursday		Office Routine morning and evening. Inspected horses of 14 Bn Inf. Bde, Divl Troops Signal Coy. Mobile Section. Rode over to RAINBERT and delivered a lecture on Horse Mastership to Officers + N.C.Os of Divisional Train dealing with all points in connexion to the highest efficiency.	

Army Form C. 2118.

WAR DIARY
or
INTELLIGENCE SUMMARY.
(Erase heading not required.)

Instructions regarding War Diaries and Intelligence Summaries are contained in F. S. Regs., Part II. and the Staff Manual respectively. Title pages will be prepared in manuscript.

Place	Date	Hour	Summary of Events and Information	Remarks and references to Appendices
Hq. 47th Lon. Divn. LILLERS.	25th February 1918. Friday		Usual Office Routine. Mobile Section. Inspected horses of Signal Coy. Above to 142nd Infantry Bde at ALLOUAGNE. Interviewed D.D.M.S. 1st Army at office upon Mallein report slight addition suggested, and the method adopted by us in the evacuation of Lords and the notification of same induding those from other Divisions. Received weekly anti-rabies from Vety Operations of animal nowadays comparatively low.	
Hq. 47th Lon. Divn. LILLERS.	26th February 1918. Saturday		Office Routine morning and evening. Mobile Section. Inspected horses of Divl. Engineers in following Tuesday. Again informed D.D.V.S. at office with regard to a result of Mallein test at Base Reception Hospital, and to have been sent from 47th Divisions, but investigation proved that such was not the case.	
Hq. 47th Lon. Divn. LILLERS.	27th February 1918. Sunday		Usual Office Routine. Visited horses of our non Field Ambulance, who are Bde. Divl. Trans. Signal Coy. Mobile Section.	

Army Form C. 2118.

WAR DIARY
OF
INTELLIGENCE SUMMARY.
(Erase heading not required.)

Instructions regarding War Diaries and Intelligence Summaries are contained in F. S. Regs., Part II. and the Staff Manual respectively. Title pages will be prepared in manuscript.

Place	Date	Hour	Summary of Events and Information	Remarks and references to Appendices
Hq.47th Lon.Divn. LILLERS.	28th February 1916 Monday		Office Routine morning and evening. Mobile Section. Inspected all transport horses of 1/4th Infantry Bde, 5th and 6th London Field Ambulances. Divnl. Supp. Signal Coy.	
Hq.47th Lon.Divn. LILLERS.	29th February 1916 Tuesday		Usual Office Routine. Mobile Section. Inspected horses of Divl. Hqrs. Signal Coy. at MENSECQ from thence to Divl. Ammn. Column at PICHEM. Rode over to LAPUGNOY and delivered a lecture on Horse Maclarship. Watering. Feeding. Disease, cause of prevention of etc., to Officers and N.C.Os of Field Companies R.E.	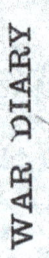

Joseph Alison
A.D.V.S. 47th London Division

Vol IV
XIII

D.A.G.,
G.H.Q.,
3rd Echelon.

Herewith please, Diary for Month of March 1916!

Joseph Abson
Major.
A.D.V.S. 47th (London) Division.

Hdqrs.,
47th Divn.
April 1st 16.

WAR DIARY
INTELLIGENCE SUMMARY.

Army Form C. 2118.

Place	Date	Hour	Summary of Events and Information	Remarks and references to Appendices
Hq. 47th Lon. Divn. LILLERS	1st March 1916 Wednesday		Office routine morning and evening. Made inspection of all horses of Divisional Train at RAINBERT also Divl. Headquarters and Signal Coy at MENSECQ. Gave lecture to Officers, N.C.Os and men of Signal Coy about stores. Mastistips. Visited Mobile Section + arrangements about treatment of motor vans.	
Hq. 47th Lon. Divn. LILLERS	2nd March 1916 Thursday		Usual office routine. Mobile Section. Interviewed P.C. 47th Mobile Section the Divisional with reference to moving 2nd Cavalry base cases into Mv Mobile Section. Inspected Transport horses of 142nd Infantry Bde with 142nd T.R.O. D.C. Headquarters Signal Coy. Order a convocation of Several	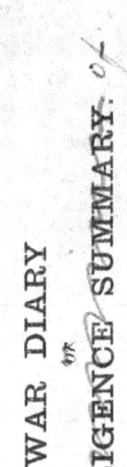
Hq. 47th Lon. Divn. LILLERS	3rd March 1916 Friday		Office routine. Visited Mobile Section. Inspected horses of 6th Field Ambulance, Judges Remarks. Held conference in afternoon at office with all Tpt. Officers discussing all questions pertaining to the efficiency of the animals under their charge.	

Army Form C. 2118.

WAR DIARY
or
INTELLIGENCE SUMMARY. of
(Erase heading not required.)

Instructions regarding War Diaries and Intelligence Summaries are contained in F. S. Regs., Part II. and the Staff Manual respectively. Title pages will be prepared in manuscript.

Place	Date	Hour	Summary of Events and Information	Remarks and references to Appendices
Hq 47th Lon Divn LILLERS	4th March 1916 Saturday	9am	Office routine morning and evening. Mobile Section. Inspected horses of Divl. Engineers at LAPUGNOY and 4th Bn Royal West Surreys at MARLES-LES-MINES: have given orders specified with Lt.-Col. Sidebottom 7.D.H. upon return, indicating schedule of passing sick at Mo Field Ambulance Inspections.	J.R.
Hq 47th Lon Divn LILLERS	5th March 1916 Sunday	9am	Routine office work. Rode over to ERNY-ST.JULIEN to inspect several cases left behind by various units during manoeuvres, and arranged for removal to Mobile Section. Inspected horses of Mo Field Ambcd., Signal Coy & Divl. Hqrs. Mobile Section.	J.R.
Hq 47th Lon Divn LILLERS	6th March 1916 Monday	9am	Usual Office routine, morning and evening. Mobile Section. Lopus & Signals. Rode over to AUCHEL and gave lecture on Horse management to Officers of Divl. Ammun. Column. Made inspection of whole of horses of Sn Lon Bde R.F.A. – also at AUCHEL.	J.R.

2353 Wt. W3544/1454 700,000 5/15 D. D. & L. A.D.S.S. Forms/C. 2118.

WAR DIARY
INTELLIGENCE SUMMARY

Army Form C. 2118.

Place	Date	Hour	Summary of Events and Information	Remarks and references to Appendices
Hq. 47th Div. Dn. LIFTERS	7th March 1916 Tuesday		Office routine morning & evening. Visited Mobile Section. Rode over to AUCHEL & inspected Lorries & Desl. Amm. Column. Found condition of same to be satisfactory. Drove thence to LAPUGNOY and inspected 3 Companies Royal Engineers, also 4th Battn. Royal Welsh Fus. at MARLES-les-MINES.	J.
Hq. 47th Div. Dn. LIFTERS	8th March 1916 Wednesday 10.00 a.m.		Usual Office routine. Mobile Section stages & signals. In afternoon rode over to BRUAY, to arrange for billeting of horses and men. Selected site for Mobile Section, ordered & thorough examination of same. Returned here to Div.l Hags. for mobilisation in D.Routine Orders, including all units to thoroughly overhaul + all stables & horse stalling before inoculation in view, as to be taken over in view of prevalence of mange in French Lorries. Received to D.D.V.S. 1st Army as to action taken with reference to above.	J.

Army Form C. 2118.

WAR DIARY
or,
INTELLIGENCE SUMMARY of.
(Erase heading not required.)

Instructions regarding War Diaries and Intelligence Summaries are contained in F. S. Regs., Part II. and the Staff Manual respectively. Title pages will be prepared in manuscript.

Place	Date	Hour	Summary of Events and Information	Remarks and references to Appendices
Hd.Qrs. 47th Divn. BRUAY.	9th March 1916 Thursday		Office now in MONTEBOMMAIN Co. The office moved from LILLERS to BRUAY. 16. Rifles, Mobile Section, superintended inspection of stables later morning. Arrival of horse lamp. Inspected horses at HEADQUARTERS of 2nd Bn Col. Remainder of day spent at Office.	JR
Hq 47th Divn. BRUAY.	10th March 1916 Friday		Usual office routine. Visited horses at Signal Coy & Divl. Engrs. Hence to King Edward's Horse: no cases here & horses in splendid condition. Held conference at office with Vety Officers, received weekly pit returns. Interviewed Capt. STUART. 16. re. lecture with Malleine horses of Reserve Col. In London Bus. R.F.A. by request from D.D.V.S. 1st Army.	JR
Hq. 47th Divn. BRUAY.	11th March 1916 Saturday		Office routine morning and night. Visited Mobile Section, conversed upon treatment of cases here. Inspected horses of 141st Infantry Bde in and around neighbourhood of BRUAY. Condition fair considering rigours of past few months.	JR

2353 Wt. W2544/1454 700,000 5/15 D. D. & L. A.D.S.S. Forms/C 2118.

Army Form C. 2118.

WAR DIARY
or
INTELLIGENCE SUMMARY. of
(Erase heading not required.)

Place	Date	Hour	Summary of Events and Information	Remarks and references to Appendices
Hqrs. 47th Divn. B.R.H.Q.	12th March 1916 Sunday		Office routine as usual. Rode over to LILLERS, NOYELLOBE and EBUN/6oMINES to inspect several Loces left behind by London Bar R.F.A. sign London Batts. rearranged for their removal to nearest Mobile Section.	
Hqrs. 47th Divn. B.R.H.Q.	13th March 1916 Monday		Office routine Rode over to CAMBLAIN-CHATELAIN and made inspection of metals of 7th London Bde. R.F.A: all her mules sent to Mobile Section for evacuation. Reported same in evening to D.D.R. of Army. Trained Mobile Section. Dud. Shops Signal Coy.	
Hqrs. 47th Divn. B.R.H.Q.	14th March 1916 Tuesday		Office routine right morning. Rode over to DIEVAL inspected horses of French Col. Tr. No.646 and 22nd Battery; from there to Dud. French Column at LABUISSIERE. Mobile Section. Instructions received to move to new forward area 15.3.16.	

Army Form C. 2118.

WAR DIARY
or
INTELLIGENCE SUMMARY of

(Erase heading not required.)

Instructions regarding War Diaries and Intelligence Summaries are contained in F. S. Regs., Part II. and the Staff Manual respectively. Title pages will be prepared in manuscript.

Place	Date	Hour	Summary of Events and Information	Remarks and references to Appendices
Hq 47th Div. SAVEUCOURT	15th March 1916 Wednesday		Two Officers went to SAVEUCOURT: also to relieve 26/ Major V.G.P. Mobile Section also. Inspected lorries and platoons plotting in the area immediately surrounding installing upon all T.S.S. Tech. Offrs. the urgent necessity of investigation remainders of any spare an Mobile Section + attending to emergencies at once. 	JR
Hq 47th Div. SAVEUCOURT	16th March 1916 Thursday		Received communication from A.D.S.S. 23rd Division that he was going to inspect stabling at RATEAU-to FRESNICOURT by invitation of D.D.S.S. 1st Army, and he was visiting the area later on by me. Inspected new horses disinfection carried out, place put out of bounds + organized duty to D.D.S.S. Office continued work + Mobile Section.	JR
Hq 47th Div. SAVEUCOURT	17th March 1916 Friday		Usual Office work in morning and evening. Rode over to RATEAU-RE-10-SAIE 16 see horses of Dark Hy Retreat Coy when when pressing indented animals of 142nd Inf. Bde, 3 Companies Engineers and Signal Company at various places where camped on the way.	JR

2353 Wt W2544/1454 700,000 5/15 D. D. & L. A.D.S.S. Forms/C 2118.

WAR DIARY
INTELLIGENCE SUMMARY
(Erase heading not required.)

Army Form C. 2118.

Place	Date	Hour	Summary of Events and Information	Remarks and references to Appendices
Hq. 47th Divn. & HULLUCH	18th March 1916 Saturday		Office routine. Visited Mobile Section: Inspected 3 French telephones lent to Govt. Service, sent them to Mobile Section for examination. Made general reading round of N.C.O. Infy. Bde. Transport 2/3rd Signal Co., R.E. Signal Coy., r Artillery units, advising A.M. D.T.'s, Transport Officer & Field Ord. with regard to condition & erection of Breeches have new their charge. Weekly act returns rendered to D.D.T.S. (Army) much slow smallest borrowings of messages. Howest rate of returns since Bureau's period in the country, two only were received.	J.A.
Hq. 47th Divn. & HULLUCH	19th March 1916 Sunday		Office routine nothing noted. Visited Sgnl. Tropp. Signals: undertook drive to D.H.Q. HAPPE BATTERY R.G.A. at ESTRE-TROUCHIE, pilot attached to Bureau: received has various hour requiring attention. Rode over to FREVILLERS, halted by pilot a chapter with puncture just below my 2nd Bureau. Line to King Avenue Street at MARNICOURT. No circuit was	J.A.

WAR DIARY
INTELLIGENCE SUMMARY

Army Form C. 2118.

Place	Date	Hour	Summary of Events and Information	Remarks and references to Appendices
Hq. 47th Lon. Div. CAUCOURT	20th March 1916 Monday		Office routine morning and evening. Visited 2nd Reserve Park OLHAIN; having just formed Divisional 6th London Bde. R.F.A. at GAUCHIN-LEGAL; 140th Inf. Bde. Headquarters and Divl. Trans. Signal Corp. Made appointment for inspection of 5th Batt. R.F.A. for 22nd inst. Mobile Section.	J.A.
Hq. 47th Lon. Div. CAUCOURT	21st March 1916 Tuesday		Usual office routine. Inspected 4 horses of Divl. Ammn. Column at CAUCOURT recommended with T.O.E. Rode over to ESTREE-CAUCHIE. To see horses of 5th Siege battery; ordered destruction of bad case of open shirt fetlock. Sent others to Mobile on arrival. Instructions received from Divl. Trans. to Leave to move to HERMIES and two officers to MESNIL-BOUCHE on 22nd inst.	J.A.
Hq. 47th Lon. Div. MESNIL BOUCHE W.10.B.	22nd March 1916 Wednesday		Attended to correspondence at office. Inspected photo of horses of 6th London Bde. R.F.A. in and around replacement at GAUCHIN-LEGAL; denoted 200 cases evacuated to Base for rest. Office and Mobile Section move as above. Joined 4/4-5/4-6/4 Field Ambulances.	J.A.

Army Form C. 2118.

WAR DIARY
or
INTELLIGENCE SUMMARY.
(Erase heading not required.)

Instructions regarding War Diaries and Intelligence Summaries are contained in F. S. Regs., Part II. and the Staff Manual respectively. Title pages will be prepared in manuscript.

Place	Date	Hour	Summary of Events and Information	Remarks and references to Appendices
HQrs 47th Divn MESNIL-BOUCHE	23rd March 1916		Routine office work morning and evening. Interviewed B.A.A.D. A.L.B. at Gnl. Hqrs, with regard to a more suitable site for Mobile Section at FRESNICOURT: Suggested house of Sig.ad Coy. Received and examined a 167 Reinforcements at HERSIN Station. Instructed by D.D.V.S. to render R.F.A. 2000 for No 2 Reserve Park OLMAIN to previous Thursday. Rode over to OLMAIN to gather necessary information and return remarks. Visited Mobile Section at HERIPRE.	J.A.
HQrs 47th Divn MESNIL-BOUCHE	24th March 1916		Office routine. Gnl. Hqrs Signal Coy. Interviewed with Sig. Officers of Office in addition, discussing their various charges and progress of reinforcements treatment; re-allotted units for attendance. Received from him their weekly return when. Visited Corps Troops Signals Lines at RANCICOURT, now under my charge for Holy observance. Inspected out lines of 56th Brig. R.F.A. with Capt. J. GOSLING.	J.A.

WAR DIARY of INTELLIGENCE SUMMARY.

Army Form C. 2118.

Place	Date	Hour	Summary of Events and Information	Remarks and references to Appendices
Hd. Qrs. Mob. Sect. MESNIL BOUCHE	25th March 1916		Morning and evening Office routine. General inspecting tour of the Field Ambces: ESTREE-CAUCHIE, DIEVAL and FRESNICOURT. Mobile Section HERIPRE and St. NICHOLAS Chatham. Return at 18h.COURT. Saw horses of Ind. Bde. Signal Coy. and 16th London Battery at Chelers. Mr Lt. JAHIE in afternoon. Went in a/c to rehearse headers to D.D.V.S. St. Pol.	J.R.
Hd. Qrs. Mob. Sect. MESNIL BOUCHE	26th March 1916		Office routine. Twelve horses of 141st Infantry Bde. at GRAND SERVINS with T.O.K. Capt. BRYDEN. From there to 5th London bde R.G.A. at ESTREE-CAUCHIE also 115th Siege Battery R.G.A. there. Also, Signal Coy. and 16th London Battery.	J.R.
Hd. Qrs. Mob. Sect. MESNIL BOUCHE	27th March 1916		Routine Office work. Inspected site for Mobile Section at FRESNICOURT and made final arrangements for occupation. Inspected all horses of 2 Lorbardie Ind. Engineers at GOUY-SERVINS No 2 Reserve Park and No 2 G.S. Troops and Cycle at RANZICOURT. Mobile Mobile Section.	J.R.

Army Form C. 2118.

Instructions regarding War Diaries and Intelligence Summaries are contained in F.S. Regs., Part II. and the Staff Manual respectively. Title pages will be prepared in manuscript.

WAR DIARY
or
INTELLIGENCE SUMMARY.
(Erase heading not required.)

Place	Date	Hour	Summary of Events and Information	Remarks and references to Appendices
Luzeary Hqrs 47th Lon. Divn. MESNIL-BOUCHE	28th March 1916 Tuesday		Office routine: Visited FRESNICOURT and made final arrangements for removal of Mobile Section there. Inspected horses of No 2 Reserve Park at OBLAIN and 4th Field Ambulance GAUCHIN-LEGAL, also 6th Lon. Bde. R.F.A. at ESTREE-CAUCHIE.	J.A.
Hqrs 47th Lon. Divn. MESNIL-BOUCHE	29th March 1916 Wednesday		Office routine morning & evening. Visited horses of Divl. Hqrs. Signal Coy. & 15th & 16th Lon. Batteries R.F.A. Rode over to OBLAIN to obtain 10 sick horses of No 2 Reserve Park from there to RANCOURT. to 4 Lon. Loco Signals. Visited Mobile Section FRESNICOURT.	J.A.
Hqrs 47th Lon. Divn. MESNIL-BOUCHE	30th March 1916 Thursday		Usual Office Routine. Met D.D.V.S. at 10am at Office, and spent day with him in inspecting horses of Divl. Ammn. Column and various other units for the purpose of reading those too heavy for Artillery, most others requiring rest. Arranged for Divisional inspection to take place on Monday and Tuesday April Third & Fourth. Mobile Section	J.A.

WAR DIARY
INTELLIGENCE SUMMARY.

Place	Date	Hour	Summary of Events and Information	Remarks and references to Appendices
3rd Army Hq. 47th Lon. Divn. MESNIL-BOUCHÉ	31st March 1916		Office routine. Communicated with all units of Division with regard to forthcoming inspection of gas helmets and gloves for same. Inspected lines of 4 Field Companies R.E. at PETIT-SERVINS also 2nd/2nd French Stores at GOUY-SERVINS, no storage case has been located there, necessary precautions taken. Visited Mobile Section. Conferred with Sely. Officers at Office, hoping in view of wet weather and influenza sickness modernly low, no particular complaint predominating.	

Joseph Adam
Major R.A.M.C.
A.D.M.S. 47th (London) Division.

adVs 47 Dw

Vol XLV

Army Form C. 2118.

WAR DIARY
or
INTELLIGENCE SUMMARY.
(Erase heading not required.)

Instructions regarding War Diaries and Intelligence Summaries are contained in F. S. Regs., Part II. and the Staff Manual respectively. Title pages will be prepared in manuscript.

Place	Date	Hour	Summary of Events and Information	Remarks and references to Appendices
Hq. 47th Lon. Divn. MAISNIL-BOUCHÉ	1st April 1916 Saturday		Office routine morning and evening. Visited Mobile Section. Programme of inspection for following Monday forwarded to D.D.M.S. 1st Army. Weekly return returns also rendered to D.D.M.S. Inspection horses of Divl. Hq. Signals & 6th Lon. Bde. R.F.A. in vicinity of CHATEAU-DE-LA-HAIE.	JA
Hq. 47th Lon. Divn. MAISNIL-BOUCHÉ	2nd April 1916 Sunday		Usual office routine. Visited lines of 5th London F.A.B. at ESTRÉE-CAUCHIE also 4th Lon. Field Ambulance, thence to Mobile Section FRESNICOURT. Inspected transport horses of Units Supplied at GRAND-SERVINS.	JA
Hq. 47th Lon. Divn. MAISNIL-BOUCHÉ	3rd April 1916 Monday		Routine office work. Met D.D.V.S. and D.D.R. at SAULCOURT and commenced inspection of Artillery lines as follows: 10.30 a.m. 6th Lon. B.A.C.: 10.20 a.m. 7th Lon. B.A.C. 11 am 8th Lon. F.A.B. complete: 2pm 6th Lon F.A.B. Battery horses: 3.30 pm 5th Lon F.A.B. complete. 5pm: 5th Lon. F. Ambce. 5.30pm 4th Lon. F. Ambce. Heavy units in and around SAULCOURT : ESTRÉE-CAUCHIE and GROUCHIN-LES-AB.	JA

Army Form C. 2118.

WAR DIARY
INTELLIGENCE SUMMARY.

(Erase heading not required.)

Place	Date	Hour	Summary of Events and Information	Remarks and references to Appendices
Hq. 47th Lon. Divn. MAISNIL-BOUCHÉ	4th April 1916 Tuesday		Usual Office routine. Again met D.D.M.S. and D.D.V.S. in an inspected lines of Divisional units as follows:- 10.30, 7th Lon. F.A.B. Battery horses: 11 am, 6th Lon. F. Ambce. S: 12 noon 1/3rd, 2/3, 4/4 &1/3/8 N.M.S. Roy. Engineers; 2.30 pm, 140th Infantry Bde: 3.15 pm, 141st Infantry Bde: 4 pm, 142nd Inf. Bde: 6.15 pm Divisional train & Signal Coy. Field units in and around VERDREL · GRAND-SERVINS · GOUY-SERVINS and PETIT-SERVINS. Thus completing the entire Division: most satisfactory result, all horses looking well and in first rate condition.	JL
Hq. 47th Lon. Divn. MAISNIL-BOUCHÉ	5th April 1916 Wednesday		Office routine morning and evening. Visited Mobile Section, Divisional Ammun. Column and Divl. train conferring with Sup. Officers in charge & sending up new cases to Mobile for evacuation. Informed D.A.D.M.G. with regard to Remount cases to be exchanged as a result of the recent inspection	JL

Army Form C. 2118.

WAR DIARY
or
INTELLIGENCE SUMMARY
(Erase heading not required.)

Instructions regarding War Diaries and Intelligence Summaries are contained in F. S. Regs, Part II. and the Staff Manual respectively. Title pages will be prepared in manuscript.

Hour, Date, Place	Summary of Events and Information	Remarks and References to Appendices
6th April 1916. Thursday. Hq 47th Divsn MAISNIL BOUCHE.	Office routine sight and morning. Visited Mobile Section and 5th Lon. F.A.B. 2 & 4 Lon. Field Ambulance ESTREE CAUCHIE. In afternoon mobilised Letters of London F.A.B. Instructed Capt. CRAIGBANE to render assistance to these units during my absence on leave.	[signature]
7th April 1916. Friday. Hq 47th Lon. Divn MAISNIL BOUCHE.	Proceeded on leave to England for ten days. Capt. J. SOUTHALL, O.C. Mobile Section Officiating during that time. Received weekly sick reports from July Officers and dealt with correspondence at Office.	[signature]
8th April 1916. Saturday. Hq 47th Lon. Divn MAISNIL BOUCHE.	Visited Hosps of am Corps Hq and Signalling. Usual office routine. Own duties at Mobile Section, which are included in Diary for that unit.	[signature]

Army Form C. 2118.

WAR DIARY
or
INTELLIGENCE SUMMARY.
(Erase heading not required.)

Instructions regarding War Diaries and Intelligence Summaries are contained in F. S. Regs., Part II. and the Staff Manual respectively. Title pages will be prepared in manuscript.

Place	Date	Hour	Summary of Events and Information	Remarks and references to Appendices
Hq 47th Dn MRLSNL BOUDME	9th April 1916 Sunday		Routine office work and own duties at Mobile Section	J.S.
	10th April 1916 Monday		Ditto	J.S.
	11th April 1916 Tuesday		Do	J.S.
	12th April 1916 Wednesday		Do	J.S.
	13th April 1916 Thursday		Do	J.S.
	14th April 1916 Friday		Do	J.S.
	15th April 1916 Saturday		Do	J.S.

WAR DIARY
or
INTELLIGENCE SUMMARY of.

(Erase heading not required.)

Army Form C. 2118.

Place	Date	Hour	Summary of Events and Information	Remarks and references to Appendices
	16th April 1916 Sunday		Usual Office Routine town duties at Mobile Section.	JP
	17th April 1916 Monday		Do	JP
	18th April 1916 Tuesday		Do A.D.V.S. returns from leave in evening. Reported arrival to D.D.V.S.	JP
	19th April 1916 Wednesday		Resumed duties and dealt with work at Office and dealt with all outstanding correspondence. Visited Mobile Section inspected mobilized cases prior to evacuation, which included 13 from 34th Battery R.F.A. This unit having recently joined this Division. Inspected horses of 7th Lon. F.A.B VERDREL and surrounding district.	JP
	20th April 1916 Thursday		Usual Office routine morning and evening. Visited Mobile Section, and discussed cases under treatment with O.C. Afternoon rode over to LA CONTE and inspected with C.R.E. 34/1 - 34/2 and 93rd Batteries. Langfurst arrived to be permanently attached. Horses of 1 Former Battery in somewhat poor condition, but later, exceptionally good. Report upon same rendered to D.D.V.S	JP

Army Form C. 2118.

WAR DIARY
or
INTELLIGENCE SUMMARY.
(Erase heading not required.)

Instructions regarding War Diaries and Intelligence Summaries are contained in F. S. Regs., Part II. and the Staff Manual respectively. Title pages will be prepared in manuscript.

Place	Date	Hour	Summary of Events and Information	Remarks and references to Appendices
	21st April 1916 Friday		Usual Office Routine. Inspected horses of 4th Lon. Field Amb'ce. ESTREE TRUCHIE, thence to Mobile Section, and Battery horses of 5th Bde upon return. Interviewed Telg. Officers at Office in afternoon, bringing in their weekly report returns, and discussed with them all questions bearing upon the efficiency of the animals under their charge. Visited Headquarters L. Signal Coy.	J.H.
	22nd April 1916 Saturday		Office routine early morning. Inspected transport horses of 140th Infantry Bde at GOUY-SERVINS and the 10th R'l Welsh Fus. & advised upon some stirrup cases &c. Visited Mobile Section: 4th Lond. E. Ambce at FAUCOURT.	J.H.
	23rd April 1916 Sunday		Usual Office routine. Visited horses of Divl. Hdqrs. Signal Coy, also 16th London Battery and "R" Battery R.F.A. in the rear vicinity.	J.H.

T2134. Wt. W708—776. 500000. 4/15. Sir J. C. & S.

WAR DIARY
or
INTELLIGENCE SUMMARY.
(Erase heading not required.)

Army Form C. 2118.

Place	Date	Hour	Summary of Events and Information	Remarks and references to Appendices
	24th April 1916 Monday		Office Routine Morning and night. Visited Mobile Section and detailed all cases for evacuation to Base. Advised treatment of others. Inspected 3 Batteries R.F.A. at LA COMTE, and 15th Battery at ESTREE-CAUCHIE. Arranged with C.R.A. 16 Divn. course of lectures on Horsemanship to Officers N.C.O.'s & men under his command.	J.A.
	25th April 1916 Tuesday		Usual Office routine. Visited Divl. Sig. Signals, 16th & "R" Batteries R.F.A.: cases in these units almost nil but general notes in both contained for when cases of Enteric are recommended. Conducted post-mortem on Published & severe led bowel case of Bde. Hd. Qrs. in afternoon & demons trated to Officers men upon same. Inspected horses of JA 3rd Bde F Ambce in evening.	J.A.

WAR DIARY
or
INTELLIGENCE SUMMARY
(Erase heading not required.)

Army Form C. 2118.

Place	Date	Hour	Summary of Events and Information	Remarks and references to Appendices
	26th April 1916 Wednesday		Office routine during morning. Visited Hqs of Signal Coy. Horses to 4 Companies Royal Engineers at GOUY-SERVINS. These horses in excellent condition. Rode over to OLSAIN and gave lecture on horsemanship to Officers N.C.Os & men of 1st London Battery Mobile Section.	JR
	27th April 1916 Thursday		Usual Office routine. Visited 16th "R" Battery R.F.A. at VILLERS-au-BOIS - also on 16 Mobile Section. Inspection horses of 5th & 6th Field Ambulances at GRAND-SERVINS & SIFREE and 5th Bde Amm. Col. at NEUVCOURT. Again visited 16th Battery to see horse case admitted lameness	JR

Army Form C. 2118.

WAR DIARY
or
INTELLIGENCE SUMMARY
(Erase heading not required.)

Instructions regarding War Diaries and Intelligence Summaries are contained in F. S. Regs., Part II. and the Staff Manual respectively. Title pages will be prepared in manuscript.

Place	Date	Hour	Summary of Events and Information	Remarks and references to Appendices
	27th April 1916 Thursday		Office routine morning and evening. Visited 16th L'R Batt. in Divl Hq Signals Lines, and to M.M.P. at Gouy-Servins and Mobile Section. After gunnery lecture on Lorettoensberg to officers, N.C.O. and men of 3/k Lon R.F.A. at Estree-Cauchie. Afterwards inspecting lines of this unit. Proceeded to Gouchin-Legal and saw lines of Divl. Train, also N-London Field Ambce, arranged for Bath to be picked up in open.	J.A.
	29th April 1916 Saturday		Usual office routine. Visited lines of Headquarters 6th Nor, F.A.B, in 2015 A.L.H. Haig D.H.Q. Signals, and lines of M.G. Coy 142nd Inf. Bde Gouy-Servins. Mobile Section. Again listened to transport N.C.O. men of his Lon. F. Bakes on Horsemanship.	J.A.
	30th April 1916 Sunday		Office routine, troops, part of morning in clearing up business for monthend. Visited Mobile Section, and lines of 141st Inf. Bde at Grand-Servins. Joseph Atton. M of N R.D.V.S. 47th Division	J.A.

D.A.G.,
    G.H.Q.,
        3rd Echelon.
————————————

    Herewith please War Diary for month of May 1916.

                                    Joseph Abson.
                                        Major,
Hq., 47th Divn.   A.D.V.S., 47th (London) Division.
31-5-16.

WAR DIARY
INTELLIGENCE SUMMARY.
(Erase heading not required.)

Army Form C. 2118.

Place	Date	Hour	Summary of Events and Information	Remarks and references to Appendices
Hq. 47th Div. / MAISNIL-BOUCHE	1st May 1916		Office routine morning and evening, including instructions to all "Officers and m.d's" to arrange to send Tetj. Cooks NCO + R&Fs to Mob. Section now being without one owing to reduction of establishment. Visited lines of 'R'/7 Battery, 16th Battery, Div. Sig. Signal Coy in and around CHATEAU-DE-LA-HAIE. Hence to 4 Companies Engineers at Govy-SERVINS. Met D.D.V.S. at Mobile Section re proposed upon the number of Sepsis to be made for cavalry with Artillery Brigades.	
INDANY	2nd May 1916		Usual office routine. Met D.D.R. and D.D.V.S. of ESTRÉE-CAUCHIE and with him inspection lines of 36/6, R/6 and 'R'/7 Batteries R.F.A. Gave lecture on Horsemastership to Officers NCO's and men of 16th and 'R'/7 Batteries at VILLERS au BOIS, instilling upon the minds of all the absurdly necessity and economic value of Veterinary preventive medicine by keenness of interest in the animals under their charge.	

Army Form C. 2118.

WAR DIARY
or
INTELLIGENCE SUMMARY.
(Erase heading not required.)

Instructions regarding War Diaries and Intelligence Summaries are contained in F. S. Regs., Part II. and the Staff Manual respectively. Title pages will be prepared in manuscript.

Place	Date	Hour	Summary of Events and Information	Remarks and references to Appendices
	3rd May 1916 Wednesday		Office routine morning and night. Visited horses of Divl. Sig. Coy. and transport horses of 144th Infantry Bde. at GD. BERVINS, & of 16 Motor Section at FRESNICOURT. Dealt with and advised treatment of cases seen. Inspection lines of 5th London Field Ambulance QUATRE-VENTS.	J.R.
	4th May 1916 Thursday		Daily office routine. Made general inspecting tour of 7th Kn. F.A.B. Divl. Ammn. Col. and S.A.A. and 6" Battery at MAGNICOURT and surrounding districts enquiring the advisability of picketing the horses on hard or soft ground now that the weather is more favourable. Twice a horse of Signal Coy. in evening & found had case of laminitis. Ordered horse to be removed & horse to be turned into paddock afterwards.	J.R.
	5th May 1916 Friday		Usual office routine. Troubled Mobile Section. Telephone interviewed Telip. Officer at Divl.H.Q. respecting all matters of direct importance. Inspecting horses of "R/D" Battery at VERDREL, and incidentally discovered the Heavy Battery newly administered to 2nd Div. with 13 cases strangles to Reinforce frames R.D.V.S., 2nd Div.	J.R.

T2134. Wt. W708—776. 500000. 4/15. Sir J.C. & S.

WAR DIARY
or
INTELLIGENCE SUMMARY.
(Erase heading not required.)

Place	Date	Hour	Summary of Events and Information	Remarks and references to Appendices
	6th May 1916 Saturday		Office routine: Monthly vet returns rendered to D.D.V.S. Afternoon employed on Mobile Section in clearing with case & noting examination of 30 Tely. Regts. received from Divisional units reporting condition to D.D.V.S. Cases for invalidism as to disposal. Gave lecture on Horsemastership to Officers N.C.O. men of "R/16 Battery at ESTRÉE CAUCHIE.	J.
	7th May 1916 Sunday		Usual office routine morning and evening. Visited horse of Divl Hq. Signals. Proceeded at 12 noon with A.D.V.S. 2nd Division to RIRE to attend a conference of A.D.'s V.S. there, discussing all questions of local interest.	J.
	8th May 1916 Monday		Office Routine. Day devoted to lecturing to Officers N.C.O. men & farriers of Divl Ammn Column upon Horse management and farriery, demonstrating in latter case to the infantile care to be exercised with the feet of the horse both in shoeing and in detecting the onset of lameness.	J.

Army Form C. 2118.

WAR DIARY
or
INTELLIGENCE SUMMARY.
(Erase heading not required.)

Instructions regarding War Diaries and Intelligence Summaries are contained in F.S. Regs., Part II. and the Staff Manual respectively. Title pages will be prepared in manuscript.

Place	Date	Hour	Summary of Events and Information	Remarks and references to Appendices
	9th May 1916 Tuesday		Office routine morning and evening. Inspected horses of Divl. Hq and Signal Coy; 16th Battery and R.F.A Battery. Visited Mobile Sections and horses of 15th London Battery at LES M. VENTS upon return.	JL
	10th May 1916 Wednesday		Usual Office routine. Visited Divl Amn Column at MAGNICOURT. Conferred with T.O.i/c upon cases there. Inspected horses of 15th 19th 20th Batteries R.F.A. at LA CONTE. Mobile Section: Gave lecture on Horse management to N.C.O's and men of 15th London Battery, impressing upon all the essentiality of conciliating their horses and to be exercised in preventing Disease accidents.	JL
	11th May 1916 Thursday		Office Routine. Visited Horses of Divl Hq. & Signal Coy horse 16 Coln. Serving to see Remounts of R.F.M. reported upon same to D.A.D.M.S. Lectured 15 Officers N.C. & men of 21st and 22nd Battns at CAUCOURT Mobile Section.	JL

T2134. Wt. W708-776. 500000. 4/15. Sir J. C. & S.

Army Form C. 2118.

WAR DIARY
or
INTELLIGENCE SUMMARY.
(Erase heading not required.)

Instructions regarding War Diaries and Intelligence Summaries are contained in F. S. Regs., Part II. and the Staff Manual respectively. Title pages will be prepared in manuscript.

Place	Date	Hour	Summary of Events and Information	Remarks and references to Appendices
	12th May 1916 Friday		Office routine morning and night. Visited Mobile Section Superintended evacuation of horses to base. Rode on to VERDREL saw horses of 121st-24th and R/6 Batteries. Interviewed Vet. Officer at Office in afternoon conferred with him generally upon all questions pertaining to the efficiency of the animals under their care. In evening listened to Opr. N.C.O.'s exam of 5th London Bde Am. Col. at ESTRUCOURT.	J.A.
	13th May 1916 Saturday		Usual Office routine. Visited Divl. Sig. Sqdrn horses; also 1460 Inf. Bde transport horses at BOUVIGNY-LE-RUINS; went to Mobile Section. Inspected several remount cases at Divl. Train, unsuitable for their work	J.A.
	14th May 1916 Sunday		Office Routine occupying all morning. Visited horses of Divl. Sig. Sqdron Coy. Mobile Section	J.A.

T2134. Wt. W708—776. 500000. 4/15. Sir J.C. & S.

WAR DIARY
INTELLIGENCE SUMMARY

Army Form C. 2118.

Place	Date	Hour	Summary of Events and Information	Remarks and references to Appendices
	15th May 1916 Monday		Office routine morning and evening. Wired C.R.E.s of Divl Sig Signal Coys, + interviewed A.A.D.M.S. with regard to provision of heel ropes for all horses, owing to the number of casualties from kicks. Lesberlis Remounts at GONNEHEM Depot Mobile Section.	A
	16th May 1916 Tuesday		Usual Office routine. Rode over to Mobile Section, + studied cases for evacuation to base returned treatment of others. Hence to No 2 Reserve Park at OLHAIN. Conferred with O.C. upon advisability of getting the horses on duty 6 days provn. & exercise. Heel rop for all. Afternoon gave lectures on Horsemanship to Officers noncom men of 1st Inf. Bde at 60 SERVINS. also to noncom men of 34th Battery R.F.A at VERDREL.	A
	17th May 1916 Wednesday		Office routine Lesberli horses of Divl Sig Signls, 5th Fgan Amb and R/236 Battery R.F.A. Practically no sickness and great improvement in appearance and condition of both animals and [...] Lines of horses and Gy SERVINS.	A

T2134. Wt. W708-776. 500000. 4/15. Sir J. C. & S.

WAR DIARY
INTELLIGENCE SUMMARY
(Erase heading not required.)

Army Form C. 2118.

Place	Date	Hour	Summary of Events and Information	Remarks and references to Appendices
	18th May 1916 Thursday		Office routine morning & evening. Visited Mobile Section. Rode over TARHUN Cavalry. Rode over only requiring attention of "B" Squadron R.E.H. Corps Cavalry, the rear only requiring attention of Proceeded to LA CONTE & inspected horses of 3 Batteries of 29th Brigade R.F.A. & discussed matters with the O.C.s after which I gave a lecture on Horse management generally & prevention of disease to all Officers N.C.Os & men of these Batteries.	JR.
	19th May 1916 Friday		Office routine. Visited horses of Divl Hq Signal Coy, & Sig. Bde Hqrs. 6.23 B/r Batteries on (?) Mobile Section, addressed batch of Sergts just arrived from England re duty with their units touching their duties. Afternoon received Teleg. Offrs at office & conferred upon all questions pertaining to the horses with their charge.	JR.
	20th May 1916 Saturday		Office routine. Visited horses of 14th Inf Bde at 50 SERVINS and 3 Companies Engineers at GOUY-SERVINS. They a few minor injuries in these units due for tics at G.9.V.SERVINS they a few minor injuries in these units due for tics at inspected transport horses of 140th Inf Bde at CAMBLAIN L'ABBE	JR.

WAR DIARY
INTELLIGENCE SUMMARY
(Erase heading not required.)

Army Form C. 2118.

Place	Date	Hour	Summary of Events and Information	Remarks and references to Appendices
	21st May 1916 Sunday		Office routine morning and evening. Rode over to HERNON to inspect horses of 123th Bde R.F.A. arranges for isolation & dressing of 0.5 skin cases, on to PERNES & and got motor on horse of Div. trans. thence to "B" Sq. T.E.H. at TRAISON to SPERLES all horses done with O.C. Selected a few lame cases for evacuation & isolated a suspected foot case. Proceeded to NOEUX LCOURT in evening. T.O. in charge of Div. Tr. Col. Called at Mobile Section examined all cases	J.
	22nd May 1916 Monday		Usual office routine. Visited horses of Div. Hq. Signal Coy. Hence to Govt. Servins to transport of 142nd Infantry Bde. Several horses seriously wounded some and 7 killed as a result of previous days shelling. Report upon same rendered to Div. Hq. Inspected horses of 140th Infantry Bde at PETIT SERVINS and visited Mobile Section.	J.

Army Form C. 2118.

WAR DIARY
or
INTELLIGENCE SUMMARY.
(Erase heading not required.)

Instructions regarding War Diaries and Intelligence Summaries are contained in F. S. Regs., Part II. and the Staff Manual respectively. Title pages will be prepared in manuscript.

Place	Date	Hour	Summary of Events and Information	Remarks and references to Appendices
	23rd May 1916 Tuesday		Office routine morning and evening. Visited Divl. Hq. Signals and again inspected transport lines of 12th & 13th Lond. reporting unit to 7.6.% as to treatment and disposal of wounded cases. Mobile Section	JR
	24th May 1916 Wednesday		Usual office routine. Visited B/236 Battery at ESTRÉE-CAUCHIE, and 5th London Fd. Ambulance at ESTRÉE-CAUCHIE, and 5th London Fd. Amb. Rode on to TERREL and inspected 34th and B/235th Batteries. Afternoon went in Mobile Section meeting with cases for communion to Base.	JR
	25th May 1916 Thursday		Office routine. Visited lines of Divl. Hq. Signal and informed A.A. & Q.M.G. with regard to retaining more Mtr. for Mobile Section and a place for my own office. Rode on to CAMBLAIN-L'ABBÉ and inspected lines of 142nd Inf. Bde. and 22th Bde R.F.A.	JR

WAR DIARY
INTELLIGENCE SUMMARY.
(Erase heading not required.)

Army Form C. 2118.

Place	Date	Hour	Summary of Events and Information	Remarks and references to Appendices
LA-COMTE	26th May 1916 Friday.		This office moves with Divl. Hq. to LA-COMTE. O.15.a (Map reference 1/40,000 Sheet 36 b.). Inspected arrival of units in this area and ascertained various positions to be taken over. In pursuance of with routine work at office: notified D.DT.S. of change of units to A.D.T.S. 2nd Division arranging for their attendance upon units left in area taken over by that Division.	J.R.
	27th May 1916 Saturday.		Office routine. Weekly ack. returns rendered to D.D.T.S. Visited HQrs. of 3 Field Companies Royal Engineers in LA-COMTE also Signal Coy. R.E. and Divl. Hqrs. Mobile Section moves from FRESNICOURT to BRUAY.	J.R.
	28th May 1916 Sunday.		Usual office routine morning. Visited Divl. Hq. Col. with D.A.Q.M.G. met D.D.R. and D.D.T.S. Rene. 130 horses selected for evacuation being surplus owing to reorganization of Artillery. D.DT.S. requested cancellation of Capt. Souter's leave at present. Inspected Battery of Horses at LA-THIEULOYE. 3 Field Companies Signal Coy R.E. at LA-COMTE.	J.R.

WAR DIARY
INTELLIGENCE SUMMARY of

Army Form C. 2118.

Place	Date	Hour	Summary of Events and Information	Remarks and references to Appendices
29th May 1916 Monday			Office routine morning & evening. Again visited D.A.D.S. to make final arrangements for evacuation of horses; proceeded to BRYAS to inspect horses of 23/Div. R.F.A. Thence to "B" Squadron K.E.H. at TALMON. Percentage of sickness in all units abnormally low. Condition of horses good. Rode over to Mobile Section BRRAY instructed O.C. with regard to evacuation of horses.	J.A.
30th May 1916 Tuesday			Usual office routine. Visited lines of April By. R.E. Rode over to BARLIN and ascertained from the R.A. position of all Artillery units, same having moved frequently during last few days. Inspected lines of B/238 Battery and C/234 Battery. Slight outbreak of purpuric mange in latter not reported to D.D.V.S. 139 horses evacuated to Base including 129 mm Divl. Am. Colum. Visited Mobile Section.	J.A.

Army Form C. 2118.

WAR DIARY
or
INTELLIGENCE SUMMARY.
(Erase heading not required.)

Place	Date	Hour	Summary of Events and Information	Remarks and references to Appendices
	31st May 1916 Wednesday		Usual office routine, morning and evening. Inspected horses of two Bdes. of Artillery in and around BARLIN and MAISNIL: found under arrangements inadequate & reported this to C.R.A. Visited horses of 1/4 1st Bn. (Infantry) at DIEVAL and Mobile Section BRUAY. Joseph Hogan, Major A.V.C. A.D.V.S. 47. London Div. 31/5/16	JH

Army Form C. 2118.

WAR DIARY
or
INTELLIGENCE SUMMARY.
(Erase heading not required.)

Place	Date	Hour	Summary of Events and Information	Remarks and references to Appendices
4th Division HQrs Northern div. LA COMTE.	1st June 1916		Office routine morning and evening. Inspected all Artillery wing horses in BARLIN. Also HQ Field Coy R.E. HQrs. Signals at LA COMTE. Visited the Mobile Veterinary Section.	ga
	2nd June 1916 Friday		Usual office routine. Inspected B/237 Battery R.F.A. horses with D.D.V.S. re outbreak of Sarcoptic mange and discussed the treatment for same. Visited VALHUON and inspected the horses of "B" Squadron 16th King Edward's horse. Also inspected HQ Field Coy & H.Q.R.E.	ga
	3rd June 1916 Saturday		Office routine morning and evening. Moved from LA COMTE to CHATEAU ANTIGNEUL map reference FRANCE	
CHATEAU: ANTIGNEUL			Sheet 36B. 1:40,000 square N.17.D. Visited HQrs. Signals & 3 boys R.E. also inspected all horses of B/237 Battery and arranged dressing of all horses against "Skin Disease" (Mange). Inspected horses of 236 Brigade R.F.A. at MAISNIL. Visited Mobile Veterinary Section	ga

WAR DIARY
or
INTELLIGENCE SUMMARY

Army Form C. 2118.

Place	Date	Hour	Summary of Events and Information	Remarks and references to Appendices
	4th June 1916. Sunday		Usual office routine morning and evening. Inspected all horses of the regiment of King Edward's Horse at VALHUON. Attended A.D.V.S. Conference at AIRE.	J.
	5th June 1916. Monday		Office routine morning and evening. Visited Signals and Headquarters. Inspected all horses of B/237 and B/238 Batteries at BARLIN. re Mange, and advised isolation for all return cases and suspects.	J.
	6th June 1916. Tuesday		Usual office routine morning and evening. Visited Mobile Veterinary Section at BRUAY prior to Capt. Southall going on leave to England, and arranged for veterinary attendance of all units under his charge. Handed the Mobile Section to IV Corps Cavalry, and saw suspected and returned case Tetanus and advised as to treatment of same. Inspected O.B. 76 Squadron King Edward's Horse at VALHUON belonging	J.

WAR DIARY
INTELLIGENCE SUMMARY

Army Form C. 2118.

Place	Date	Hour	Summary of Events and Information	Remarks and references to Appendices
	7th June 1916. Wednesday		Usual office routine morning and evening. Inspected horses of A/B/C Squadrons 16mg (Bowmans Horse (IV Corps Cavalry) at Valhuon, and gave instruction as to how to deal with suspected mange. Visited Headquarters and Signals, thence to Division, meeting the V.O. of. and inspected all horses of 142nd Inf. Bde.	J.A.
	8th June 1916 Thursday		Office routine morning and evening. Interviewed Captain Craig, and arranged with him to render Veterinary attendance to the Mobile Veterinary Section at BRUAY, also inspected all horses there, and chem horses of the Divisional Train. I then went in to Barlin when I inspected the horses of 137 and 238 Batteries R.F.A. Inspected 3 Coys of Divisional Engineers and gave Lecture on Horsemanship in the evening.	J.A.
	9th June 1916. Friday		Usual office routine morning and evening. Called at the M.V.S. BRUAY, thence to Col. JA Ambulance and inspected all horses there. Inspected all horses at the D.A.C. Signals and A/B/C Squadrons 1C.R.H.	J.A.

Army Form C. 2118.

WAR DIARY
or
INTELLIGENCE SUMMARY.
(Erase heading not required.)

Instructions regarding War Diaries and Intelligence Summaries are contained in F. S. Regs., Part II. and the Staff Manual respectively. Title pages will be prepared in manuscript.

Place	Date	Hour	Summary of Events and Information	Remarks and references to Appendices
	10 June 1916. Saturday		Office routine morning and evening. Went to see two horses suspected of Mange belonging to 33rd R Div. at HOUDAIN, and advised as to treatment of same. Visited H Qrs.	
	11th June 1916. Sunday		Usual office routine morning and evening. Inspected horse of Signals, 3 boys of Engineers and Headquarters. Also inspected all horses belonging to 16 ing Edwards Horse at JALHOON.	
	12th June 1916. Monday		Office routine morning and evening. Visited mobile Veterinary Section at BRUAY, inspecting the horses there, thence to mobile Veterinary Section 23rd Division at BARLIN when I made arrangement for the transfer of the units, Received instruction from A.D.V.S. 23rd Division regarding the units which were being left in the area vacated by him, and instructed him as to the units being left in the area vacated by me	

T2134. Wt. W708—776. 500000. 4/15. Sir J.C. & S.

Army Form C. 2118.

WAR DIARY
or
INTELLIGENCE SUMMARY.
(Erase heading not required.)

Instructions regarding War Diaries and Intelligence Summaries are contained in F.S. Regs., Part II. and the Staff Manual respectively. Title pages will be prepared in manuscript.

Place	Date	Hour	Summary of Events and Information	Remarks and references to Appendices
	13th June 1916 Tuesday		Usual office routine morning and evening. Attended the evacuation of several horses from mounted Veterinary Section at BRUAY, also received 69 Remounts at BRUAY Station. Inspected all horses at Army Tramways Horse VALHUON.	JA.
	14th June 1916 Wednesday		Moved from CHATEAU ANTIGNEUL to 16 Rue de Hallicourt, BARLIN, where I inspected the proposed office and billet and found them suitable. Visited mobile Veterinary Section on their arrival, the O.C. being on leave. Office routine in the evening.	JA.
BARLIN	15th June 1916 Thursday		Office routine morning and evening. Inspected the horses of the No. 1.V.S. previous to evacuation, also inspected horses of Divisional Train, Headquarters and Signals. Visited advanced units at HERSIN to obtain the exact location of their whereabouts.	JA.

Army Form C. 2118.

WAR DIARY
of
INTELLIGENCE SUMMARY.
(Erase heading not required.)

Place	Date	Hour	Summary of Events and Information	Remarks and references to Appendices
	16th June 1916. Friday.		Usual office routine morning, pitching in several hours in evening. Overhead preparation of horses at the D.S. as it was back to duty. Interviewing the Veterinary Officers with their Weekly Reports, and arranging taking over many attached units. Inspected several horses of 2nd Reserve Park at HERSIN and arranging removal of sick. Dealing with several lame horses at Headquarters	A/
	17th June 1916. Saturday.		Inspected number of horses D.A.C. arranging with D.D.V.S. & Section of D.F.I.C. units to be removed from St Eloy to BARLIN and there arrange for testing of Mallein. As these animals had been in indirect contact with Glandered animals belonging to 25th Division. Interviewing V.C.O. and O.C. D.A.C. respecting same. Very much office work getting out Weekly Report etc.	A/
	18th June 1916. Sunday.		Office routine morning and evening. Inspected horses of Mobile Section thence to D.A.C. inspecting all the horses thus Inspected several Battery horses at COUPIGNY and HERSIN	A/

WAR DIARY or INTELLIGENCE SUMMARY

Army Form C. 2118.

Place	Date	Hour	Summary of Events and Information	Remarks and references to Appendices
	19th June 1916. Monday		Usual office routine morning and evening. Visited the stable to see some sick cases, which came in early morning, superintending the dressing of same. Inspected the horses of 5th London Field Ambulance BARLIN thence to COUPIGNY, when I inspected the horses of A.P.M. also inspected horses of the 20th and 24th Bn. London Regt. at HERSIN, also visited him of 2 Batteries R.F.A.	Sgd.
	20th June 1916. Tuesday		Office routine morning and evening. Inspected horses of D.A.C. also visited teams of 4 Batteries of F.F.A. Examined A.H.Q. re inspection of artillery horses by DDVS and DDVS on 22nd & 23rd June, attending to refer for one week. Visited the mobile section afternoon, inspecting the horses of MPs and of Signals.	Sgd.
	21st June 1916. Wednesday		Office routine morning and evening, attending to much correspondence. Inspected horses of 4th London Field Ambulance at FOSSE,10. thence to BOYEFFLES, when I inspected horses of Kent Heavy Battery (ATTACHED) also C/226 of Battery R.F.A., viewing the mobile section on return.	Sgd.

/ WAR DIARY /
INTELLIGENCE SUMMARY.

Army Form C. 2118.

Place	Date	Hour	Summary of Events and Information	Remarks and references to Appendices
	22nd June 1916. Thursday		Usual office routine morning and evening. Inspected the horses of the 4th London Field Ambulance BARLIN, thence to CHATEAU COUPIGNY, when I inspected the horses of the Col J. Field Ambulance, Supercar horses of the 4th & Cd Hervilly Battery (attached) at BOYEFFLES also B/236 and B/235 Batteries at HERSIN.	J.R.
	23rd June 1916. Friday		Usual office routine morning and evening. Inspected several Artillery units' horses at HERSIN also at COUPIGNY, when I visited the horses of several infantry units. Reviewed officers in the afternoon with Weekly Report. Superintended the evacuation of horses at the M.V.S.	J.R.
	24th June 1916. Saturday		Office routine morning and evening. Inspecting horses of the 235th Brigade R.F.A. at HERSIN, COUPIGNY and BARLIN also several horses of the Royal Engineers and Signal Coy. Visited the Mobile Section. Attending in the evening to several urgent cases.	J.R.

WAR DIARY or INTELLIGENCE SUMMARY.

Army Form C. 2118.

Place	Date	Hour	Summary of Events and Information	Remarks and references to Appendices
	25th June 1916. Sunday.		Usual office routine morning and evening. Met Captain Stewart in morning and inspected all horses of the D.A.C. at BARLIN and HERSIN, also inspected horses of B/236 Battery and 2 Battery A/236 at Saint ELOY. Visited the Mobile Section to make arrangements for evacuation on Monday.	JR.
	26th June 1916. Monday.		Usual office routine morning and evening. Met Capt. Ewing A.V. in the morning and proceeded with him to HERSIN, where I inspected all the horses of five units of Artillery, giving strict attention to see that there was no suspected mange prevalent, and instructed V.O. to give immediate attention, as soon as a case was suspected. Visited Mobile Section and experimental evacuation of horses, also visited and inspected horses of Headquarters.	JR.
	27th June 1916. Tuesday.		Office routine morning and evening. Inspected five lines of Artillery horses under the charge of Capt. Edwards A.V. at SAINS-EN-GOHELLE, HERSIN and COUPIGNY. Also inspected the horses of the 2/3rd and H.Q. 9th Corps R.E. Visited the V.S. and thence to inspect mules D.A.C. returned from St. ELOY, where they were detained owing to outbreak of Glanders in the lines of D.A.C. 25th Division.	JR.

Army Form C. 2118

WAR DIARY
or
INTELLIGENCE SUMMARY
(Erase heading not required.)

Place	Date	Hour	Summary of Events and Information	Remarks and references to Appendices
	28th June 1916 Wednesday		Office routine morning and evening. Visited and inspected all horses of four Batteries of Artillery at HERSIN and COUPIGNY and two Battalions of Infantry. Also inspected the horses of Hq and Signals. Visited M.DS in the afternoon also inspected Mallimus huts of D.A.C. BARLIN	J.A.
	29th June 1916 Thursday		Usual office routine morning and evening. Inspected the horses of four Artillery Batteries at HERSIN and SAINS-EN-GOHELLE also 2/3rd & 4th boys C.Bs. Visited M.DS, and inspected Mallimus huts. D.A.C. BARLIN	J.A.
	30th June 1916 Friday		Usual office routine morning and evening. Inspected horses of four Artillery Batteries at Cité de COUPIGNY, Cité LIAUTEY, BOYEFFLES and BARLIN, 2 Sections of D.A.C. also horses of the D.A.C. headquarters. In afternoon visited M.DS & arrange for inoculation on Saturday, also inspected horses of Headquarters and Signals.	J.A.

Joseph Aaron. Major.
A.D.V.S., 47th (London) Division.

Headquarters,
    47th London Division.

> A.D.V.S.,
> 47th (LONDON)
> DIVISION.
> No. V.74.
> Date 2.8.16

Herewith please War Diary for Month of July 1916.

August 2nd 16.

Joseph Aston
Major,
A.D.V.S., 47th London Division.

Army Form C. 2118.

WAR DIARY
INTELLIGENCE SUMMARY of
(Erase heading not required.)

Instructions regarding War Diaries and Intelligence Summaries are contained in F.S. Regs., Part II. and the Staff Manual respectively. Title pages will be prepared in manuscript.

Place	Date	Hour	Summary of Events and Information	Remarks and references to Appendices
47. W.L. Mn. Bde. BARLIN	1st July 1916 Saturday		Office routine morning and evening. Met by appointment at 9.30 a.m. B.D.R. and A.D.M.S. First Army and with them inspected in site of horses of Divl. Artillery; condition of same satisfactory with exception of Divl. Am. Column, to which went a number of remounts. Had been pulled from other Divisions upon re-organization of Artillery in 1st condition. 30 of these preferred for evacuation to base, to be replaced by much superior horses and mules of D.A.C. Motorised having been in contact with Glanders in mules of 25th Division at MOUNT ST.ELOY. No reactors.	[signature]
BARLIN	2nd July 1916 Sunday		Usual office routine. Visited Mobile Sections and arranged for proceedure on following day. Inspected horses of Divl. Train at BARLIN. Attended conference of A.D'sV.S. of 1st ARMY with A.D.V.S. of 2nd and Royal Naval Divisions.	[signature]

Army Form C. 2118.

WAR DIARY
or
INTELLIGENCE SUMMARY. of
(Erase heading not required.)

Instructions regarding War Diaries and Intelligence Summaries are contained in F. S. Regs., Part II. and the Staff Manual respectively. Title pages will be prepared in manuscript.

Place	Date	Hour	Summary of Events and Information	Remarks and references to Appendices
	3rd July 1916 Monday		Office routine morning and evening. Rode over to HERSIN and superintended distribution of horse shoes of B/23 & B/238 Batteries. No apparent to spread of mange. Inspected arrival of 223 horse trunks. Bde. R.F.A. recently attached to Division returning general to Mobile Section. Reported unfavourable condition of the same to D.D.V.S. & suggested an inspection by him. Visited horses of Sig. Train and Divl. Sig. & Signals in BARLIN. Tested Mobile Section.	J.A.
	4th July 1916 Tuesday		Usual office routine. Received report from D.D.V.S. upon inspection of unit. Supervised disinfecting horse lines of batteries at HERSIN: rode on to COUPIGNY. Inspected horses of No. 1 Gordon Park: 2 horses of D.R.C. Divl. Sig. & Signal Coy upon return to BARLIN. Visited Mobile Section, & conferred with O.C. upon treatment of skin cases & erection of shed for same.	J.A.

WAR DIARY
or
INTELLIGENCE SUMMARY of

Army Form C. 2118.

Place	Date	Hour	Summary of Events and Information	Remarks and references to Appendices
	5th July 1916 (Wednesday)		Office routine as usual. Arranged with units for inspection on Friday by D.D.R. and D.D.V.S. Inspected 25th & 26th Field Cos. R.E. at SAINS-EN-GOHELLE, & paid monthly service money to Field Cashier. Met Capt. NEILL R.V.C. at lines of 233 Bde R.F.A. HERSIN & discussed progress of horse units re charge, isolated pans unit him.	J.R.
	6th July 1916 (Thursday)		Office routine morning. Visited all Artillery units in neighbourhood of HERSIN to see disposition of horse lines carried out by Sermant [?] horses and cased [?] evolution. Inspection lines of Divl. Train [?] called upon Mobile Section.	J.R.
	7th July 1916 (Friday)		Attended to Office routine. Visited Divl. Hq. Noyelles. Met D.D.R. & D.D.V.S. at NOEUX with them inspecting horses of 223 1.00 R.F.A, 4, 5, 16th Lon. Field Ambces. & 1/3, 2/3 14th Field Cos. R.E. arranged exchange of H.D. type animals for L.D.s from Remount Depot. Received weekly Cust return from V.Os & discussed with them concerning then charges.	J.R.

Army Form C. 2118.

WAR DIARY
or
INTELLIGENCE SUMMARY.
(Erase heading not required.)

Instructions regarding War Diaries and Intelligence Summaries are contained in F. S. Regs., Part II. and the Staff Manual respectively. Title pages will be prepared in manuscript.

Place	Date	Hour	Summary of Events and Information	Remarks and references to Appendices
	8th July 1916 Saturday		Office routine morning and evening. Visit from D.D.R. 1st Army, conferred with him with regard to movements for field Remount Section reevacuation for base, cast at previous days inspection. Inspected horses of an later R.I.Batch Two. at Govt. SERVINS, who unit unable owing to shortage of transport of horses. Interviewed D.A.D.M.S. for same to be supplied. Visited "Lord" baths at VERDREL and Mobile Section upon return.	J.R.
	9th July 1916 Sunday		Office routine. Inspected animals of D.A.C. with 7.D.R. Visit a Mobile Section selecting cases for evacuation rearranging with O.C. in all equipment to be in readiness should move take place.	J.R.
	10th July 1916 Monday		Usual Office routine. Received & examined 56 Remounts at BARLIN Station; Tractor Mobile Section. Superintend disinfection of horse lines of Artillery units.	J.R.

Army Form C. 2118.

WAR DIARY
or
INTELLIGENCE SUMMARY.
(Erase heading not required.)

Place	Date	Hour	Summary of Events and Information	Remarks and references to Appendices
	11th July 1916 Tuesday.		Office routine morning and evening. Inspected section of No 2 Reserve Park BARLIN just attached. Has been sent to Mobile Section. Made inspection of whole of Transport Lorries of Motor Amb. Cars. at LAPUGNY and HERSIN, also 176 Travelling Forge and 33m Lorry. Two. Condition of all units favourable. Visited No 2 Section 47th D.A.C. and Mobile Section.	JR
	12th July 1916 Wednesday.		Usual office routine. Received and examined 56 Remounts at BARLIN Station. Inspected Lorries of D.A.C. and 2nd Reserve Park BARLIN arranging for disinfection of remaining 3 sections of former. Hence to No 1 Coy Train, D.Sub, Hq, Signals & Mobile Section.	JR
	13th July 1916 Thursday.		Office routine morning & evening. Inspected Lorries of 47th Sup. Park with Capt. CRAIG F.V.C. + am to No 2 Section 47th D.A.C. at HERSIN. Mobile Section.	JR

T2134. W. W708—776. 500000. 4/15. Sir J. C. & S.

WAR DIARY
INTELLIGENCE SUMMARY

Army Form C. 2118.

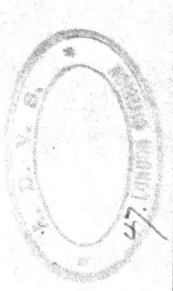

Place	Date	Hour	Summary of Events and Information	Remarks and references to Appendices
	14th July 1916 Friday		Usual office routine. Visited Mobile Section; saw case there - advised treatment. Met Capt. BRYDEN, R.V.C. at 10.15 am who had then inspected transport horses of 140th Inf. Bde. at BOYEFFLES; found in good condition; reported to D.A.D.V.S. I Corps. 9 A.D. of 6th Div. Regiment over establishment. Conferred with T.O. in afternoon bringing in their weekly sick return.	JL
	15th July 1916 Saturday		Office routine. Visited Mobile Section & selected cases for evacuation. Inspected whole of transport horses of 141st Inf. Bde. with 7.04s also 223 Bde. R.F.A. at HERSIN. Inspected horses of section D.A.C. BRAIN.	JL
	16th July 1917 Sunday		Usual Office routine: Wrote to A.D.V.S. Royal Naval Division arranging for him to render Veterinary administration to units left behind in ar[e]a to be vacated by 2nd Divn. Received list of units left in area vacated by 2nd Divn. Visited Mobile Section & instructed O.C. with regard to move in near area. Made general inspection of all horses of D.A.C.	JL

T2134. Wt. W708—776. 500000. 4/15. Sir J. C. & S.

WAR DIARY
INTELLIGENCE SUMMARY

Army Form C. 2118.

Place	Date	Hour	Summary of Events and Information	Remarks and references to Appendices
	17th July 1916 Monday		This Office moved to CAMBLIAN TREE, M.22.B. Map reference 36C.1 & 2000. Remainder of day spent in making with matters at Office. Arrangements made with A.D.V.S. of 2nd & 23rd Divisions with regard to changing over Mobile Sections. Labourers at O.C. 12.20 London M.V.S. at office.	JH
CAMBRIAN TREE.	18th July 1916 Tuesday		Usual Office routine. Visited lines of R & B Batteries at MT. ST. ELOY & worked upon correction of forms to D.D.V.S. Inspected horses of 24th Coy. Divl. Train. Divl. Sig. Signals, & 140th Bde. M. Gun Coy. at CAMBRIAN TREE.	JH
	19th July 1916 Wednesday		Office routine morning and evening. Inspected horses of D.A.C. in BARLIN. also 14th Div. Decl. Train. Rode on to Head Quarters 5th Div. GONNEHEM to debt charges for Liaison Officer staff. Visited horses of train & 140th M. Gun Coy upon return.	JH
	20th July 1916 Thursday		Office routine as usual. Rode over to VILLERS-au-BOIS & saw horses of 1st Sussex R.T. Coy. R.E. R & B/236 Battery R.F.A. Visited Mobile Section & selected cases for evacuation. Inspected horses of B/235 & C/237 Batteries.	JH

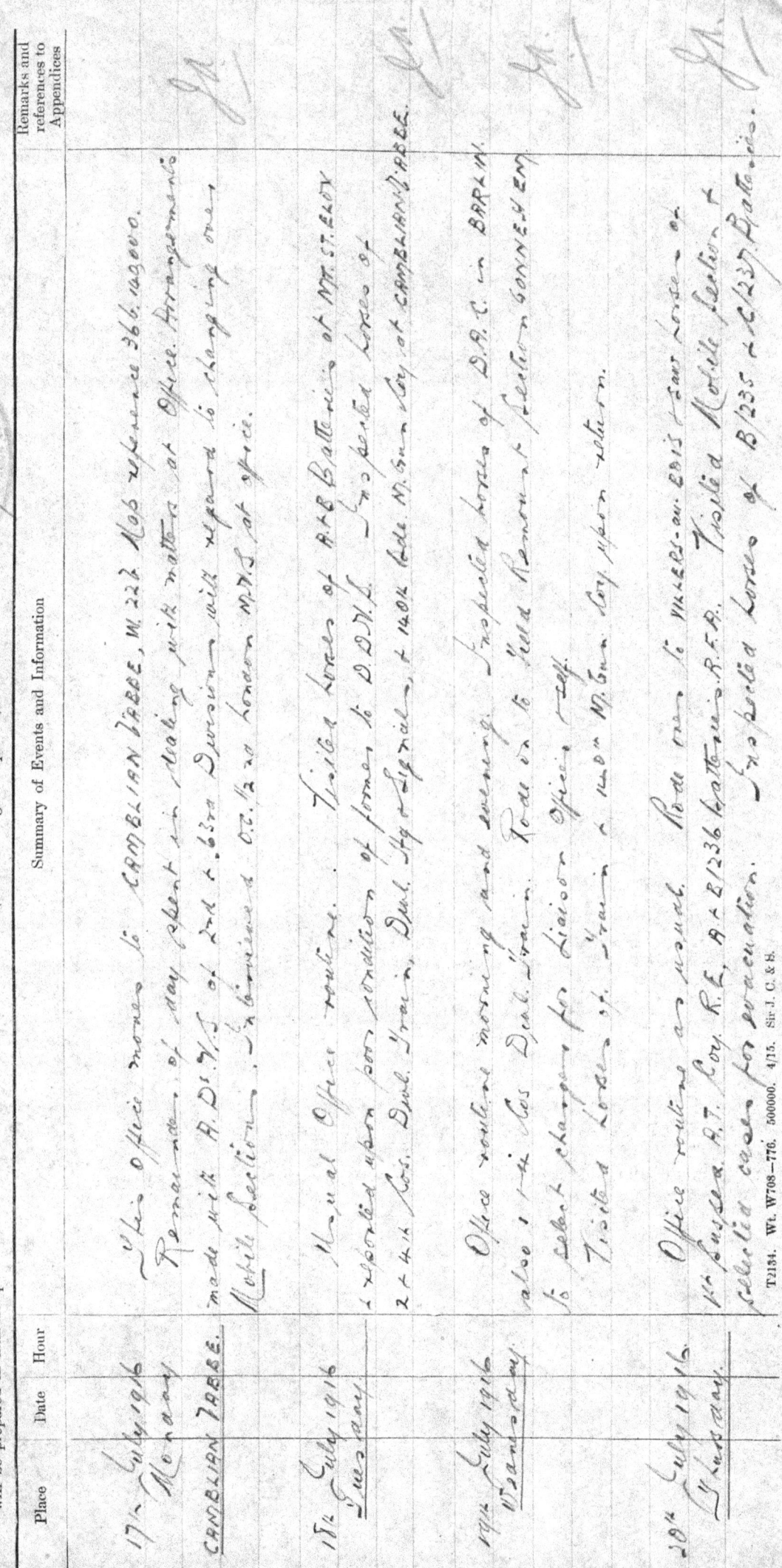

Army Form C. 2118.

WAR DIARY
or
INTELLIGENCE SUMMARY.
(Erase heading not required.)

Place	Date	Hour	Summary of Events and Information	Remarks and references to Appendices
	21st July 1916 Friday		Usual Office Routine. Visited No 4 Coy Lines & attended to matters there. Rode over to 182nd Ind. Coy at MINGOLAH & inspected horses. re internees. In afternoon conferred with Telg. Officers at Office & discussed all questions relating to efficiency of animals under their charge. Inspected horses of No 2 Coy lines.	J.A.
	22nd July 1916 Saturday		Office routine. Weekly act. returns rendered to D.D.V.S. 1st Mob. Remount & distress shewn quite normal, mostly the unavoidable due to hides. Inspected all lines of units in CAMBRIAN LINES - Dul. typ. Signals 27th Res. Train 140th Fd. Lb. M. Inns Coy. Moved office from Rue d'Azara to 79 Rue de Place.	J.A.
	23rd July 1916 Sunday		Usual office routine. Made general round of inspection of Artillery units in and around BAHRIN, saw cases under treatment in Mobile Section & visited the Lot Field Ambc. Horses of No 1 & 2 Section D.A.C. shewing signs of improvement in condition. Visited horses of M.H. Inns 4th Division.	J.A.

Army Form C. 2118.

A.D.V.S.,
47th (LONDON)
DIVISION.

No....................
Date..................

WAR DIARY
or
INTELLIGENCE SUMMARY.
(Erase heading not required.)

Instructions regarding War Diaries and Intelligence Summaries are contained in F. S. Regs., Part II. and the Staff Manual respectively. Title pages will be prepared in manuscript.

Place	Date	Hour	Summary of Events and Information	Remarks and references to Appendices
	24th July 16 Monday		Routine office work nothing of enemy. Confined to his room of day with sudden illness.	
	25th July 16 Tuesday		Usual office routine. Instructions received from D.D.V.S. in event of movement by train. Acknowledged reply passed to M.O. on London M.T.S. Visited horses of Divl. Hq. Signals. No + hay found + M.M. Pouch. Interviewed O.C. Mobile Section & instructed him with regard to noting inspections for marcy=trans.my one of races & forwns at that kind. Interviewed D.A.D.M.S as to result of inspection previous day by D.D.R. + D.S.S.	
	26th July 16 Wednesday		Dealt with office routine. Visited horses of Mob. Vety. Secn. Hq Signal Coy. Rode over to BRUAY & inspected huts of Remounts arriving. Home 16 L.A. COMTE arranging listing over of office huttst. Take a at Mob. Section. Rode to F.D.U. 37th Divn upon being re akanpet one. of sectons rebbed to rayany inspecting latter on on this ploan for subs_qube of horses.	

T2134. Wt. W708—776. 500000. 4/15. Sid. C. & B.

Army Form C. 2118.

A.D.V.S.,
47th (LONDON)
DIVISION.
No............
Date............

WAR DIARY
or
INTELLIGENCE SUMMARY.
(Erase heading not required.)

Instructions regarding War Diaries and Intelligence Summaries are contained in F.S. Regs., Part II. and the Staff Manual respectively. Title pages will be prepared in manuscript.

Place	Date	Hour	Summary of Events and Information	Remarks and references to Appendices
	27th July 1916 Thursday		Usual office routine. Visited Horse of A. & C. Train Dublin Fusiliers Hence to D.A.D.C at HERSIN and BARLIN. Rode over to GUY-SERVINS Inspected Horse of 4th London R.W. Fus & Engrs. Instructions received for move on following day; A.D.V.S. of incoming Division notified of units being left behind for Vet: administration.	JM
	28th July 1916 Friday		This office moves from CAMBRIAN-L'ABBÉ to LA-COMTE via Mobile Section from FRESNICOURT to LA-THIEVLOYE. Remainder of day occupied by visit at Office. All Vet. Ovendentials as to care Supervision to be exercised by him during forthcoming List of Divn.	JM
LA-COMTE	29th July 1916 Saturday		Inspected Horse of Engineers Duty (Signals) in LA-COMTE & rode over to Mobile Section. Attended to office routine; all Weekly etc returns rendered to D.D.V.S. 4th Army. Instructions received for move to commence following day, same conveyed to Mobile Section.	JM

T2134. Wt. W708—776. 500000. 4/15. Sir J. C. & S.

Army Form C. 2118.

A.D.V.S.,
47th (LONDON) DIVISION.

No..............
Date............

WAR DIARY
or
INTELLIGENCE SUMMARY.

(Erase heading not required.)

Place	Date	Hour	Summary of Events and Information	Remarks and references to Appendices
	30th July 1916 Sunday		This officer and Mobile Section reno unit often units of Division to FLERS. During into Fourth Army Area. March commenced at 7 am and destination reached at 1.30 pm.	
FLERS	31st July 1916 Monday		Dealt with matters at Office. Inspected all horses in vicinity of FLERS road on to MONCHEL to investigate means of water supply to units stationed there. Same reported inadequate. Orders received to continue march on following day.	

Joseph Khan
Capt. A.V.C.
A.D.V.S. 47th (London) Division.

SECRET

47th Division.

Herewith please War Diary for month of August 1916.

Joseph Abson
Major,
A.D.V.S., 47th (London) Division.

A.D.V.S.,
47th (LONDON)
DIVISION.
No. V.93.
Date 1-9-16

Army Form C. 2118.

WAR DIARY
or
INTELLIGENCE SUMMARY.
(Erase heading not required.)

A.D.V.S.,
47th (LONDON)
DIVISION.

No. ....
Date ....

829

Place	Date	Hour	Summary of Events and Information	Remarks and references to Appendices
FREHEN-LE-GRAND.	1st August 1916 Monday		Continued march with Divl. Hd.Qrs at 5 am and proceeded to FREHEN-LE-GRAND, arriving at 12.30 p.m. All horses in good condition & no casualties. D.D.V.S. THIRD ARMY notified of arrival in this area and position of Mobile Section. All T.V.O. officers also notified of same.	J.R.
FREHEN-LE-GRAND.	2nd August 1916 Tuesday		Dealt with usual office routine. Visited Mobile Section. Inspected horses of Divl. Hd. Qrs. Signal Coy & 2/3rd Field Coy R.E. Rode over to OCCOCHES & saw all animals of Divl. Am. Col. there. Went to BARLY and VILLERS L'HOPITAL & inspected horses of Infantry units around that neighbourhood.	J.R.
	3rd August 1916 Thursday		Visited horses of 236 Bde. R.F.A. at BEAUVOIR-RIVIERE and 236 Bde. at BERGICOURT ordering 6 bad cases to Mobile Section for evacuation. Inspected horses of Signal Coy & Field Coy. R.E. upon return. Instructions received from Divl. Hq. to move off next morning.	J.R.

T.J134. Wt. W708—776. 500000. 4/15. Sir J. C. & S.

Army Form C. 2118.

WAR DIARY
or
INTELLIGENCE SUMMARY.

A.D.V.S.,
47th (LONDON)
DIVISION.

Place	Date	Hour	Summary of Events and Information	Remarks and references to Appendices
	4th August 1916 Friday		Again commenced march at 5 am arriving at YVRENCH at 1 pm. Afternoon visited office in dealing with sick and went round selecting more suitable position for Mobile Section.	
YVRENCH E-7	5th August 1916 Saturday		Rode over to RE-PONCHEL inspected Lines of 337 Coy R.E.A.S. conferred with O.C. upon care of his animals. Mange having been prevalent in this brigade. Visited Lines of Epuil Bty Sproule & Mobile Section.	
	6th August 1916 Sunday		Usual office return. Proceeded to YVRENCHEUX + valley lines of 1st bn. R. Welsh Fus. conducting two other cases to Mobile. Afternoon made general inspection round of all lines of Divl. Artillery + Am. Column, ending in the valley of River BRUTHIE from TOLLENT to VITZ-VIKEROY. All animals in excellent condition + improvement marked by plentiful supply of good water + grazing. Distress nil; only few injuries from fields. Discussed matter with Captains EDWARDS, STUART and GEEKING. Y. Crampeyre.	

T2134. Wt. W708—776. 500000. 4/15. Sir J. C. & S.

WAR DIARY
or
INTELLIGENCE SUMMARY.

(Erase heading not required.)

Army Form C. 2118.

A.D.V.S.,
47th (LONDON)
DIVISION.

No. ....
Date ....

Place	Date	Hour	Summary of Events and Information	Remarks and references to Appendices
	7th August 1916 Monday		Usual Office routine morning & evening. Visited Mobile Section. Inspected horses over to procuration. Rode over to VYRENCHEUX. Saw horses of 1/1st Batn. R. Welch Fusiliers. Hence to GUESCHART. Inspected horses of 13m, 2 Bn 144, 1st & 6th R.E. Delivered lecture on Horsemastership to Officers of these Companies. Visited Signal Coy. & Divl. Hq. Dull fg. horses upon return.	A.
	8th August 1916 Tuesday		Dealt with Office Routine. Rode over to ST RIQUIER Inspected transport animals of 1/4th & Inf. Bde and 6th Lon. field Ambce with Capt. CRAIG M. in charge. Condition of all favourable. Saw horses of No 3 Coy. Train at HAUTVIN upon return journey. Visited Mobile Section. Divl. Hq. Signal Coy.	A.
	9th August 1916 Wednesday		Office routine as usual. Visited a Mobile Section. Inspected horses of 1/4 1/5t Infantry Battns. 5t Lon. F. Ambce or GRPENNES, and 4th Batn. R.W. Fus. or VYRENCHEUX Divl. Hq. Signals.	A.

Army Form C. 2118.

Instructions regarding War Diaries and Intelligence Summaries are contained in F.S. Regs., Part II. and the Staff Manual respectively. Title pages will be prepared in manuscript.

WAR DIARY
or
INTELLIGENCE SUMMARY
(Erase heading not required.)

Place	Date	Hour	Summary of Events and Information	Remarks and references to Appendices
	10th August 1916 Thursday		Office routine morning and evening. Mobile Section. Inspection lines of 110th Companies R.E. at GUESCHART. Pending General to Mobile Section in preparation. There is not long leave.	J.A.
	11th August 1916 Friday		Usual office routine. Rode over to ST. RIQUIER to see horse of wire Lydda 2nd or 110th Ambce. General condition of all good and reliable. Reviewed Telephones at office in afternoon bringing 7 a.m. weekly audit returns compared with them upon all matters pertaining to horses of units under their charge.	J.A.
	12th August 1916 Saturday		Office routine morning. Mobile Section. Did by I Signal Coy. Made general inspection of 110th Infantry Bde. at BRUCAT, NEUF-MOULIN - CROUY - and MILLENCOURT. Discussed cases with O.C. 110th M. Gun Coy. Inspected No 4 boy train and 6th No F. Ambce at ST. RIQUIER upon return journey. Weekly audit returns rendered to D.D.V.S. Fourth Army and D.D.V.S. Third Army notified re the opening.	J.A.

Army Form C. 2118.

A.D.V.S.,
47th (LONDON)
DIVISION

No.............
Date............

WAR DIARY
or
INTELLIGENCE SUMMARY.

(Erase heading not required.)

Instructions regarding War Diaries and Intelligence Summaries are contained in F. S. Regs., Part II. and the Staff Manual respectively. Title pages will be prepared in manuscript.

Place	Date	Hour	Summary of Events and Information	Remarks and references to Appendices
	13th August 1916 Sunday		Proceeded with D.A.D.M.S. at 7am to recce mains back of Reserves at VIGNACOURT. Visited Mobile Section, where evacuation of personnel and destruction of 2 anons oder kratzwar + kradschützen. Saw horses of A.S.M. Div. Hq. Signal Coy. Office routine, officers + allotted above Generals to visits from Mobile Section in evening.	A
	14th August 1916 Monday		Office routine. Visited 3 Field Companies R.E. at GUEZZART and Mobile Section Signal Coy upon return. Instructions received from Div. to move with Headquarters 1st on following day.	A
	15th August 1916 Tuesday		Move from YVRENCH to NEUF-MOULIN. Map reference FREVILLE Sheet 14 A.5. Mobile Section at same place.	A

Army Form C. 2118.

WAR DIARY
or
INTELLIGENCE SUMMARY.
(Erase heading not required.)

Instructions regarding War Diaries and Intelligence Summaries are contained in F. S. Regs., Part II. and the Staff Manual respectively. Title pages will be prepared in manuscript.

A.D.V.S.
47th (LONDON)
DIVISION.
No. ....
Date ....

Place	Date	Hour	Summary of Events and Information	Remarks and references to Appendices
Wailaan	16th August 1916		Dealt with routine work at office. Visited Mobile Section Sunday Signals Horse. Rode on to ST. RIQUIER, saw horses of No 2 Coy Signals and 6th on Field Ambce.	JA
Lindsay	17th August 1916		Usual office routine. Rode over to GUESCHART and inspected horses of 13rd 2/3rd Field Co. R.E. Saw horses of typical any cases in Mobile Section whose return. In afternoon proceeded to ABBEVILLE conferred with D.D.V.S. Also called at Advanced Remount Depot and arranged exchange of number of unsuitable horses.	JA
the day	18th August 1916		Routine office work morning and evening. Inspected horses of 142nd Coy Bn in and around neighbourhood of ST. RIQUIER. All Mobile and in satisfactory condition. Conferred with I.O. at office in afternoon discussing arrival of units, made their charge, and all questions relating to sick.	JA

T2134. Wt. W708-776. 500000. 4/15. Sir J. C. & S.

Army Form C. 2118.

A.D.V.S.
47th (LONDON)
DIVISION.

No..........
Date..........

WAR DIARY
or
INTELLIGENCE SUMMARY.
(Erase heading not required.)

Instructions regarding War Diaries and Intelligence Summaries are contained in F.S. Regs., Part II. and the Staff Manual respectively. Title pages will be prepared in manuscript.

Place	Date	Hour	Summary of Events and Information	Remarks and references to Appendices
	19th August 1916 Saturday		Inspected horses of Divl. Sig. Signals mobile Section. Dealt with usual office routine. Weekly vet. return rendered to D.D.V.S. Second Army. Wastage return 16 of total of 2617.	JR
	20th August 1916 Sunday		Sub office and Mobile Section move with Headquarters - move to AILLY-LE-HAUT CLOCHER Map appendix. Chief in ABBEVILLE, A.B. Selected site for Mobile Section in a walled in field mounted. Received particulars of horses left behind on the line of march and forwarded same to D.D.V.S. for action, together with location of sick in M.	JR
	21st August 1916 Monday		Sub office and Mobile Section move with Headquarters - move to VRONECOURT map appendix sheet 11 LENS, C.B. Ross with chemist to visit condition of horses. D.D.V.S. enquires of location. Arrival of Regnal Coy and the field ambce kept behind on line of march. Particulars forwarded to D.D.S. for action.	JR

T2134. Wt. W708—776. 500000. 4/15. Sir J. C. & S.

Army Form C. 2118

A.D.V.S.,
47th (LONDON)
DIVISION.
No.........
Date........

WAR DIARY
or
INTELLIGENCE SUMMARY
(Erase heading not required.)

Instructions regarding War Diaries and Intelligence Summaries are contained in F.S. Regs., Part II. and the Staff Manual respectively. Title Pages will be prepared in manuscript.

Place	Date	Hour	Summary of Events and Information	Remarks and references to Appendices
	22nd August 1916 Tuesday		March again continued to BRIZIEUX. Not reference AMIENS sheet 17 - G.1 arriving at 7.30 p.m. Arrangements for Mobile Section room for office.	A.
	23rd August 1916 Wednesday		Dealt with usual office routine. Rode over to ALBERT and made general inspection of Lorries of 235 and 236 Res. R.F.A. two horses sent to Mobile Section for evacuation.	A.
	24th August 1916 Thursday		Mobile Section office routine. Interviewed D.D.V.S. 4th Army at office and discussed with him matters generally relating to Veterinary administration of Division in new area. Later afternoon rode over to D.R.C. on outskirts of ALBERT. Inspected horse lines of horse-mulepales 235 & 236 Res. R.F.A. and found conditions all favourable, also noticing absent to nothing.	A.

1875 Wt. W593/826 1,000,000 4/15 J.B.C. & A. A.D.S.S./Forms/C.2118.

Army Form C. 2118

A.D.V.S.,
47th (LONDON)
DIVISION.

No. ....
Date ....

WAR DIARY
or
INTELLIGENCE SUMMARY of
(Erase heading not required.)

Instructions regarding War Diaries and Intelligence Summaries are contained in F.S. Regs., Part II. and the Staff Manual respectively. Title Pages will be prepared in manuscript.

Place	Date	Hour	Summary of Events and Information	Remarks and references to Appendices
	25th August 1916 Friday		Usual Office Routine. Visited Horse of 1/3-2/3 Field Cos. R.E. at BEHENCOURT in morning and Signal Coy & Divl. Hq. in afternoon. Interviewed Vety. Officers of Divnl. Engrs., Divl. wet by put rebums. 8 Casualties in 236 has reported by Capt. GOSLING by hostile aeroplanes. All horses of Divnl. interest concerning losses under their charge discussed.	J.A.
	26th August 1916 Saturday		Ordinary Office routine morning and evening. Visited Mobile Section and Horses of Water Wagon Section 3rd Corpt. & Divl. Signal Coy. Got returns rendered to D.D.V.S. in pm shewing wastage of 27 out of total of 5,390.	J.A.
	27th August 1916 Sunday		Office routine morning & evening. Saw horses of Divl. Hq. & Signal Coy.	J.A.
	28th August 1916 Monday		Proceeded to FRESHENCOURT Station at 7.45 am received rollotted Lottes at BRESLE in morning arrived at 14.15. 67 Bn. and Remounts with D.R.Q.M.S. NO. 3 Coy train. Dealt with Office routine visited Mobile Section	J.A.

Army Form C. 2118

A.D.V.S.,
47th (LONDON)
DIVISION.
No. ....
Date ....

WAR DIARY
or
INTELLIGENCE SUMMARY
(Erase heading not required.)

Instructions regarding War Diaries and Intelligence Summaries are contained in F. S. Regs., Part II. and the Staff Manual respectively. Title Pages will be prepared in manuscript.

Place	Date	Hour	Summary of Events and Information	Remarks and references to Appendices
	29th August 1916 Tuesday		Usual office routine. Tested Mobile Section in method race prior to evacuation, also showing Descriptive Roll of animals. Rode over to ALBERT and inspected all horses of 4th D.A.C. conferred with Vety. Officer. Is upon treatment of cases in hand, also with O/C Echelons upon general condition of animals. Inspected all horses of 235, 236, 237 & 238 Ides R.F.A on plain beyond ALBERT, eliminating a number of Debilitated cases. Discussed matters with Captains EDWARDS & HASTING. T.O.½. Returned to D.A.D.V.S. on return upon two animals in D.A.C. Submitted for casting.	JA
	30th August 1916 Wednesday		Routine Office work. Mailed horses of Divl.Hq. Signal Corps. Met D.D.V.R. at Mobile Section in afternoon & brought before him notice several cases for casting as Remounts.	JA
	31st August 1916 Thursday		Inspected horses of 22nd & 24th Battns. at BEHEN COURT also 1/2nd, 1/2/3 Field Co. R.E. at Pot Place. Visited Mobile Section, horses of Divl.Hq. Signal Corps.	JA

Joseph Abron
Major, A.V.C.
A.D.V.S. 47th Division

SECRET.

Headquarters,
47th (London) Division.

       Herewith please War Diary for month of SEPTEMBER 1916.

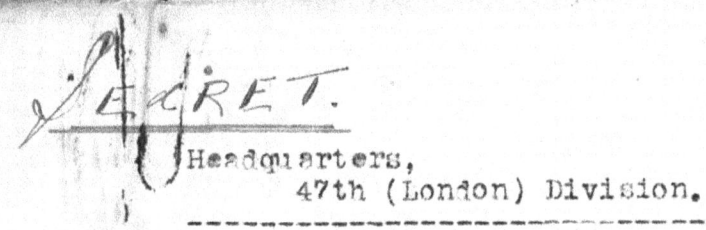

                                      Major,
                        A.D.V.S., 47th (London) Division.

Army Form C. 2118.

A.D.V.S.
47th (LONDON) DIVISION.
No..........
Date..........

WAR DIARY or INTELLIGENCE SUMMARY.
(Erase heading not required.)

Instructions regarding War Diaries and Intelligence Summaries are contained in F.S. Regs., Part II. and the Staff Manual respectively. Title pages will be prepared in manuscript.

Place	Date	Hour	Summary of Events and Information	Remarks and references to Appendices
BRIZEUX	1st September 1916 Friday		Office routine morning and evening. Visited Noris Jetton Lieut. Hy. H. & 2nd Lr. Horses. Rode over to MAILLENCOURT and inspected horses of 140th Infantry Bde. Hence to 13th & 2/3 Field Cos. R.E. at BEZIENCOURT	JA
	2nd September 1916 Saturday		Office Routine only, owing to indisposition, unable to leave bed. Report received from Captain GOSLING A.V.C. upon "GASSING" of 53 animals of D.238 Battery at 10.30 previous night. In wheel being exercised near MAMETZ Wood whilst transporting Ammunition. Wire sent to D.D.V.S. Fourth Army asking for action to be taken under circumstances.	JA
	3rd September 1916 Sunday		Attended to office routine only. still unfit for duty. Visited by D.D.V.S. Fourth Army, who included a report made above mentioned, who conferring upon various matters.	JA

Army Form C. 2118.

A.D.V.S.,
47th (LONDON)
DIVISION.

No..............
Date............

WAR DIARY
or
INTELLIGENCE SUMMARY.
(Erase heading not required.)

Instructions regarding War Diaries and Intelligence Summaries are contained in F. S. Regs., Part II. and the Staff Manual respectively. Title pages will be prepared in manuscript.

Place	Date	Hour	Summary of Events and Information	Remarks and references to Appendices
	4th September 1916. Monday		Dealt with office routine only owing to continued sickness. Further report received from Capt. GOSKIN giving full details; copy forwarded to D.D.V.S. in Army.	A.
	5th September 1916 Tuesday		Routine office work only.	A.
	6th September 1916 Wednesday		Resumed ordinary duties. Notified D.D.V.S. to this effect. Inspected horses of Infantry Bde in BEHENCOURT and district. Visited Mobile Section & horses of Divl. Sig. Signal Coy & C.R.E.	A.
	7th September 1916 Thursday		Office routine as usual. Rode over to FRESHENCOURT at 9 a.m. with D.R.A.M.S. to receive & allot batch of Remounts - 50. In afternoon visited R.D.V.S. 1st Division to arrange taking over his quarters & to select site for Mobile Section at ALBERT. Called at D.A.C. Hqrs., saw Lewis & conferred with Captains STUART and EDWARDS, R.A.S.C. upon question relating to issue no soldiers' rations.	A.

Army Form C. 2118.

WAR DIARY
or
INTELLIGENCE SUMMARY.
(Erase heading not required.)

A.D.V.S.,
47th (LONDON)
DIVISION.

No............
Date............

Instructions regarding War Diaries and Intelligence Summaries are contained in F.S. Regs., Part II. and the Staff Manual respectively. Title pages will be prepared in manuscript.

Place	Date	Hour	Summary of Events and Information	Remarks and references to Appendices
	8th September 1916 Tuesday		Office routine morning and evening. Made inspection of horses of "N" Battery R.H.A. & D.R.C. 2nd & 3rd Cav. Divs. attached to this Divn. at BEDENCOURT sending several to Mob. Section for examination. Visited Lines of Horse Cy. & Sub. Hq. r. Mob. Section. Interviewed Vety. Officers of these in afternoon.	J.R.
	9th September 1916 Saturday		Usual Office Routine. Rode over to FRANVILLERS & inspected mules of transport horses of 141th Inf. Bde. Condition generally good. 1st returns rendered to D.D.V.S. 4th Army; of the 53 "cases" cases, 50 have been returned to duty, & remaining 3 nothing from progress journals recovery. Made a No 3 Roy. R.L.T. at BRESLE, & Mob. Section upon return.	J.R.
	10th September 1916 Tuesday		Office routine as usual. Mob. Section. Dual hq. of Central Cav. Rode over to BRESLE tow. Hors. of 4th Batt. R.W. Fus. + 4th Field Co. R.E. Conclusion received & to move on following day	J.R.

Army Form C. 2118.

A.D.V.S.
47th (LONDON) DIVISION.
No.................
Date................

WAR DIARY
or
INTELLIGENCE SUMMARY.
(Erase heading not required.)

Instructions regarding War Diaries and Intelligence Summaries are contained in F. S. Regs., Part II. and the Staff Manual respectively. Title pages will be prepared in manuscript.

Place	Date	Hour	Summary of Events and Information	Remarks and references to Appendices
	11th September 1916 Monday		Dealt with office routine & supplied Mobile Section. Three offices moves with Divl. - Hq. to E.G. Central, on outskirts of ALBERT. & Mobile Section to E.V.D. D.D.V.S. and all Bdg. Officers notified of change of positions.	St.
	12th September 1916 Tuesday		Attended to office routine. Made general working round of the lines of Divl. Arty. + 3 Infantry Bdes., wagon lines being adjacent to each other outside ALBERT. Number of Artillery Mules losing condition in consequence of work demanded of them. Conferred with all Bdg. Officers, impressing upon them the necessity of maintaining the highest possible efficiency in animals under their charge, always proving a unit where any lead to attain this end. Applied to A.D.O. on behalf on B/235 Battery for increase in forage for horses passed to enable them to regain lost condition.	St.

2353 Wt. W5344/1454 700,000 5/15 D. D. & L. A.D.S.S./Forms/C. 2118.

WAR DIARY or INTELLIGENCE SUMMARY

Army Form C. 2118.

A.D.V.S.
47th (LONDON) DIVISION.

Place	Date	Hour	Summary of Events and Information	Remarks and references to Appendices
	13th September 1916 Wednesday		Usual office routine morning & evening. Inspected horses of 13/7/8 4th Yorks Lt.R.E. and 8 sections of D.R.C. in remainder of R.E.B.E.R.T. Visited Mobile Section & horses of Divl. Sig. Coy.	Sgd.
	14th September 1916 Thursday		Office routine & Mobile Section. Attended Conference of A.D's.V.S. by D.D.V.S. Fourth Army at QUERRIEU. Call from Capt. MACONACHIE R.A.V.C. i/c of Shead Corps. Heavy Artillery, & discussed with him generally upon condition of animals under his care. Capt. BRYDEN. R.A.V.C. visits his return to duty.	Sgd.
	15th September 1916 Friday		Ordinary office routine. Visited horses of 221 A.T. Co. R.E. now attached to this Division. Thence to A.D.V.S. Guards Divn. & arranged with him conjointly for evacuation of casualties. Jones horse killed by shell-fire in D.A.C. Interviewed T.O. of office emerging in weekly sick returns. Visited horses of Signal Coy. & A-hooks C. Sqn. Surrey Yeomanry.	Sgd.

Army Form C. 2118.

A.D.V.S.,
47th (LONDON) DIVISION.

No..........
Date..........

WAR DIARY
or
INTELLIGENCE SUMMARY.
(Erase heading not required.)

Instructions regarding War Diaries and Intelligence Summaries are contained in F. S. Regs., Part II. and the Staff Manual respectively. Title pages will be prepared in manuscript.

Place	Date	Hour	Summary of Events and Information	Remarks and references to Appendices
	16th September 1916 Saturday		Usual Office routine. Went by motor relieves rendered to D.D.M.S. 4th Army. Made general working round of Divl. Artillery, and three Infantry bdes on plateau between ALBERT and FRICOURT. Home to 5th Lon. Field Ambulance in FRICOURT. Visited Mobile Section & horses of Divl. Hq. Signal Coy upon return.	J.S.
	14th September 1916 Sunday		Visited horses of R.E. near FRICOURT & sent two roll-worn cases to Mobile Section. Proceeded to Artillery horse lines & there met Capts EDWARDS, GOSLING & CRAIG. Rvt. & arranged re. abatement of units for Vety attendance, necessitated by moves forward. Saw horses of Divl. Hq. Signals cases at Mobile Section. Dealt with office work: Wire received from Capt. CRAIG reporting lineless casualties by shell fire in horses of Divl. Train & 220 Coy Lon. Regt. MAMETZ WOOD.	J.S.
	18th September 1916 Monday		Attended Conference by D.D.M.S. 4th Army at MEAULTE under question of Casualty Clearing Station for this area was discussed. Arrangements to be organised forthwith, each Mobile Section contributing two men for staff. Visited Mobile Section.	J.S.

WAR DIARY
INTELLIGENCE SUMMARY

Army Form C. 2118.

A.D.V.S.
47th (LONDON) DIVISION.

Place	Date	Hour	Summary of Events and Information	Remarks and references to Appendices
	19th September 1916 Tuesday		Whole office moved with Divl. Hq. from E.g central to BRIZIEUX. Dealt with office matters: list of attached units in area just vacated handed over to A.D.M.S. 1st Div. F.D. ambulances. Instructions received from D.D.M.S. Fourth Army to admin. 1st Divl. Arty. All F.O's and D.D.V.S. notified of change of location	Sd.
	20th September 1916 Wednesday		Usual office routine. Nothing evening. Reported that Capt. GOSLING R.A.V.C. admitted sick to Hospital. Application made to D.D.V.S. for relief. Working horses of 5 & 76 London Field Ambces at MILLENCOURT also. Divl. Hq. & Signals. Upon return.	Sd.
	21st September 1916 Thursday.		Attended to office routine. Visited lines of Divl. Artillery in neighbourhood of FRICOURT with D.A.D.V.S. – Inspection of horses occupying private front of stay. Instructed Capt. EDWARDS to give attention to Capt. GOSLING'S animals pending arrival of relief.	Sd.

Army Form C. 2118.

A.D.V.S.,
47th (LONDON)
DIVISION.

No. ....
Date ....

WAR DIARY
or
INTELLIGENCE SUMMARY.
(Erase heading not required.)

Instructions regarding War Diaries and Intelligence Summaries are contained in F. S. Regs., Part II and the Staff Manual respectively. Title pages will be prepared in manuscript.

Place	Date	Hour	Summary of Events and Information	Remarks and references to Appendices
	22nd September, 1916 Friday		Office routine as usual. Proceeded to FRENCHEN COURT Station with D.A.D.M.S. & inspected 3 palletted of remounts - 49. Visited horses of 2, 3, 4th Corps train at BRECLE also 141st Infantry Bde. & H.Q. Section 1st D.A.C. Interviewed M.O. i/c office bringing in weekly sick returns.	A.
	23rd September, 1916 Saturday		Weekly statistics rendered to D.D.V.S. 4th Army. Weekly light awning to attachment of 1st D. Rly. Casualties by death from 32 of which 17 were fillies at remounts, somewhat. Visited & interviewed by request D.A.D.V.S. Fourth Army upon general matters at GUERRIEU. Inspected with D.A.D.V.T.O.M.G. horses of 236 & 224 Bdes. R.F.A. between FRICOURT and MAMETZ.	A.
	24th September, 1916 Sunday		Made thorough inspection of all horses of Signal Co. R.E. Reconnais to Mobile Section. Dealt with correspondence at office.	A.

Army Form C. 2118.

A.D.V.S.
47th (LONDON)
DIVISION.

No............
Date..........

WAR DIARY
or
INTELLIGENCE SUMMARY.
(Erase heading not required.)

Instructions regarding War Diaries and Intelligence
Summaries are contained in F.S. Regs., Part II.
and the Staff Manual respectively. Title pages
will be prepared in manuscript.

Place	Date	Hour	Summary of Events and Information	Remarks and references to Appendices
	25th September 1916 Monday		Attended to office routine. Rode over to BRESLE and inspected 2 horses of 141st Infantry Bde. Interviewed Capt. R.D. WILLIAMS, A.R.M.C. having just arrived for temporary duty during absence of Capt. A.G.G. OSLIN G.R.Bartlet arrived to D.D.V.S. 4th Army. Saw horses of Signal Coy R.E. and Divl. Sig.	JG
	26th September 1916 Tuesday		Usual office routine. Morning was pouring. Communication from A.D.V.S. 1st Division to effect that he would nominate 1st Divl. Rely. train estab. Rode over to Mobile Section: about unit cases 7 debated Horse for evacuation; hence to nos 2,3,3 & 4 Cos. Divl. Train & inspected all animals; condition very satisfactory and dressed ret. Saw. D.R.B.M.L. and made application to him for remounts to be expected for 236 and 234 toles R.F.R. in consequence of casualties from shell fire and extra work demanded of those remaining.	JG
	27th September 1916 Wednesday		Office routine. Rode over to MILLEN COURT and inspected all transport animals of 142nd Infantry Bde: conferring with Vety. Officer in charge. Saw horses of Signal Coy & Divl. Sig. upon return.	JG

2353 Wt. W2344/1454 700,000 5/15 D.D.&L. A.D.S.S./Forms/C. 2118.

Army Form C. 2118

WAR DIARY
or
INTELLIGENCE SUMMARY
(Erase heading not required.)

Instructions regarding War Diaries and Intelligence Summaries are contained in F. S. Regs., Part II. and the Staff Manual respectively. Title Pages will be prepared in manuscript.

47th (LONDON) DIVISION.

No. ....
Date ....

Place	Date	Hour	Summary of Events and Information	Remarks and references to Appendices
	28th September 1916 Thursday		Summoned by G.O.C. Division to conference previous to his departure upon relinquishing command. Dealt with usual Office Routine. Rode over to FRANVILLERS and inspected horses of 4th Lon. Field Ambulance. Horse to HAPPENCOURT to 6th Lon. F. Ambulance. Visited Mobile Section. Instructions received to move on following day.	A.
	29th September 1916 Friday		This office moved from BRIZIEUX to E. G. Central, near ALBERT, with Divl. Hq. at 9.30 am. Visited Mobile Section. Interviewed Telg. Officers at office bringing in their Weekly vet reports.	A.
	30th September 1916 Saturday		Usual office routine: re-allotting units for Telg. attendance necessitates for some: instructions received from D.D.V.S. to direct Capt. R.O. Williams Vett. to proceed to FREEVILLE upon arrival of Capt. GOSSIP G. sick return rendered to D.D.V.S. Casualties - 5 only. Made general visiting round of all Artillery horses in vicinity of MAMETZ and FRICOURT. CONTALMAISON: conferring with Telg. Officers in charge and evacuating cases requiring rest so far as circumstances would permit.	A.

Joseph Hobson
Major. A.V.C. A.D.V.S. 47th London Division

47th Division 'Q'

       Herewith please War Diary for Month of OCTOBER 1916.

Joseph Abson
Major,
A.D.V.S., 47th (London) Division.

```
A.D.V.S.,
47th (LONDON)
DIVISION.
No. ..................
Date. ..................
```

A.D.V.S.
47th (LONDON)
DIVISION

WAR DIARY

Vol XI

Place	Date	Hour	Summary of Events and Information	Remarks and references to Appendices
ALBERT. E.9.Central	1st October 1916 Sunday		Office routine morning and evening. Visited Mob. Section, inspected cases prior to evacuation. Saw horses of 221 F.T. Co. R.E. Divl. Hq. and Signal Coy.	/s/
	2nd October 1916 Monday		Usual office routine. Mob. Section: conducted O.C. to arrange for floating of several Left wound shell wounded cavalries from MAMETZ WOOD. Made general inspection of horses of 47th D.A.C. and Artillery Bde., eliminating several debilitated cases, these occupying greater part of day.	/s/
	3rd October 1916 Tuesday		Office routine as usual. Inspected animals of 1/3rd 2/3rd 7th Yeld. Co. R.E. rgt. BELLEVUE FARM - ALBERT. Hence to transport lines of 141st Inf. Bde. at F.A.D. conferring with 70% I dealing with cases under treatment. Visited Mob. Section. Capt. J.R.G. GOSLING. A.V.C. returns to duty.	/s/

WAR DIARY or INTELLIGENCE SUMMARY

Army Form C. 2118

A.D.V.S.
47th (LONDON) DIVISION.

Place	Date	Hour	Summary of Events and Information	Remarks and references to Appendices
	4th October 1916 Wednesday		Usual office routine:- dealt with correspondence. Captain R.D. WILLIAMS. A.V.C. returned to No.14 base Veterinary Hospital for duty. To select site for No. W.S.I. eventually decided upon position near BECOURT WOOD. Visited FRICOURT and district with D.t. Mobile Section. To report to No. W.S.I. eventually decided upon position near BECOURT WOOD. Inspected horses of Divl. Hq. Reserve and those in Mobile Section.	A.
	5th October 1916 Thursday		Office routine as usual. Mobile Section moves to BECOURT WOOD. All F.O.s and D.D.V.O. notified. Visited all horses of 13th 23rd 4th Field Cos R.E. at BELLEVUE FARM and 221 A.T. Co. R.E. near ALBERT making inspection of all.	A.
	6th October 1916 Friday		Dealt with office routine. This office moves with Divl. Hq. to FRICOURT-FARM. Visited Mobile Section. Afternoon interviewed Vety. Officers bringing in their weekly sick returns & conferred upon all matters involving the care of the animals under their charge.	A.
	7th October 1916 Saturday		Office routine. Made general visiting rounds of animals of Divl. Artillery located in area of MAMETZ and MANTAUBAN arranging with V.O.s evacuation of many sore faced horses day absent in looking over the pens base and D.A.C. Condition of all favourable, attributing to exposure of past few weeks.	A.

WAR DIARY or INTELLIGENCE SUMMARY

Army Form C. 2118

A.D.V.S.
47th (LONDON) DIVISION.

Place	Date	Hour	Summary of Events and Information	Remarks and references to Appendices
	8th October 1916 Sunday		Dealt with office routine & correspondence. Inspected lines of Divl. Sig. & Signals & visited Mobile Section, opening cables from rearwards to evacuation. Proceeded to ALBERT Station at 3.30 pm to receive 12th Removals: arrived at 12.30 am 9th inst: examined all & distributed to various units, finishing by 3.30 am.	JR
	9th October 1916 Monday		Usual office routine. Saw lines of Divl. Hq. & Signal Coy. Visited 20th R.T. Co. R.E. 1st Division & attended to cables there being called in by R.E. Interviewed A.D.T.P.S. 9th Division and arranged for taking over of office and all connected by Mobile Section upon vacation of same by 47th Divn. Visited Mobile Section.	JR
	10th October 1916 Tuesday		Usual office routine with Divl. Sig. to BRIZIEUX: also Mobile Section. Advanced Collecting Station established at F.I.D. in lines of D.A.C. Visited Mobile Section prior to moving, also lines of D.A.C. in all west lines. Proceeded hence to FRANVILLERS & saw lines of 141st Inf. Bde. Saw lines of Signal Coy. & Divl. Hq. upon arrival at BRIZIEUX.	JR
	11th October 1916 Wednesday		Usual office routine & Mobile Section. Visited lines of 142nd Inf. Bde at MILLENCOURT and to Horse F. Amb at FRANVILLERS attending to post care of batts. Saw lines of Signal Coy upon return.	JR

WAR DIARY or INTELLIGENCE SUMMARY

Army Form C. 2118

A.D.V.S., 47th (LONDON) DIVISION.

Place	Date	Hour	Summary of Events and Information	Remarks and references to Appendices
	12th October 1916 Thursday		Daily office routine. Visited Mobile Section. Rode over to ALBERT & inspected area of HQrs & infantry Bde with Capt. BRYDEN, T.O. Went to 3 Field Companies R.E.s at BELLEVUE FARM.	JA
	13th October 1916 Friday		Usual office routine. Rode area of Divl. Hq. & Signal Coy. before commencing trek en route to SECOND ARMY area. March started at 12.30 p.m. went ST. SAUVEUR reached by 10 p.m. (map reference AMIENS 17). Rode ahead to OVERRIEU to D.D.R. 4th Army and warned 6 Remounts en route to replace casualties on road, and joined column at that place. Also interviewed D.D.V.O. FOURTH ARMY.	JA
	14th October 1916 Saturday		March continued at 9.30 a.m. and AILLY-LE-HAUT-CLOCHER reached by 3.20 p.m. Mobile Section proceeding to BRUCOURT (map ref. ABBEVILLE sheet 44). Instructions received for billeting of Division on 16th and 17th insts. Weekly sick return sent to D.D.V.S. 4th Army with notification of departure from his area.	JA
	15th October 1916 Sunday		Dealt with office routine and visited horses of Divl. Hq. & Signal Coy. also Mobile Section. Only 3 animals left behind on line of march. Left AILLY at 9 a.m. for PONT-REMY and superintended billetting of horses.	JA

Army Form C. 2118

WAR DIARY
or
INTELLIGENCE SUMMARY

(Erase heading not required.)

A.D.V.S.
47th (LONDON)
DIVISION

No..........
Date..........

Instructions regarding War Diaries and Intelligence Summaries are contained in F.S. Regs., Part II. and the Staff Manual respectively. Title Pages will be prepared in manuscript.

Place	Date	Hour	Summary of Events and Information	Remarks and references to Appendices
	16th October 1916 Monday.		Left PONT-REMY at 3.28 am and arrived at GODEWAERSVELDE at 3.20 pm, proceeding thence to destination at HOOGGRAAF Camp near POPERINGHE. D.D.V.S. Second Army notified of arrival in area.	A.1
	17th October 1916 Tuesday.		Dealt with usual office routine. Visited Mobile Section and Horses of Divl. Hq. & Divnl Sigl Coy: arranged for loading of Horses of Batta. units Hqrs. at detrainment platform with punctured feet.	A.1
	18th October 1916 Wednesday.		Attended to office work only, being unable to ride owing to foot which is still extremely painful.	A.1
	19th October 1916 Thursday.		Ditto.	A.1
	20th October 1916 Friday.		Usual office routine. Visited Mobile Section; arranged with C.R.E. for supply of material to inner sheds for sick horses. Inspected horses of Divl. Hq. & Signal Coy. Not 2/4th Corps Divl. Train and 6th Lon F. Amb.c. Interviewed A.D.S. at 6 pm in afternoon, bringing in him Weekly Sick returns.	A.1

1875 Wt. W593/826 1,000,000 4/15 J.B.C. & A. A.D.S.S./Forms/C. 2118.

Army Form C. 2118

WAR DIARY
or
INTELLIGENCE SUMMARY
(Erase heading not required.)

A.D.V.S.
47th (LONDON) DIVISION.

No ....
Date ....

Place	Date	Hour	Summary of Events and Information	Remarks and references to Appendices
	21st October 1916 Saturday		Office Routine as usual. Interviewed DDMS. SECOND ARMY at office & discussed with him all questions relating to my administration in this area & notes on evacuating by rail. Visited Rolic Section. Visited Yutte Remount Section re: HAZEBROUCK - were to remount to rabbay urgent casualties.	J.R.
	22nd October 1916 Sunday		Office routine: dealt with correspondence. Inspected horses of Divl. Amm. Column who being examined many being in debilitated condition also extremely lame & continuous work on somme and subsequent fast to this area. 6 horses of 523rd Howitzer Battery of BOSSCHEPE, having recently arrived from England; whole battery more or less affected with form of ringworm. Inducted O.C. 2nd London M.T.O. to proceed with battering & all animals & renewed report of general condition to DDVS Reserve Army. Visited Stores of Divl. Sup. & Signal Coy.	J.R.
	23rd October 1916 Monday		Office routine as usual. Inspected horses of two batteries of Divl. Arty. upon arrival in area. Visited Mobile Section, Divl. Sup. Depôts, and No 4. Coy. Train, and 522nd Battery.	J.R.

Army Form C. 2118.

WAR DIARY
or
INTELLIGENCE SUMMARY
(Erase heading not required.)

A.D.V.S.
47th (LONDON) DIVISION.

No. ....
Date ....

Instructions regarding War Diaries and Intelligence Summaries are contained in F. S. Regs., Part II. and the Staff Manual respectively. Title Pages will be prepared in manuscript.

Place	Date	Hour	Summary of Events and Information	Remarks and references to Appendices
	24th October 1916 Tuesday		Usual office routine, morning meeting. Met D.D.V.S. at 523 Battery & with him made examination of all horses and mules & decided upon treatment of same. Arranged for evacuation to Base Sick on Thursday of 74 horses from D.A.C. and number others from artillery units. Expected losses of 5 Lon. Field Ambulance.	A.
	25th October 1916 Wednesday		Office routine. Visited units of Divl. Arty. Signals & Motor Section. Hors to D.A.C. making final elimination of Debility cases with M.O.V.S. and O.C. Visited 523 Battery: no cases of pneumonia apparent: average treatment.	A.
	26th October 1916 Thursday		Road over to _____ and received collected Remounts with D.A.D.R.R.G. 39 in number. Proceeded to 523 Battery: Evacuated cases of debility. Ringworm progressing favbly & hely. Visited B/235 & A 4/235 Batteries, selecting him cases for evacuation. Visited Divl. Arty. Signal horses: N.T.R. 99 cases despatched to base.	A.
	27th October 1916 Friday		Office routine as usual. Wire received from D.D.V.S. asking for inspection of Artillery units to be arranged, if possible, for 25th inst. Informed Staff Capt. Divl. Artly upon same. Wire to D.D.V.S. suggesting postponement until 30th inst.— concurred. Visited remnant of 523 Battery morning and evening. Conference with Divl. Officers at 6 o'clock in afternoon.	A.

2449 Wt. W14957/M90 750,000 1/16 J.B.C. & A. Forms/C.2118/12.

WAR DIARY
or
INTELLIGENCE SUMMARY

Army Form C. 2118.

A.D.V.S.
47th (LONDON) DIVISION.

Place	Date	Hour	Summary of Events and Information	Remarks and references to Appendices
	28th October 1916 Saturday		Office work. Inspected a horse of four Batto men of 236 Bde R.F.A. relating to evacuation. Visited 523rd Battery lines, to attend pneumonia case. Noted horses of Divl Cy Signal Coy, and Mobile Section. Weekly act returns to D.D.V.S. 2nd Army: percentage of wastage higher on account of this Division, due to evacuation from Rolling subsequent on their return from Somme + front village in short time. Report of Losses rendered to D.D.V.S.	J.M.
	29th October 1916 Sunday		Office routine. Continued inspection of batteries with M.O. I recommended to D.D.V.S. numbers available for evacuation on 2.11.16 about one linen being arranged. Visited horses of 523rd Battery BOESCHEPE; numerous cases of strangles + arranged special isolation with D.D.V.S. on subject. Visited Mobile Section Dickebusch, Ypres.	J.M.
	30th October 1916 Monday		Usual office routine. Completed inspection of batteries: Completed inspection of batteries: the animals seem in good condition: interviewed Staff Captain 47th D.A. with regard to inspection by D.D.V.S. on 31st inst. Visited 523 Battery, Mobile Section, Divl Cy Signals.	J.M.

SECRET.

Hq., 47th (London) Division.

        Herewith please War Diary for month of December 1916.

Southael

Captain,
A/A.D.V.S., 47th (London) Division.

```
A.D.V.S.,
47th (LONDON)
DIVISION.
No. V.100/103
Date. 1  1  07
```

Army Form C. 2118

WAR DIARY
or
INTELLIGENCE SUMMARY
(Erase heading not required.)

A.D.V.S.,
47th (LONDON) DIVISION.

Place	Date	Hour	Summary of Events and Information	Remarks and references to Appendices
	24th October 1916		Dealt with office routine	A/.
	July day		Whole day spent in inspection of Div. Artillery horses with D.D.V.S. and D.D.R. 2nd Army. Inspection of H.Q. units being completed by 6.30 pm.	

Joseph Moore
Major A.V.C.
A.D.V.S. 47th (London) Division.

SECRET.

Hq., 47th (London) Division.

        Herewith please War Diary for Month of NOVEMBER 1916.

Joseph Aboon.

Major,
A.D.V.S., 47th (London) Division.

A.D.V.S.,
47th (LONDON)
DIVISION.

No. V.180/44
Date 1.12.16

WAR DIARY
or
INTELLIGENCE SUMMARY

(Erase heading not required.)

Army Form C. 2118.

A.D.V.S.
47th (LONDON)
DIVISION.

No. ....
Date ....

Place	Date	Hour	Summary of Events and Information	Remarks and references to Appendices
	1st November 1916 Wednesday		General Office Routine: final arrangements made for evacuation on following day. Rode over to BOESCHEPE to see horses of 523 Battery: all skin cases nothing more. Inspected Mobile Section & advised treatment of patients there. Paid visit to Divl. Hq. & Signal Coy.	J.H.
	2nd November 1916 Thursday		Usual Office routine. Rode over to WIPPENHOEK. Horse Riding & supervised entrainment of 162 mules. Hence to 523 battery BOESCHEPE. Again inspected animals of 47th D.A.C. with Captain STUART A.V.C. F.O. i/c. The unit having suffered considerably by severe hard continuous work followed by long trek. Paid visits to Divl. Hq. & Signal Coy.	J.H.
	3rd November 1916 Friday		Office routine: met Capt. BRYDEN. A.V.C. by appointment & met him unloading of 140th Infantry Bde, 3, 5th & 6th London field ambces., hence to 523 Battery. In afternoon conferred with A.D.M.S. at office, all matters pertaining to Div. respective charges being exhausted. Paid visits to Divl. Hq. & Signal Coy.	J.H.

WAR DIARY
or
INTELLIGENCE SUMMARY

(Erase heading not required.)

Army Form C. 2118.

A.D.V.S.
47th (LONDON)
DIVISION.

Place	Date	Hour	Summary of Events and Information	Remarks and references to Appendices
	4th November 1916 Saturday.		Office routine morning and evening. Met D.D.V.R. record group at Ham in lieu of D.A.D. with a number of unsuitable, unserviceable & vicious animals of Division were brought before him and dealt with. D.A.D.V.S. arranging distribution of those transferred within Divn. Visited 523 Battery Dvl. Hq. & Signals.	A.
	5th November 1916 Sunday.		Usual office routine. Capts. ARRIG and BRYDEN are summoned to duties & programme drawn up for inspection of draught horses of Infantry bdes by D.D.V.S. on 6th inst. for re-classification of same for relieving purposes. Visited 523 Battery, Dvl. Hq. 1 Signal Coy. and 1/3rd and 2/3rd Field Cos. R.E. upon return.	A.
	6th November 1916 Monday.		Office routine: in morning visited 523 Battery; arranged for isolation of pneumonia cases, the remainder of battery horses having never ub typhoid Dval. A.V. Visited Mobile Section & local Sick Lines. In afternoon commenced inspection of Infantry bdes with D.D.V.S. at 2 p.m. finishing at 5.30 p.m. decided that all H.D. animals then and above establishments should be relieved accordingly.	A.

Army Form C. 2118.

A.D.V.S.,
47th (LONDON) DIVISION.
No. ....
Date ....

WAR DIARY
or
INTELLIGENCE SUMMARY
(Erase heading not required.)

Instructions regarding War Diaries and Intelligence Summaries are contained in F. S. Regs., Part II. and the Staff Manual respectively. Title Pages will be prepared in manuscript.

Place	Date	Hour	Summary of Events and Information	Remarks and references to Appendices
	7th November 1916 Tuesday		Usual Office routine. Rode over to BOESCHEPE. Interviewed Lieut Ryan & hot lines recently occupied by 528 Battery but out of 4 sounds would light pneumonia cases isolated there. Three new convalescent Homes to open Battery. Interviewed Staff Captain 47th D. about where & arranged for through disinfection of lines and clothing at BOESCHEPE. Visited lines of 6th Lon Field Ambulance and 2 batteries of 235th R.F.A.	JN
	8th November 1916 Wednesday		Daily Office routine. Visited Koele Perion & Devk 5th J Lionel Coy. Report rather poor form. A.D.V. of general condition of all A.Vet. equipment with units and walker with Capt. Att. Farriers. Visited lines of 236 Bde R.F.A.? stabled horse lines for evacuation. Interviewed A.D.V.S. 55th Division at office & arranged for pneumonia cases from his Division through my Koele Perion.	JN
	9th November 1916 Thursday		Office Routine. Visited BOESCHEPE: attended a case flow & superintended operation: saw horses of no 3 Coy Train; Lieut & Signal Coy on return journey. Rode over to 2nd Field Remount Perion & selected two charges. Interviewed A.A. & Q.M.G. when various matters	JN

Army Form C. 2118

WAR DIARY
or
INTELLIGENCE SUMMARY

(Erase heading not required.)

A.D.V.S.
47th (LONDON)
D[IVISION]

Place	Date	Hour	Summary of Events and Information	Remarks and references to Appendices
	10th November 1916 Friday		General office routine. Confidential report called for from all V.Os. on the Regtl. A.V.C. under their charge as to reliability and efficiency. Visited Mobile Section. Dul. Sgt. & Signals. in afternoon - not there. Officers at office bringing in their weekly returns & discussed with them all questions of topical interest. Visited cases of No 2 Coy. train. & main Sig. & rec'd data these for delivery to N.C.O.'s & men on horsemastership.	J[initials]
	11th November 1916 Saturday		Routine office work. Evacuation arrangements learned from D.D.V.S. for 13th inst. Proceed to RENINGHELST riding with D.A.D.V.S. returns from of returns 185 in number - all horses enlisted to units. Visited Mobile Section to inspect animals for evacuation.	J[initials]
	12th November 1916 Sunday		Usual office routine. Visited transport animals of 1/42nd. Infantry Bde. with Colonel IRWIN, 7/V.C. Visited noses of Divl. Hq. & Signal Coy. Informed A.D.R.H.J. reporting to him necessity of all A.D. horses and establishment of mules being returned as such owing to impossibility of their dealing on A.D. rations at present allowed.	J[initials]
	13th November 1916 Monday		Routine office work. Visited Mobile Section & noses of No 6 Coy. train. Hence to BOESCHEPE to see remount mares of 523 Battery. & progress being made with disinfection. Visited Signal Coy. & noses of Divl. Hq. & unsuitable farriers with regard to fitting of tin plate to sole for displaced frog.	J[initials]

1875 Wt. W593/826 1,000,000 4/15 J.B.C. & A. A.D.S.S./Forms/C. 2118.

Army Form C. 2118

A.D.M.S.
47th (LONDON) DIVISION

WAR DIARY or INTELLIGENCE SUMMARY

(Erase heading not required.)

Place	Date	Hour	Summary of Events and Information	Remarks and references to Appendices
	14th November 1916 Tuesday		Routine office work morning & evening. Made general walking round of four beds of Artillery, attending two hot cases to Mobile Section for evacuation, & arranging bulling up of other doubting case and M.O. to attend this case by advice. In afternoon met D.D.R. at Mobile Section & brought him down roads for sending & time for transfer to Remount Station. Visited Lotto of Divl. Hq. & Signal Coy.	J.A.
	15th November 1916 Wednesday		Usual Office routine. Diagrams arranged for inspection by D.D.R. of M.D. Lobo & Labouring Teams and Field Ambulance R.E. on 17th inst for inspection & re-classification. Visited lines of Field Companies R.E. and 4th Bn R.W.S. Fus. Mobile Section & 6th London F. Ambulance.	J.A.
	16th November 1916 Thursday		Office Routine. Visited lines of 4 Artillery Batteries, & No 2 Coy Train. Rode over to BOESCHEPE & saw Drenchings made & stabled horse ordered there. Called upon burnt down removal to Battery lines. all having now recovered. Called upon Lieut Lolliss recently invalided to arrange completion of inscription of Stables & noted marker circular letter distributed to all Divl. units explaining the method of Preservation of Litter up trail & provided for by Hen flap fixed to flap Questioning for usual to be given.	J.A.

1875 Wt. W593/826 1,000,000 4/15 J.B.C. & A. A.D.S.S./Forms/C. 2118.

Army Form C. 2118

A.D.V.S.,
47th (LONDON)
DIVISION.

No..................
Date.................

WAR DIARY
or
INTELLIGENCE SUMMARY of
(Erase heading not required.)

Instructions regarding War Diaries and Intelligence Summaries are contained in F. S. Regs., Part II. and the Staff Manual respectively. Title Pages will be prepared in manuscript.

Place	Date	Hour	Summary of Events and Information	Remarks and references to Appendices
	17th November 1916 Friday	10h a.m.	Dealt with usual office routine. Inspection by D.D.V.S. postponed to 18th inst. Visited 5 Batteries of 236 & 237 bdes R.F.A. inspecting animals. Met Capt EDWARDS M.O.Vc at Front. Debilitated mare to M.VO for evacuation. Visited horses of Divl Sig. Coy and Mob Section going through all patients there previous to evacuation. Interviewed Maj Owen at office in afternoon conferring with him generally.	A.
	18th November 1916 Saturday		Routine office work. Weekly vet return rendered to D.D.V.S. Met D.D.R. at 9.15 and proceeded to Hd Qrs bde Waggoners at Bn. R.W Fus. & 3 Field Companies R.E. raising in all forty N.C.O.s seven establishment to be replaced by N.C.O. Interviewed O.C. Mobile Section at others also several matters concerning his unit. Began for 24.11.16 tournament to D.D.V.S. supporting contributions from Officers & N.C.O.'s men W.H.C. for Lord Kitchener Memorial Fund.	A.
	19th November 1916 Sunday	10h a.m.	Office routine as usual. Visited 3 Batteries of 237 bde R.F.A. near BURDEDOM. Visited Mobile Section & Mob Section D A.C.s & & Coy, Divl Train Divl Hq & Originals.	A.

1875 Wt. W593/826 1,000,000 4/15 J.B.C. & A. A.D.S.S./Forms/C. 2118.

Army Form C. 2118.

A.D.V.S.
47th (LONDON)
DIVISION.

No. ....
Date............

WAR DIARY
or
INTELLIGENCE SUMMARY
(Erase heading not required.)

Instructions regarding War Diaries and Intelligence Summaries are contained in F.S. Regs., Part II. and the Staff Manual respectively. Title Pages will be prepared in manuscript.

Place	Date	Hour	Summary of Events and Information	Remarks and references to Appendices
	20th November 1916 Monday		Routine Office work. Received call from Major Officer 7th Corps + arranged to administer mits matters pro change whilst absent on leave. Lt. Capt. Edwards + inspection with him horses of No 1 Coy R.F.A. Visited Mobile Section Vet. Hosp + Signal Coy Horses.	J.R.
	21st November 1916 Tuesday		Usual office routine. Visited animals of Signal Coy + reported to D.A.D.V.S. upon suitability of pack horses for L.D. work. Inspected horses of 225 Fd. R.F.A. conferring with O.C. upon matters tending to improve condition. Interviewed ADVS 23rd Division arranging for him to see another Mobile Section now being busily occupied in erection of standings.	J.R.
	22nd November 1916 Wednesday		Dealt with routine office work morning and evening. Inspected horses of 528th Fd. R.F.A. advising generally and urging clipping to save time. Visited No 4 Section D.A.C. Hence to No 1 Coy. saw and addressed Farriers on horsemastership to Officers N.C.Os and men. Visited Horses of Divl. Hq.	J.R.
	23rd November 1916 Thursday		Office work. Inspected and checked with that no. 40 L.D. Horses from R.E.s, 1st London Field Amb. and No RMS Engineers cavity by D.D.R. and addressed by L.D. Two sent to Mobile Section and remainder to Field Remount Depôt. In afternoon received 198 Remounts at Pointe Station with D.D.R. and D.A.R.M.V. examining and allotting them	J.R.

2449 Wt: W14957/M90 750,000 1/16 J.B.C. & A. Forms/C.2118/12.

Army Form C. 2118.

A.D.V.S.,
47th (LO:DON)
DIVISION.

No.............
Date............

WAR DIARY
or
INTELLIGENCE SUMMARY

(Erase heading not required.)

Instructions regarding War Diaries and Intelligence
Summaries are contained in F. S. Regs., Part II,
and the Staff Manual respectively. Title Pages
will be prepared in manuscript.

Place	Date	Hour	Summary of Events and Information	Remarks and references to Appendices
	24th November 1916 Friday		Moral office work. Submitted scheme to Div. Vety. for piking off Anglo ARC, under reorganization. No. of Cast GUNS, by abbreviation & inspected with him Battery horses of 235 T.M. Bde. An awaiting treatment of sores & general rest. In afternoon conference with Vety. Officers at this upon his changes. Eight establishment of Infirmary and Green Stable recommended upon, and progress made with collection of gathered nails by tin pots attached to stable. Visited Kettle Section to see through horses awaiting evacuation.	JR
	25th November 1916 Friday		Office routine. Sick returns rendered to D.D.V.S. Visited No. 1 Sub. Country at BOULOGNE. Made with (illegible) arrangements all required reorganizing treatment. Observed exclusion of horses with frostbitten shins. Visited now Section B.Ve. No. 3 Bac. Stores and Mobile Section.	JR
	26th November 1916 Sunday		Routine office work. Failure of No. 2 Employment Commissariat horses & arranged out & home for delivery of Mules not 29th Section D.A.C. condition of horses too (illegible) but some already improved. Visited by Sub. or Saddlings and (illegible) Chipping. Visited transport lines of 23rd (illegible) Bn. Rpt. of ARTIFERY Lamb. D.A.C 149th Bde. R.F.A. writing to D.C. of latter upon uberm unsatisfactory condition of stable, standings for horses.	JR

Army Form C. 2118.

A.D.V.S.,
47th (LONDON)
DIVISION.

No. ....
Date ....

WAR DIARY
or
INTELLIGENCE SUMMARY
(Erase heading not required.)

Instructions regarding War Diaries and Intelligence Summaries are contained in F.S. Regs., Part II. and the Staff Manual respectively. Title Pages will be prepared in manuscript.

Place	Date	Hour	Summary of Events and Information	Remarks and references to Appendices
	27th November 1916 Monday		Routine office work from Windens. Rode general visiting round as follows:- D/235 Battery: Losses improving in condition; 4th Field Amb.? sore horse - would go.o for supply horses same. C/235, B/235. Losses of R.H. batteries good: B/235 hy. but one horse: 523 Battery done clear of pneumonia: hence to 2/3 wr. Field Co. R.E.: found management of horse lines bad: 50% animals mange ridden: pointed out defective points to O.R.E. under return. No. 1 & 3 Sections D.A.C. animals improving here but shaping progressing favorably. Saw charges of O.C. 235 bde path anaboli? trachines packs.	Sgd.
	28th November 1916 Tuesday		Royal Office routine. Continued visiting rounds as follows:- C/235 hy: nearly all animals clipped & management of horse extremely good. B/235 hy: horses good & keeping progressing well; 4th Batt. R.W.? hyes. +15 Km. Rly. Regt. In evening gave lecture to Officers, N.C.O.s & men of no. 3 Ser. Sub. train on horse management generally, instructing them in elementary duties.	Sgd.
	29th November 1916 Wednesday		Routine Office work. Visited Mobile Veterinary Section: inspected cases there awaiting evacuation, directing treatment of several. Visited horses of Signal Coy. + Sub. Hq.	Sgd.

2449 Wt. W14957/M90 750,000 1/16 J.B.C. & A. Forms/C.2118/12.

WAR DIARY
or
INTELLIGENCE SUMMARY
(Erase heading not required.)

Army Form C. 2118

A.D.V.S.,
47th (LONDON) DIVISION.

Place	Date	Hour	Summary of Events and Information	Remarks and references to Appendices
	30th November 1916 Thursday		Usual Office routine. Man & Draft Horses detailed to proceed to Farenep. Continued general inspecting animals & units as follows:- 4th Bn. Lon. Regt. Horses in fair condition; 16 Battn. water good; B.258 Battery - good; 21st Bn. Lon. Regt. good; 18th Bn. Batt. Hq. satisfactory; Machine Gun Co. 142nd good; 22nd Bn. Lon. Regt. animals usually improved in condition; A/235 Battery horses also in good condition. In evening delivered a lecture on Horsemastership to N.C.Os and men of No 2 Hery. Sub. train. This application for one month's General leave received & duly approved by DMS. L.D. L.B. Reinfts. Camps herewith forwarded 1026.	✓

Joseph Aitken
Major A.V.C.(T)
A.D.V.S. 47th London Division.

Army Form C. 2118.

A.D.V.S.,
47th (LONDON)
DIVISION.

No. ....
Date. ....

WAR DIARY
or
INTELLIGENCE SUMMARY

(Erase heading not required.)

Vol 13

Instructions regarding War Diaries and Intelligence Summaries are contained in F. S. Regs., Part II. and the Staff Manual respectively. Title Pages will be prepared in manuscript.

Place	Date	Hour	Summary of Events and Information	Remarks and references to Appendices
	1st December 1916 Friday		Dealt with usual office routine Correspondence. Met Capt. Edwards A.V.C. at 10.30 am & with him inspected horses of 236 Coy. R.F.A. with in fair condition - evidence of over work. In afternoon conferred with Veti: Officers of office discussing all matters connected with their charges and impressing upon them necessity of reporting at once made to suddenness power outbreak of mange.	JR
	2nd December 1916 Saturday		Office routine: Visited lines of 13th Div. Am. Sub Col. R.E. Dental Sp. & Signal Coy. Inspected horses of 235th Bde. R.F.A. & invalided horse section. Went by rect returns rendered to D.D.V.S. wastage only .291 %.	JR
	3rd December 1916 Sunday		Visual office work. Visited horses of Deal. Sp. Signals, and no.4 Section D.A.C. Interviewed Capt. Louttall, & arranged with him to perform vet duties whilst absent on leave & during general situation. Reported to D.D.V.S. upon (1) trade progress of Mange; now very to unsatisfactory Loud ?? of Mackinnes. (2) Result of Trial Essen to problem of Protection of horses not by addition of lin Bali. (3) General outbreak of Mange in Division.	JR
	4th December 1916 Monday		Attended to office routine work: Visited horses of Signal Coy & Dental Sp. Proceeded on Special leave for one month. Capt. Louttall A.V.C. D.C.2nd London M.V.S. officiating during that period.	JR

2449 Wt. W14957/M90 750,000 1/16 J.B.C. & A. Forms/C.2118/12.

Army Form C. 2118.

WAR DIARY
or
INTELLIGENCE SUMMARY
(Erase heading not required.)

A.D.V.S.,
47th (LONDON)
DIVISION.

Place	Date	Hour	Summary of Events and Information	Remarks and references to Appendices
	5th December 1916 Tuesday		Usual office routine and men duties at Mobile Section.	J.S.
	6th December 1916 Wednesday		Ditto. Visited horses of Divl. Hq. Signal Coy.	J.S.
	7th December 1916 Thursday		Ditto	J.S.
	8th December 1916 Friday		Ditto. Interviewed Vety. Officers at office hospital in ten weekly sick returns. Total sick: 16 Horses 9 Mules Inf. Base: 16 2000 in all.	J.S.
	9th December 1916 Saturday		Usual office routine & men duties at Mobile Section. Weekly sick return rendered to D.D.V.S. Wastage for week: Nil. Visited horses of Divnl. Inf. Bns. Conferred with Capt. CRAIG, inspected Influenza cases, and arranged for all precautions to be taken.	J.S.
	10th December 1916 Sunday		Office Routine: Visited horses of Divnl. Hq. Signal Coy. Men duties at Mobile Section.	J.S.
	11th December 1916 Monday		Ditto.	J.S.

Army Form C. 2118.

A.D.V.S.,
47th (LONDON)
DIVISION.

No. ....
Date. ....

WAR DIARY
INTELLIGENCE SUMMARY
(Erase heading not required.)

Instructions regarding War Diaries and Intelligence Summaries are contained in F. S. Regs., Part II. and the Staff Manual respectively. Title Pages will be prepared in manuscript.

Place	Date	Hour	Summary of Events and Information	Remarks and references to Appendices
	12th December 1916 Tuesday		Book work, usual office routine. Instructions received from D.D.V.S. to send Cuart of Enquiry on loss of Microscope by Mobile Section: passed to D.D.V.S. on arrival. Visited horses of Divl. Sig. & signal Co. & attended to sick duties at Mobile Section.	J.S.
	13th December 1916 Wednesday		Office routine & own duties at Mobile Section.	J.S.
	14th December 1916 Thursday		Ditto.	J.S.
	15th December 1916 Friday		Do. Lath: Drew no 349 Received a new W.O. Record notifying that all W.O. personnel with Divison transferred to Regular Forces vide under Army Council Instruction 185. Weekly sick reports rendered to D.D.V.S. 2nd Army. Wastage 559.	J.S.
	16th December 1916 Saturday		Usual Office routine & own duties at M.V.S. Attended a Court of Enquiry on loss of Microscope at A.R. 47th Divl. Train.	J.S.
	17th December 1916 Sunday		Usual office routine & own duties at M.V.S.	J.S.

Army Form C. 2118.

WAR DIARY
or
INTELLIGENCE SUMMARY

(Erase heading not required.)

A.D.V.S.
47th (LONDON)
DIVISION.

No..................
Date..................

Instructions regarding War Diaries and Intelligence Summaries are contained in F. S. Regs., Part II. and the Staff Manual respectively. Title Pages will be prepared in manuscript.

Place	Date	Hour	Summary of Events and Information	Remarks and references to Appendices
	18th December 1916 Monday		Usual office routine and own duties at Mobile Section. Visited Lorries of Divl. Hq. and Signal Coy. R.E.	
	19th December 1916 Tuesday		Ditto.	
	20th December 1916 Wednesday		Ditto.	
	21st December 1916 Thursday		Ditto. & Visited Lorries of 5th Lon. Field Ambce. and 6th Lon. Field Ambce.	
	22nd December 1916 Friday		Usual routine office work & own duties at Mobile Section. Visited Lorries of Divl. Hq. Signal Coy.	
	23rd December 1916 Saturday		Do. Weekly sick returns rendered to D.D.M.S. 2nd Army. Wastage 188	
	24th December 1916 Sunday		Do.	

Army Form C. 2118.

WAR DIARY
or
INTELLIGENCE SUMMARY

(Erase heading not required.)

A.D.V.S.
47th (LONDON)
DIVISION.

Place	Date	Hour	Summary of Events and Information	Remarks and references to Appendices
	25th December 1916 Monday.		Draft visit routine office work and attended to own duties at Mobile Section.	
	26th December 1916 Tuesday.		Do. Visited horses of Dvl. Hq + Signal Coy.	
	27th December 1916 Wednesday.		Do. + own duties at Mobile Section	
	28th December 1916 Thursday.		Do.	
	29th December 1916 Friday.		Do.	
	30th December 1916 Saturday.		Do. Do. /Sankh sick returns received to D.D.V.S. Wantage 13th 10 horses killed + one wounded by shell fire at CAFE-BELGE night of 29th inst.	
	31st December 1916 Sunday.		Usual office routine + own duties at Mobile Section.	

Ken Foster A.M.C.(T)
A.D.V.S. 47th London Division

SECRET.

Hq., 47th Division.

　　　　　Herewith please War Diary for Month of January 1917.

```
┌─────────────────┐
│   A.D.V.S.,     │
│ 47th (LONDON)   │
│   DIVISION.     │
│  V.100/130.     │
│ No.             │
│ Date 1. 2. 17.  │
└─────────────────┘
```

　　　　　　　　　　　　　T. Hibbard
　　　　　　　　　　　　　　　Major,
　　　　　　　　　　A.D.V.S., 47th (London) Division.

Army Form C. 2118.

A.V.S.
47th (LONDON)
DIVISION

WAR DIARY
or
INTELLIGENCE SUMMARY
(Erase heading not required.)

Instructions regarding War Diaries and Intelligence Summaries are contained in F. S. Regs., Part II. and the Staff Manual respectively. Title Pages will be prepared in manuscript.

Place	Date	Hour	Summary of Events and Information	Remarks and references to Appendices
	1st January 1917 Monday		Dealt with usual routine office work. Inspected horses of Divl. Hq. & Signal Coy. was attended to own duties at Mobile Section.	
	2nd January 1917 Tuesday		Routine office work: visited horses of Divl. Hq. & Signal Coy. Horse over to WINNIZEELE and inspected horses of 236 Bde. R.F.A. all in good condition and up this message. Own duties at Mobile Section.	
	3rd January 1917 Wednesday		Office routine & own work at Mobile Section. Met Capt. Goshy OVC by appointment with him inspected animals of 235 & 236 Bde. R.F.A. actress their slight outbreak of mange in two batteries of 235 Bde. demonstrated cases sent to Mobile Section for evacuation and arrangements made for treatment & isolation of remainder.	
	4th January 1917 Thursday		Usual routine office work & own duties at Mobile Section. Visited animals of Divl. Hq. & Signal Coy. & transport horses of Useful Coy. & 2/3 Lon. York & R.E. Arrangements made for evacuation of animals by road, & L. of C.	
	5th January 1917 Friday		Office Routine. Own duties at Mobile Section. Interviewed Mil. Agers at office in afternoon, & discussed with them all matters concerning new changes, impending upon them urgency of coping with mange situation. Moved horses of Divl. Hq. Signal Coy.	

2449 Wt. W14957/Mg0 750,000 1/16 J.B.C. & A. Forms/C.2118/12.

Army Form C. 2118.

A.D.V.S.
47th (LONDON)
D[IVISIO]N.

No. ....
Date ....

WAR DIARY
or
INTELLIGENCE SUMMARY
(Erase heading not required.)

Instructions regarding War Diaries and Intelligence Summaries are contained in F.S. Regs., Part II. and the Staff Manual respectively. Title Pages will be prepared in manuscript.

Place	Date	Hour	Summary of Events and Information	Remarks and references to Appendices
	6th January 1917 (Saturday)		Dealt with office routine + own duties at Mobile Section. Act. returns rendered to D.D.V.S. unchanged but to inc. returns by last five: Leave for Capt. Bolling cancelled owing to return return of A.D.V.S. Mobile animals of 140th Section D.A.C. + Divl. Hq. Signal Coy. + 2.M.R.	
	7th January 1917 (Sunday)		Usual office work and Mobile Section routine. Saw horses of 1/19th Inf. Bde. + of held Cos R.E. condition of all good.	
	8th January 1917 (Monday)		Office routine + own work at Mobile Section. Saw horses of Divl. Hq. Signal Coy. Visited 1/235 Battery; again wounded range cases: Reported made to D.D.V.S. Remy. Rode to 228 Coy R.F.R. Singerled Farm.	
	9th January 1917 (Tuesday)		Usual office routine and Mobile Section duties. Inspected animals of D.A.C. + of 235 Battery. Divl. Hq. Signal Coy. Rode over to WINNEZEELE saw horses of 236 Brigade R.F.A. Received and examined batch of Remounts 45 at HOPOUTRE arriving 4.30 p.m. came sent to lines of D.A.C. for distribution next morning.	
	10th January 1917 (Wednesday)		Attended to office routine + own duties at M.V.O. own return of Major QUINN, reported. Distribution Remounts at D.A.C. Again visited 1/235 Battery: met Capt. GOLDING, A.V.C. inspected + walk with him horses.	

Divl. Hd Qrs. 47th Div.

WAR DIARY
or
INTELLIGENCE SUMMARY

Army Form C. 2118.

A.D.V.S.
47th (London)
Division

Place	Date	Hour	Summary of Events and Information	Remarks and references to Appendices
	11th January 1917 Thursday		Routine office work and Mobile Section duties; Evacuation of animals by road arranged. Mobile Lines of D.A.A. Signals.	
	12th January 1917 Friday		Usual routine office work & Mobile Section duties. Vet. Officers at office in afternoon received sick reports & discussed matters generally. Mobile Lines of D.A.A. Signal Co.	
	13th January 1917 Saturday		Office routine; sick returns rendered to D.D.V.S. Arrangements made with D.D.V.S. for collection of sick ones by Mobile Ambulance, post & left wounds. Afternoon occupied with duties at Mobile Section.	
	14th January 1917 Sunday		Office routine & Mobile Section duties. Rode over to 226 Coy at WINNIZEELE & inspected animals, on return visited M.Gun Huts & R.E. Base Lines & reported to D.A.D.M.S. upon two mules for casting in that unit. Notification received from D.D.V.S. that Major T. HIBBARD A.V.C.(T.F.) attached A.V.M.S. 47th Division, arriving from England, arrived to rejoin.	
	15th January 1917 Monday		Office Routine & own duties at Mobile Section. Mobile Lines of Divl. Hq & Signal Co, Mobile animals of no 4 Section D.A.C. and No Echelon of 235 Bde. R.F.A.	

WAR DIARY or INTELLIGENCE SUMMARY

Army Form C. 2118.

A.D.V.S.
471...
No. ....
Date ....

Instructions regarding War Diaries and Intelligence Summaries are contained in F.S. Regs., Part II. and the Staff Manual respectively. Title Pages will be prepared in manuscript.

(Erase heading not required.)

Place	Date	Hour	Summary of Events and Information	Remarks and references to Appendices
	16th January 1917 (Tuesday)		Usual office duties: Remainder of day spent in dealing with cases at Mobile Sections & all duties in connection therewith.	
	17th January 1917 (Wednesday)		Office work & Mobile Section duties: arranged for evacuation of cases by road. Programme of inspection by Army Commander on 18th inst. received: all Sec. Officers to attend: instructed accordingly. Visited Horses at Deal. Hy. Signal Coy.	
	18th January 1917 (Thursday)		Routine Office work & Mobile Section duties: Visited Hy. Signal Horses: Visited Horses of 2nd & 3rd Bde Hvy. R.E. Attended inspection of Horses of Divl. train by Army Commander.	
	19th January 1917 (Friday)		Usual office routine: Visited 236 Emp. R.E. Coy in afternoon: received a sett report & instructed Commander especially as to Mange situation: I/c Mobile Section all cases of Mange and suspected otin Disease.	
	20th January 1917 (Saturday)		Visited 19th Corps to attend conference to discuss question of preparation of material to cope with prevalence of Mange: pending completion of Caps. Dip Bath. Instructed to attend Hors. Divl. Commander with special to Mange preparation arrangt. A. Madam A.V.C. for Eastling & civilian.	

Army Form C. 2118.

A.D.V.S.,
47th (LONDON)
DIVISION.

No. ....
Date ....

WAR DIARY
or
INTELLIGENCE SUMMARY
(Erase heading not required.)

Instructions regarding War Diaries and Intelligence Summaries are contained in F. S. Regs., Part II. and the Staff Manual respectively. Title Pages will be prepared in manuscript.

Place	Date	Hour	Summary of Events and Information	Remarks and references to Appendices
	20th January 1917 Saturday		Major T. HIBBARD A.V.C. & arrived and assumed duties as A.D.V.S. Division. Arrival notified to D.D.V.S. and Divn. Mobile Veterinary Section and remounts (horse establishment 22-0:191 issue of H.m. remounts in correspondence of 2nd Corps wire: Mobile Section - D.D.V.S. Establishment returns rendered to A.D.V.S.; remounts:22; Bud.S; Destroyed 2.	
	21st January 1917 Sunday		Attended usual Sunday routine & correspondence. Visited Mobile Section : Made & issued remounts to (1) 7th Roughriders (2) Forefront to M.V.S. and (3) to returned animals for treatment. Inspected animals of North Section 17th D.A.C.	
	22nd January 1917 Monday		Dealt with office work: Visited horse of Bund. H.Q. 1 Signal Coy. horses of shell shock inoculated sent to Mobile Section on application to Vacuum Subsection. Inspected horses of C.228 Battery R.F.A. and Col. EDWARDS DAC. An afternoon called upon D.D.V.S. at H.Q. HAZEBROUCK and him discussed all matters pertaining to my appointment.	
	23rd January 1917 Tuesday		Routine office work : Morning Inspection: at ??? Officers instructed to attend conference this other at 3pm on Tuesday 26 inst. Visited Batteries of 236 Bde R.F.A. with D.V.O. animals in good condition & free from other disease with exception of two mares. Mobile horse of Bund. Hq. Borads and North Section Moor Section transferred to the mobile H.Q. A.D.V.O. 4th Division called & complained of condition of mules & animals of Heavy Artillery Brigade of which he had returned.	

2449 Wt. W14957/M90 750,000 1/16 J.B.C. & A. Forms/C.2118/12.

WAR DIARY / INTELLIGENCE SUMMARY

Army Form C. 2118.

A.D.V.S.
47th (LONDON)
D

Place	Date	Hour	Summary of Events and Information	Remarks and references to Appendices
	24th January 1917 (Wednesday)		1st VW Officers to P.M.L. unit in pital animals returned by 41st Divn out; animals fit to return to be sent in lieu; also inspected all animals on not 343 Divisional R.A.C. conditions fair & outlook poor. Visited Lorries of 518th Cox 6th Siege R.E. Tevue to Divl Hg Signals & Mobile Sect in Visit with usual conferences with veterinary Offr. G. Billings and horses in Ser Divn trans. Reprd Corporal applies for one days special leave.	
	25th January 1917 (Thursday)		Office work & correspondence. 30 mange cases evacuated by road to 23 Vety Hosp. Rouen. one to MINNIKEELE and another LOWIE O.P. 235 by R.V.H. in not area. Four Visited Mobile Sections & horses of Divl Hg and Signal Tp.	
	26th January 1917 (Friday)		Office routine morning & evening. Inspected horses of No 2 & 4 Companies Divl Train & mules at Mobile Section. Afternoon held conference of Vety Officers at Office when all matters were discussed concerning their charges, and points conducive to his Horse efficiency. Visited Mobile Section & especially dealt with mange and skin diseases treatment. C.E.R. 2880 reached 15. 10th Corps.	
	27th January 1917 (Saturday)		Daily Office routine; Sick returns rendered to D.D.V.S. Dept 1st 2 Destroyed: figures greatly swelled by addition of 106 bde Artillery sick outbreak of mange. Visited RENINGHELST riding lines to receive Remounts which failed to arrive. Visited Mobile Section & horses of Divl Hg & Signal Coy.	

WAR DIARY
or
INTELLIGENCE SUMMARY

(Erase heading not required.)

Army Form C. 2118

Instructions regarding War Diaries and Intelligence Summaries are contained in F.S. Regs, Part II. and the Staff Manual respectively. Title Pages will be prepared in manuscript.

Place	Date	Hour	Summary of Events and Information	Remarks and references to Appendices
	28th January 1917 Sunday.		Usual office routine. Visited Mobil Section Horses at Burleigh and Signal Co. Inspected horses of 47th Field Stables Park, Belton D.A.C. Mine received from 47th Divn answering all movements by rail. Same men + first horses etc. 12 Chestnut mares received on loan for the days to assist in distributing. Range ostlered: distributed to units unsaddled.	
	29th January 1917 Monday		Rode over to HALIFAX Camp & inspected 21 transport animals of 141nd. Sgt Cdr. and 44 Bn. R.W.Fus. with Vet. Officer & Capt. R&LB. Condition on the whole satisfactory. Attended to office routine. Called upon Burl. Commandant. A.D.V.S. 62nd Div discussed unit horses, suggested attachment of D.V.S. for looks and Mobil Veterinary Section for East. Co Review for Remount base (3) leave for horses in M.T.J.	
	30th January 1917 Tuesday.		Review office work as usual. Inspected animals of 10th Lond. R.Y.R.- in men of BURBERDON and 1/3 Lon batts of R.E. Visited Mobil Section + horses of Burl. HQ Signal Coy. Instructions for use of 17th Corps Horse Dip received. altered to Res. Dumps M + Shop, Provision and for all Vet. Officers units to be advanced so exposure on live cart.	
	31st January 1917 Wednesday.		Office work correspondence. Rode over to WINNEZEELE + inspected animals of 235 Coy: R.F.A. vet. avis. Visited Mobil section + went with same there.	

T. Shippard
Maj. O.R.
A.D.V.S. 47th (London) Division

(4497) W. 4884/M680 250,000 8/16 McA. & W., Ltd. (Est. 279) Forms/W 3091/3.   Army Form W. 3091.

Cover for Documents.

Vol 15

Nature of Enclosures.

War Diary 1st – 28 February 1917.

of

Major J. Hibbard A.V.C.

A.D.V.S.

47th (London) Division

Notes, or Letters written.

Army Form C. 2118

WAR DIARY
or
INTELLIGENCE SUMMARY

(Erase heading not required.)

Instructions regarding War Diaries and Intelligence Summaries are contained in F. S. Regs., Part II. and the Staff Manual respectively. Title Pages will be prepared in manuscript.

Place	Date	Hour	Summary of Events and Information	Remarks and references to Appendices
	1st February 1917 Thursday	10 am	Office routine work. Visited a & b Company H.Q. & Divisional Train. Visited a Stu Mobile with an Officer, Isolated & discussed the defects of the authoris. Stomatitis contagious & measures to be taken — Strength of animals 5384 — Horse cases 68	
	2nd February 1917 Friday	10 am	Office routine work. Visited ——— at the mobile section. Visited H.Q. Dr. Signals, Discussed all Cy Officers. Visited in afternoon & discussed subject of Stomatitis contagiosa & precautions to be taken in regards to the chopping up of rations.	
	3rd February 1917 Saturday	10 am	Office routine work & visited ——— Visited Mobile Sn Child 1 Dis. Command & Dr. Train. Visited	
	4th February 1917 Sunday	10 am	Office routine work & visited ——— Visited Mobile Sn Child 1, 2 Batteries 104th Div. confused with a branch about animal immature	
	5th February 1917 Monday	10 am	Office routine work & visited Mobile Sn., 2 Coy Train, H.S. Field Amb. & 2/3 Field Amb. 86	1/100/15 A 82/17
	6th February 1917 Tuesday	10 am	Office routine work. Visited Mobile Sn, 2 Coy Train, & conferred with Capt. O'Brien	
	7th February 1917 Wednesday	10 am	Office routine work. Visited Signals, Head quarters Mobile Sn, Leaby Train	
	8th February 1917 Thursday	10 am	Office routine work — Strength 3466 horses 608 Mules Total 4296 — Horse 109 Visited 235 Bde R.F.A.	

1875 Wt. W593/826 1,000,000 4/15 J.B.C. & A. A.D.S.S./Forms/C. 2118.

Army Form C. 2118.

WAR DIARY
or
INTELLIGENCE SUMMARY

(Erase heading not required.)

Instructions regarding War Diaries and Intelligence Summaries are contained in F. S. Regs., Part II. and the Staff Manual respectively. Title Pages will be prepared in manuscript.

Place	Date	Hour	Summary of Events and Information	Remarks and references to Appendices
	9th February Friday		Office Routine work. Conferred with O.D.V.S. & visited 104th Bde R.F.A. Afternoon held conference of Vety Officers at which O.D.V.S read a lecture on mange	
	10th February Saturday		Office Routine work. Visited No 1 Coy Divl Train + No 1 Coy Divl Train, Had 2/c Signal Coy R.E. + Mobile Vety Sn.	
	11th February Sunday		Office Routine work. Visited No 2 + 3 Coys Divl Train	
	12th February Monday		Office Routine work. Visited Mobile Vety Sn, 6th Fd Amb, 4th Fd Amb, 5th Fd Amb, signal Coy R.E., 101st 2/c	
	13th February Tuesday		Office Routine Work. Visited Mobile Veterinary Section, No 1 + No 1 Coys Divl Train, 142nd Bde, C Battery 235 Bde R.F.A + D Battery 104th Bde R.F.A.	
	14th February Wednesday		Office Routine Work. Visited B Battery 235 Bde R.F.A. Headquarters No 1 Coy Divisional Train	
	15th February Thursday		Attended mange demonstration at St Omer given by O.D.V.S. Strength Horses 348 Mules 808 Total 4591 Marge 146 - Ride of Mounted	1/1s 0/115.9 13/42.1

WAR DIARY
or
INTELLIGENCE SUMMARY.

Army Form C. 2118.

Place	Date	Hour	Summary of Events and Information	Remarks and references to Appendices
	16th February Friday		Office Routine work. Visited Signals Coy Headquarters, mobile Vety. Sn. No 1 Cav. B.G. Conference of M.Os held in afternoon at which items of general interest were discussed.	
	17th February Saturday		Office routine work. Visited M.M.3, C/256 Battery R.F.A, mobile vety Sn. No 1 III Corps Amb. Train.	
	18th February Sunday		Office routine work. Visited Mobile Vety Section 9 London S.A.C, 2 Section S.A.C. No 1 Cav/Bde Machine Gun Coy	
	19th February Monday		Office routine work. – Evacuated two horses to No 1 Vety Ambulance. Visited mobile Vety section, I, II, III Corps Amb Train, 142 Inf Bde & Amb 762.	
	20th February Tuesday		Office routine work. – Evacuated four horses to No 1 Vety Ambulance. Visited mobile vety Sn. and Headquarters, 18/19th Battalion London Regt.	
	21st February Wednesday		Office routine work.	
	22nd February		Mobile vety section, signals Coy R.E, 6 Squadron S.A.S, 17th Batt. London Regt	
	Thursday		Office routine work – Evacuated 23 animals. Visited I An/9 Inf. Train mobile Vety Sn, N.2 Inf/Bde Machine Gun Coy.	
	23rd February Friday		Office routine work. Visited Inf Signals Coy R.E. and Hd Qy Inspected Remounts. Stoney Athoric 920 duty roue Total 405 in afternoon with evidence of Vety Officer at which forton (wound) about one thousand. Field of wounds 1 – Mange 259.	

A.D.V.S.
No. 10 b/1st?
Date 23.2.17

Army Form C. 2118.

WAR DIARY
or
INTELLIGENCE SUMMARY.
(Erase heading not required.)

Instructions regarding War Diaries and Intelligence Summaries are contained in F. S. Regs., Part II. and the Staff Manual respectively. Title pages will be prepared in manuscript.

Place	Date	Hour	Summary of Events and Information	Remarks and references to Appendices
	24th February 1917 Saturday		Office routine work. Attended III Corps Div. Vet Conf. Mobile Vety Section & C/236 Battery R.F.A.	
	25th February Sunday		Office routine work. Visited I & II Echelons A.C. & Divl Arty Hq	
	26th February Monday		Office routine work. Visited Horse Battery W.Sct, 1/6 Royal Irish Rifles & 220 Coy R.E.	
	27th February Tuesday		Office routine work. Visited Hr. Signal Coy R.E., Mobile Vety Sn.	
	28th February Wednesday		Office routine work. Visited Mobile Vety Sn, M.M.P., Hr Echelon 47th & D.A.C.	

T. Dalton
Major A.V.C.
A.D.V.S.
47th London Division
1st March 1917

Army Form C. 2118.

WAR DIARY
or
INTELLIGENCE SUMMARY.
(Erase heading not required.)

A.D.V.S.
47th (LONDON)
DIVISION.
No. ....
Date ....

Vol 16

Instructions regarding War Diaries and Intelligence Summaries are contained in F.S. Regs., Part II. and the Staff Manual respectively. Title pages will be prepared in manuscript.

Place	Date	Hour	Summary of Events and Information	Remarks and references to Appendices
G.H.Q.1st & 2nd Echelon	Thursday 1.3.17		Attended to office routine: visited Horses of Divl. Hq. & Signal Coy. and Mobile Section.	
	Friday 2.3.17		Usual office routine: visited Mobile Section & Divl. Hq. & Horses of 6th Bn. Yeld Ambce. in afternoon had conference of Vety. Officers at offices & discussed all matters bearing on animals for charge, arrangement for disposal of mange cases at 18th Lods. D.S. on 11th inst.	
	Saturday 3.3.17		Office routine work: mostly out investigating rubbing, exposed to 12.30 V.S. Record Army. Wall ammunition 4955: Inoculated 50. Deal 3. Destroyed 2: 226 remaining, including 170 mange. Visited Mobile Section. Divl. Hq. & T.M.B. Coy. train.	
	Sunday 4.3.17		Routine office work: visited Horses of D/235 battery and B/106 by.	
	Monday 5.3.17		Office routine: visited Mobile Section: Divl. Hq. & Horses of A/236 by.	

Army Form C. 2118.

A.D.V.S.
47th (LONDON)
Division

No. ....
Date. ....

WAR DIARY
or
INTELLIGENCE SUMMARY
(Erase heading not required.)

Instructions regarding War Diaries and Intelligence Summaries are contained in F. S. Regs., Part II. and the Staff Manual respectively. Title pages will be prepared in manuscript.

Place	Date	Hour	Summary of Events and Information	Remarks and references to Appendices
	Tuesday 6.3.17		Dealt with correspondence of office. Inspected animals of R.A.B.T.D. Returns 236 Coo. 520 Field Co. R.E. and Mobile Section.	
	Wednesday 7.3.17		Mobile Loads of 6th, 7th, & 8th Battalions, 440 Field Ambulance, Mobile Section & office routine.	
	Thursday 8.3.17		Usual office work. Mobile Mobile Section sent animals to be evacuated; advised treatment of others. Inspected horses of D.A.D. Signal Coy.	
	Friday 9.3.17		Office work: routine. Evening: Mobile M.V.S.q. Loads of 140, 236 Coos. ran. In afternoon had conference of Vety. Officers at office, discussed all series of weekly report concerning Men.	
	Saturday 10.3.17		Office routine: visit by sick return returned to Dmn. Loks Y Army: Total strength animals 4313: Evacuated 17: Died 3: Destroyed 3: troops remaining 108: Mobile horses of 2/236 by at WINNIZEELE: no D.P.VS. conferred with him.	

T2134. Wt. W708—776. 500000. 4/15. Sir J. C. & S.

Army Form C. 2118.

WAR DIARY
or
~~INTELLIGENCE SUMMARY~~ of:

(Erase heading not required.)

Instructions regarding War Diaries and Intelligence Summaries are contained in F. S. Regs., Part II. and the Staff Manual respectively. Title pages will be prepared in manuscript.

Place	Date	Hour	Summary of Events and Information	Remarks and references to Appendices
Sunday	11.3.17		Routine office work: Mobile Loads of Amb. Hy. Aygrots & Mobile Section. 200 Lords issued through IX Corps. Dep: Lieut EDWARDS A.V.C. to duty on leave.	
Monday	12.3.17		Inspected Loads of B.s 10/236 & B/235 followed R.V.A 9 -4p.140 loss. Re: Manual office work.	
Tuesday	13.3.17		Office routine: Visited transport Loads of 140 - of Coll.? Mobile section.	
Wednesday	14.3.17		Office work as usual. Inspected Loads of B/236 & B/235 before Sect -74 Signal Coy.	
Thursday	15.3.17		Routine office work: Veterinarians issued on Loads of 2 Bul. — rain owing to outbreak on Dinantic contagious reported. Visits Loads of 1st. Bn 9 rain. Captain L.A.E. DAWSON A.V.C arrived and posted to 47. M.A.C for duty.	
Friday	16.3.17		Visited Mobile section: LM. Composed of 7 Offy. Officer at ones in alternator.	

Army Form C. 2118.

WAR DIARY
or
INTELLIGENCE SUMMARY.
(Erase heading not required.)

Instructions regarding War Diaries and Intelligence Summaries are contained in F.S. Regs., Part II. and the Staff Manual respectively. Title pages will be prepared in manuscript.

A.D.V.S.
47th (LONDON)
D   N.
No.
Date

Place	Date	Hour	Summary of Events and Information	Remarks and references to Appendices
Salisbury	17.3.17		Office routine: Weekly sick return rendered to Divn. Civil & Army. Total strength 4292 animals: 12 evacuated: 4 died: 4 destroyed: 68 mange remaining. Inspected horses of 142 N Infantry bde. & New buy. Train. Re-allotment of animals made for 7th All-Ammn. sent to B. & BAmmunition D.R.P.	
Sunday	18.3.17		Usual office routine: Inspected horses of B/236 Battery & Mobile Section. 17 horses of 235 Bde passed through VIII Corps Disp.	
Monday	19.3.17		Office work. Visited Evak. Hy. Agred los nearest Mobile Section.	
Tuesday	20.3.17		Routine office work. Attended Conference of A.D.V.S. at BARLEUX HdQrs S.D.V.S. Second Army. Instructions issued to units and Veto Officers re disposal of serums etc. VIII Corps D.S.D on 26th inst. Allotment of 400 mules.	
Wednesday	21.3.17		Office work. Visited Mobile Section horses of New Coy-train	

T2134. Wt. W708-776. 500000. 4/15. Sir J. C. & S.

Army Form C. 2118.

WAR DIARY
or
INTELLIGENCE SUMMARY
(Erase heading not required.)

Instructions regarding War Diaries and Intelligence Summaries are contained in F. S. Regs., Part II. and the Staff Manual respectively. Title pages will be prepared in manuscript.

A.D.V.S.
47th (LONDON)
DIVISION

No. ....
Date. ....

Place	Date	Hour	Summary of Events and Information	Remarks and references to Appendices
Thursday	22.3.17		Office work. Visited Mobile Section & arranged for evacuation of sick horses from Horse pond "B" village of Mobile Section: also all horses of 235 Field R.F.A.	
Friday	23.3.17		Office routine. Visited Mobile Section. In afternoon held conference of Vety. Officers at office; arrangements for dipping of horses on 31st inst. at 13th Corps D.H.	
Saturday	24.3.17		Routine office work. Weather wet. Horses needed to Dun. Horses & Army total strength 4,313. evacuation 30. Sick and Destroyed 2. 137 remaining wastage 36 animals. Visited Mobile Section. In afternoon attended inspection by D.D.V.R. of mules + sick animals at Desl. farm. Inspected horses of Mobile Section D.A.C.	
Sunday	25.3.17		Usual office routine & Mobile Section.	
Monday	26.3.17		do. Visited Mobile Section, Dvl. Hq. & Div.nl Coy.	

Army Form C. 2118.

Instructions regarding War Diaries and Intelligence Summaries are contained in F. S. Regs., Part II. and the Staff Manual respectively. Title pages will be prepared in manuscript.

A.D.V.S.
47th (LONDON)
DIVISION.
No............ Date............

WAR DIARY
or
~~INTELLIGENCE SUMMARY~~
(Erase heading not required.)

Place	Date	Hour	Summary of Events and Information	Remarks and references to Appendices
	Tuesday 27. 3.17		Office routine: Mobile Section & umbrella horses of No.1 21.3. Companies seen. Arrangements made with 7.D. for supply of 400 lbs on 28 inst.	
	Wednesday 28. 3.17		Inspected animals of 5.68 M.T. Co R.E. 520 Field Coy R.E. C.T.D. 235. Left over R. yd. All horses in good condition and appreciation of range outbreak progressing well.	
	Thursday 29. 3.17		Routine office work. Inspected horses of 4th London Labour Coy: an exceptionally good condition. Mobile Section.	
	Friday 30. 3.17		Office Routine: Mobile Section & Divl. Sigd. Hq. and Signal Coy — In afternoon had conference of Vety. Officers at office, discussing all topics of recent interest.	
	Saturday 31. 3.17		General office work: Weekly sett. returns sent to D.W.N. Corps & Army. 16 animals, 5 men & 6 destroyed — 67 remaining, including 2 ranges. Visited Mobile Section, & horses of 4th 5th Lon. Field Armes. Batts. in excellent condition. M.G. Lorwer Division	

T2134. Wt. W708-776. 500000. 4/15. Sr J.C. & 8.

Army Form C. 2118.

WAR DIARY
or
INTELLIGENCE SUMMARY.
(Erase heading not required.)

Vol 17

A.D.V.S.
47th (LONDON)
DIVISION.

Place	Date	Hour	Summary of Events and Information	Remarks and references to Appendices
G.H.Q.	1.4 Oct 28		Dealt with correspondence & routine work at office.	
Sunday	1.4.17		Rode over to Second Army Rest Area. Inspected transport animals of 142nd Sanitary Sec. in very good condition.	
Monday	2.4.17		Office routine. Visited Mobile Section, saw all cases & selected some to evacuation. Visited horses of 236th Coy R.F.A.	
Tuesday	3.4.17		Usual office routine. Superintended entrainment of sick horses at DICKEBUSCH during Indian Mobile Section. Unable to carry out inspections owing to snow and blizzards.	
Wednesday	4.4.17		Office work. Inspected horses of 2/7th Londons Divl. Train & Mobile Section. Capt R. BRYDEN M.C. proceeds on ten days special leave.	
Thursday	5.4.17		Routine office work as usual. Inspected all horses of 236 (late R.F.A.) Total 143 Carstiansen Divl. vet.	

Army Form C. 2118.

WAR DIARY
or
INTELLIGENCE SUMMARY
(Erase heading not required.)

Instructions regarding War Diaries and Intelligence Summaries are contained in F. S. Regs., Part II. and the Staff Manual respectively. Title pages will be prepared in manuscript.

A.D.V.S.,
47th (LONDON)
D...ON.
No............
Date............

Place	Date	Hour	Summary of Events and Information	Remarks and references to Appendices
Friday	6.4.17		Office routine. Inspected animals of 140th Fd. Coy. R.E. Standings in army Road condition. Reported same to Divn: Lorries of 6th Bn: condition good; 4th Bn; 5th Bn: condition good. 140 A Tun Coy: fair. In afternoon Con: Conference of ADVs at office. Discussed all matters connected to higher efficiency in animals under their charge.	
Saturday	7.4.17		Office work: Went through sick returns rendered to Divn. Corps & Army; evacuations: 30. Deaths: 3. Destructions: 3. remounts qu. including 20 mange. Visited Mobile Section & Lines of No.2. Coy. Lorry & No.1 Coy action satisfactory.	
Sunday	8.4.17		Usual office routine: Mobile Section. Letter about D.D.T.S. Second Army. HAZEBROUCK to interview him upon various questions.	
Monday	9.4.17		Inspected horses of A B C & D Batteries R.H.A. general condition good. Visited Mobile Section.	

T2134. Wt. W708-776. 500000. 4/15. Sir J. C. & S.

Army Form C. 2118.

WAR DIARY
or
INTELLIGENCE SUMMARY. of
(Erase heading not required.)

Instructions regarding War Diaries and Intelligence Summaries are contained in F. S. Regs., Part II. and the Staff Manual respectively. Title pages will be prepared in manuscript.

A.D.V.S.
47th (LONDON) DIVISION.
No.............
Date............

Place	Date	Hour	Summary of Events and Information	Remarks and references to Appendices
	Tuesday 10.	4.17	Routine office work: Arrangements made for Dipping of 400 horses or 14th inst. at VIII Corps Dip. Visited Mobile Section of S.A.O. gave allotment for two Pres. Linseed cake forwarded to 11th inst. Names of one N.C.O. + 3 men forwarded: recommended for Mule work Corps Mobile Veterinary Detachment.	
	Wednesday 11.	4.17	Usual office routine. Visited M.V.S. + horses of 34th Companies Lair.	
	Thursday 12.	4.17	Visited M.V.S: inspected horses of 4th Canadian Labour Bn. 20th Lab. Lab. Coy: 180 Battery R.F.A. + confirmed unfit. Offr. 1st 10th Bac R. F.A. 236 Roe R.F.A. move to Rest Area equiv top horse to STEENVOORDE. COOR. EDWARDS A.V.C. E.	
	Friday 13.	4.17	Dealt with office work: visited M.V.S. inspected animals of 517 4/W. Coy R.E. + 368 A.T. Co. R.E. Called upon Capt. DAWSON A.V.C. In afternoon his Lordance Vet. Offrs at stride, discussed matters pertaining to horse changes.	

WAR DIARY
or
INTELLIGENCE SUMMARY

Army Form C. 2118.

Place	Date	Hour	Summary of Events and Information	Remarks and references to Appendices
Saturday	14.4.17		Usual office routine, sick returns rendered to Div. Cops & Army: 31 mules evacuated: 2 Died: 88. Remaining including 24 mange: Visited Mobile Section + VIIIth Corps Dep to superintend Dipping of 410 animals of Division. Inspected animals of N.T. 1, 37th Composite rams:	
Sunday	15.4.17		Office work + correspondence. Visited N.T.S.	
Monday	16.4.17		Routine office work. Visited horses of 5th Div. & horses & 57th with No. R.2.	
Tuesday	17.4.17		Office work. Called on "B" Branch for information re several matters. Inspected all horses of 38 Bn. R.F.A. at WINNIZEELE and OUDEZEELE. 1.13 & 17. Olept. 27. wounds of all farmable trench wssons. Arranged for Dipping of 120 horses at VIII Corps Dep on 18th inst.	
Wednesday	18.4.17		Usual office work. Visited N.T.S. & horses of Divl. Hq. & Signal Coy:	

WAR DIARY
INTELLIGENCE SUMMARY.
(Erase heading not required.)

Army Form C. 2118.

Place	Date	Hour	Summary of Events and Information	Remarks and references to Appendices
	Thurs May 19.4.17		Dealt with office work: Asst Veter. Officer 1/c 104 Army L. Coly. Sub. not attached to Division, + inspected all animals of Brigade: deleterious evidence of Mange from Desire. Condition of all very poor + unsatisfactory. Report to this effect rendered to D.D.V.S.	
	Friday 20.4.17		Office work + correspondence. Visited Mobile Section. Inspected lines of 1/2 Sections D.M.C. + F.M.C. at 9.10 A.M. Re submission to the Superintend't of Veli. Officers 20th Office: discussed in addition to other questions: Holdings of Any. 7.25; Dipping of 150 Lnds from 104 F.H.B. on 21st inst; issue of 104 funnshers only; care of Dogs of Royal Engs; message leaving : + issued for Veli Officrs. Evening conferred with Sub. Command.	
	Saturday 21.4.17		Office routine: sick returns rendered to Div. Cabs + Army; 2 only evacuated: 6 Dead, 4 Destroyed; 194 remaining including 19 mange. Visita M.T. Fieldembn lines under treatment: loves of D.L.B. + Supply Coly. inspected L.S.B. and V.C. Exam on issue of Forage reported for.	

WAR DIARY
INTELLIGENCE SUMMARY

Army Form C. 2118.

Place	Date	Hour	Summary of Events and Information	Remarks and references to Appendices
	Sunday 22.4.17		Attended to office routine. Inspected Mob. Section and T.S.O. and 3 men established to BOESCHEPE to join Xth Corps Mobile Vety. Detachment.	
	Monday 23.4.17		Vety. Officers instructed to pay Lectures on Horsemastership and Stable Management weekly. Usual office work: Mob. Vety. Opps instructed to secure all fats from Carcases & send to M.V.S. with hides. Visited M.V.S. saw all cases & advised treatment & disposal.	
	Tuesday 26.4.17		Ordinary office routine morning & evening. Visited horses of N.O. 4 Section D.A.C. M.V.S. licence to 5th & 6th Lon. Brokers. Sent a few cases.	
	Wednesday 25.4.17		Visited M.V.S., losses of Dul. 44 T Signals & 236 Bde. R.F.A.	
	Thursday 26.4.17		Inspected animals of 1st & 2nd Sections D.A.C. and 104 Army F.A. Col. General office routine:	

Army Form C. 2118.

WAR DIARY
or
INTELLIGENCE SUMMARY of
(Erase heading not required.)

Instructions regarding War Diaries and Intelligence Summaries are contained in F. S. Regs., Part II. and the Staff Manual respectively. Title pages will be prepared in manuscript.

Place	Date	Hour	Summary of Events and Information	Remarks and references to Appendices
	Friday 27.4.17		Office work. In morning: visited M.V.S. + Horses of 8th Dn. Lanarcan Rly Troops. attached to Divn. In afternoon, held Conference of R.V. Officers: discussed all matters of Divisional interest. Capt. L.R.Y. Dawson A.V.C. attached to 47 D.A.C. evacuated to No 10 C.C.S. as result of accident with horse.	
	Saturday 27.4.17.		Weekly vet statistics returns: 45 evacuated: one aus: 108 remaining including 16 Range invalids in Wastage and to 104 of R. to be. Normal Vet. Duel. administration. Visited Mobile Section, + VIII Corps Horse Dep. to superintend Dipping of 522 animals of Division.	
	Sunday 29.4.17		Usual office routine. Called upon D.D.V.S., + inspected Horses of 236 Coie R.F.A. in Rest Area. Capt T. CRAIG. A.V.C. attached to 4th Ambulance leaving on dinner. Shoulder injury: from kick by horse: Evacuated from has via Sep Base for course of treating at ABBEVILLE.	

Army Form C. 2118.

WAR DIARY
or
INTELLIGENCE SUMMARY of
(Erase heading not required.)

A.D.V.S.
47th (LONDON)
DIVISION.

No.
Date

Place	Date	Hour	Summary of Events and Information	Remarks and references to Appendices
	May 30.4.17.		Routine office work: 2 copies of Administrative Instructions issued for General Remount: Copy to Mobile Section. Inspected transport animals of 142nd Inf Bde at Halifax Camp. Muslim Capt CRAIG RAMC in Field Ambce.	

T. Hibbard
Major.
A.D.V.S. 47th London Division

Army Form C. 2118.

WAR DIARY
or
INTELLIGENCE SUMMARY
(Erase heading not required.)

Instructions regarding War Diaries and Intelligence Summaries are contained in F. S. Regs., Part II. and the Staff Manual respectively. Title pages will be prepared in manuscript.

A.D.V.S.
47th (LONDON)
DIVISION

Vol /8

Place	Date	Hour	Summary of Events and Information	Remarks and references to Appendices
G.H.Q.	1.5.17	Tuesday	Dealt with general office routine: Made inspection of animals of 6th York & Lancs Regt not Inf. Bde: Visited Mobile Section, & Capt. Evans, MVC in Field Ambce:	
	Wednesday 2.5.17		Annual office routine: Visited "B" Siege Medical General Hospital: Visited Section, & two Companies Divl Train, inspecting all horses. Capt. T. CRAIG MVC attended. Received remounts.	
	Thursday 3.5.17		Office routine work: Visited M.V.S. Inspection horses of B/235 Battery: Met Capt. LEONARDS MVC: inspected with him transport horses of 14370 Inf. Bde:	
	Friday 4.5.17		Usual office work: Visited M.V.S. & inspection horses of D.A.C. In afternoon held Conference of Vety. Officers: matters discussed all gone over of technical nature & Capt. J. Quick MVC returns from leave & reports to 47th D.A.C.	

T2134. Wt. W708—776. 500000. 4/15. Sir J. C. & S.

WAR DIARY
or
INTELLIGENCE SUMMARY

Army Form C. 2118.

Place	Date	Hour	Summary of Events and Information	Remarks and references to Appendices
	Saturday 5	5-17	Usual office routine. Duty by rest relieves readiness to Dvr. Coles Army. 24 evacuated, no sick. Lieut McIlroy Maj. MG remained overnight. Troops received letter of No.1 Section D.M.C. & 10th Canadian Cav. 2/6 Lieut R.J.R. returned to Dul. Lines from rest camp.	
	Sunday 6	5-17	Dealt with correspondence & office work. Gave Demonstration to this Officers in adjustment of breeching, for horses to enable him to demonstrate to remainder of Wagon line Officers.	
	Monday 7	5-17	Office routine, Mobile Section, several casualties being received in consequence of with shelling of our front lines.	
	Tuesday 8	5-17	Inspected animals of 1 & 2/2nd Lowland R.H. & 3rd South Midl. Advanced Cable Sqn. H.M.C. at 17th D.M.C. & inspected horses & that unit. Office routine & Mobile Section.	
	Wedn'day May 9	5-17	Office routine & visited Mobile Section. Inspected horses of No. 2 Sec. & all at HALIFAX Camp & 4th Canadian Labour batn.	

Army Form C. 2118.

WAR DIARY
or
INTELLIGENCE SUMMARY.
(Erase heading not required.)

Place	Date	Hour	Summary of Events and Information	Remarks and references to Appendices
	Thursday May 10	5.17.	Dealt with general routine work at office. Inspected animals of 5th Fur. Ambce. 4th Lon R.W. Fus. + 517 Field Coy R.E.	
	Friday 11.	6.17.	Inspected horses of 236th L.C.B. R.F.A. & Reserve Mobile Section. In afternoon held Conference of Veterinary Officers: all questions of Veterinary interest. Office work.	
	Saturday 12.	5.17.	Office routine. Weekly vet. returns rendered to Div. Corps. & Army: 27 cases wounded 4 Died. 2 Destroyed :10 3 remaining, including 13 mangy. Inspected transport horses of 18th-19th Battns. Met Capt. Pugh. M.T.C. at D.H.Q Inspected animals of that unit with him.	
	Sunday 13.	5.17.	Usual office routine & Mobile Section. Capt. J. McBride M.T.C. arrived & posted to 236 Bce R.F.A.	

Army Form C. 2118.

A.D.V.S.,
47th (LO DOR)
DIVISION.

No.................
Date................

WAR DIARY
or
INTELLIGENCE SUMMARY.
(Erase heading not required.)

Instructions regarding War Diaries and Intelligence
Summaries are contained in F. S. Regs., Part II.
and the Staff Manual respectively. Title pages
will be prepared in manuscript.

Place	Date	Hour	Summary of Events and Information	Remarks and references to Appendices
	Monday 14	5.P.	Visited horses of H.Q. R. Artig. Rear to 235 Bn. R.F.A. & inspected animals. Interviewed Capt. M. Lowes A.V.C. Visited M.V.S. & inspected several cells with view to occupation by Corps Mobile Vety Detachment.	
	Tues May 15	5.P.	Office routine. Inspected horses of 4th 5th & 6th Bns of Brigades & interior. Down on condition of ploughing. Again visited site for Corps M.V. Det. & informed D.D.V.S. of location.	
	Wed. May 16	5.P.	Usual office work. Met Capt Lugg A.V.C. of D.A.C. & inspected animals of that unit. Visited M.V.S.	
	Thursday 17	5-P	Visited M.V.S. & horses of 2nd Hy. Siege Coy. Visited R.E. Dump to inspect G.S. Wagon fitted with Ramps & Pulley for loading carcases. Inspected animals of 517, 518 & 520 field Cos R.E. Met D.D.V.S. at M.V.S. & unearthed him to visit selection for Corps Mobile Section.	

T2134. Wt. W708—776. 500000. 4/15. Sir J. C. & 8.

WAR DIARY
INTELLIGENCE SUMMARY

Army Form C. 2118.

(Erase heading not required.)

Place	Date	Hour	Summary of Events and Information	Remarks and references to Appendices
	Friday 18.5.17		Dealt with office work. Visited M.T.S. + Dublin St. In afternoon held Conference of Vet: Officers at office.	
	Saturday 19.5.17		Usual office routine. Monthly vet: return. Horses: Inoculation 2; Dead 0; Destroyed 4; Remaining 85 including one mange. Attended Divisional Commanders Conference: possibility of reduction in Establishment of Riding horses discussion.	
	Sunday 20.5.17		Office work. + Visited M.T.S.	
	Monday 21.5.17		Inspected horses of 22nd + 23rd Battalions + Visited M.T.S.	
	Tuesday 22.5.17		Office routine as usual. Proceeded on seven days leave of absence Duties taken over by S.C. 3rd London M.T.S. D.D.V.S. notified of departure.	

Army Form C. 2118.

WAR DIARY
or
INTELLIGENCE SUMMARY.
(Erase heading not required.)

Instructions regarding War Diaries and Intelligence Summaries are contained in F. S. Regs., Part II. and the Staff Manual respectively. Title pages will be prepared in manuscript.

A.D.V.S.
47th (LONDON)
DIVISION.
No. ....
Date ....

Place	Date	Hour	Summary of Events and Information	Remarks and references to Appendices
	Wednesday 23.	5-17	Dealt with usual office routine & attended to gun duties at Mobile Section. Chief of 47th Divn Admin attached. Instructions received in connection with recent Army Offensive.	
	Thursday 24.	5-17	Office routine & gun duties at Mobile Section. Inspected horses of 24th Bn. London Regt. at STEENVOORDE.	
	Friday 25	5-17	Office routine & duties at Mobile Section. Interviewed Lieut 9hrs at office in afternoon.	
	Saturday 26.	5-17	Office routine. Westerly act returns re mange to Corps Chief. Dispatched 2. remaining SS including two mange F.M.Ps. 96th Army Field Mulig Vet. arrived in area F.M.Ps only; reports came to his office.	
	Sunday 27.	5-17	Mobile Section moves to forward position at 8.30 & 8.10. D.O.T.S. & all Vety Officers notifying. Officers went round all pulling out points daily, Cas in area for attendance, 14 h: 64 h: 76 h & 119 h.	

T2134. Wt. W708—776. 500000. 4/15. Sir J. C. & S.

Army Form C. 2118.

WAR DIARY
or
INTELLIGENCE SUMMARY.
(Erase heading not required.)

Instructions regarding War Diaries and Intelligence Summaries are contained in F. S. Regs., Part II. and the Staff Manual respectively. Title pages will be prepared in manuscript.

A.D.V.S.
47th (LON)
D   N

Place	Date	Hour	Summary of Events and Information	Remarks and references to Appendices
	28.5.17 Monday		Inspected all animals of 140th (separating holds on a second Army running horse.	
	29.5.17 Tuesday		Dealt with Office routine work & own duties at Mobile Section. Other routine & own duties at Mobile Section.	
	30.5.17 Wednesday		Ditto	
	31.5.17 Thursday		Do.	

Sgd. ....
Captain
A.V.D.V.S. 47th London Division.

Army Form C. 2118.

A.D.V.S.,
47th (LONDON)
DIVISION.

No.................
Date................

Vol 19

WAR DIARY
or
INTELLIGENCE SUMMARY of
(Erase heading not required.)

Instructions regarding War Diaries and Intelligence Summaries are contained in F. S. Regs., Part II. and the Staff Manual respectively. Title pages will be prepared in manuscript.

Place	Date	Hour	Summary of Events and Information	Remarks and references to Appendices
C.14.c.1.4. Sheet 28.	Friday June 1st 17		General office routine & own duties at Mobile Section.	
	Saturday June 2nd 17		Do. Wastage with relieves rendered to Divisions Corps and Army. Evacuated 39. Died 65 including 60 from Gunshot Wounds. Delivered to Remounts 162. Great Wastage due to Battle Casualties & attachment of Field Artillery Bdes. (Army units wounds in very poor condition.	
	Sunday June 3rd 17	3.0.p	Dealt with routine office work & own duties at Mobile Section. A.D.V.S. returns to duty. Temporarily incapacitated owing to abrasions knee. Instructions received to move forward to E^A inst.	
	Monday June 4.17		Office moved to Mobile Section	
	Tuesday June 5.17		This office moves to WINNIPEG CAMP with Div. Hq. & Signal Coy. Inspected horses of Div. Hq: H.19.A.6.3. Sheet 28. Normal office routine.	

T2134. Wt. W708—778. 500000. 4/15. Sir J. C. & S.

Army Form C. 2118.

WAR DIARY
or
INTELLIGENCE SUMMARY
(Erase heading not required.)

A.D.V.S.
47th (LONDON)
DIVISION.
No.............
Date............

Instructions regarding War Diaries and Intelligence Summaries are contained in F.S. Regs., Part II. and the Staff Manual respectively. Title pages will be prepared in manuscript.

Place	Date	Hour	Summary of Events and Information	Remarks and references to Appendices
Westrems	May 6th 17		Office routine: Inspected animals of 64th Army Bde. R.F.A. Am. Col. & A,B,C & D Batteries; condition generally good. Visited horses of Divl. Hq. & Signal Co. R.E. Reviewed Aid Post opened at PIONEER CAMP H.26.a. about 28.	
Westrems	June 7th 17		Inspected horses of D/186 Bde. Army F.A. 30 in Debilitated condition. Inspected animals of H. & D/235 Bde. R.F.A.: H. fair; D. fair condition. D. very good; thence to 517, 518, & 520 Field Companies R.E.: great improvement in condition.	
Westrems	June 8th 17		General office routine: Instructed animals of D/186 Army Bde. R.F.A. many in poor condition: Heels being clipped; & feeding from ground in continuation of others. In afternoon the experience of Vety. Officers at offices discussed in matters of weekly animal, including treatment & evacuation of casualties during active operations.	
Westrems	June 9th 17		Office routine: Weekly exit returns rendered to Dun. Corps & Army rendered to: Div. J. Destroyed 28, Evacuated 22, including 27 valuing 22 bushes Wounds Cases strength 188 of total of 9407.	

Army Form C. 2118.

WAR DIARY
or
INTELLIGENCE SUMMARY

(Erase heading not required.)

A.D.V.S.
47th (2nd LOND)
DIVISION
No..........
Date..........

Instructions regarding War Diaries and Intelligence Summaries are contained in F.S. Regs., Part II. and the Staff Manual respectively. Title pages will be prepared in manuscript.

Place	Date	Hour	Summary of Events and Information	Remarks and references to Appendices
	Wednesday June 9th 1917		ev.tc. Inspected horses of B/104 Battery: animals much improved in condition. Also Nos 1 & 2 Sections 47" D.A.C. No cases yet reached by Advanced M.V.Sec.	
	Sunday June 10th 17		Visited horses of 6th Bn. L. Yorks: M.V.S. & office routine.	
	Monday June 11th 17		Inspected animals of C + D Batteries & B.A.C. 96th Army Field Arty Bde. condition generally improving, meeting Battery + attended parade in wire lines: Report made to ADVS. & attached at VIIIth Corps Horse Show 11.30 a.m for 2nd Div mobile bath. Visited M.V.S.	
	Tuesday June 12th 17		Usual Office routine. Inspected horses of 4 batteries of 104 Army Bde. R.F.A. fairly improvement in all. Visited M.V.S. D.D.V.S. VIII Corps telephoned reference fostering men sick for M.V.S recorded by 47th Divn.	
	Wednesday June 13th 17		M.V.S. His office moves under Deal. Sp. to WESTHOUTRE. N.9.c. about 25. M.V.S. moves to G.32.d.9.1 about 25. Dealt with Office work.	

WAR DIARY or INTELLIGENCE SUMMARY.

Army Form C. 2118.

A.D.V.S.,
47th (LONDON)
DIVISION.

Instructions regarding War Diaries and Intelligence Summaries are contained in F. S. Regs., Part II. and the Staff Manual respectively. Title pages will be prepared in manuscript.

(Erase heading not required.)

Place	Date	Hour	Summary of Events and Information	Remarks and references to Appendices
	Thursday June 14th 17		Routine office work. M.J.L.	
	Friday June 15th 17		Usual office work. Administration of 3 Army Vet: Depôt handed over to A.D.V.S. 4th Div. in consequence of sending unit to Duisans. A.D.V.S. 4th Div. in consequence of 4th Div. Op.M. Office in abeyance. All other units for the time being of 4th Div. under the attendance & discussion of questions connected with 3rd Army Vet: Depôt. Went up into rest area.	
	Saturday June 16th 17		Went out visiting various sections i.e. Divn: Coy's & Army 27 mobile Veterinaries; 7 Sany: 30 Remounts: including the troops today. This office went with Divl: Hqs to BLARINGHEM. E.V.H. also HAZEBROUCK. Called on D.D.V.S. Second Army conferred with him on arrangement of units whilst Divisions in this Area.	
	Sunday June 17th 17		Office Routine. Made arrangements for Inspection tomorrow subject to air raids & weather – arrangements of the 5 & 8th Battalions.	
	Monday June 18th 17		Inspection today of 2 Coy Train 4th & 5th Lon: Field Ambces, 6th & 15th Battns. 140th Bde & Machine Gun Coy. Usual office work routine.	

Army Form C. 2118.

A.D.V.S.
47th (LONDON)
DIVISION.
No.............
Date...........

WAR DIARY
or
INTELLIGENCE SUMMARY of
(Erase heading not required.)

Instructions regarding War Diaries and Intelligence
Summaries are contained in F.S. Regs., Part II.
and the Staff Manual respectively. Title pages
will be prepared in manuscript.

Place	Date	Hour	Summary of Events and Information	Remarks and references to Appendices
Sulainey	June 19th 17		Inspected animals of Divl. Hy. & Signal Co. A.L. Coll. not noted in charges of D.A.M.S. & went forestin. Found to be in good order. Dwit. work carried out at offices.	
Willesden	June 20th 17		Attended conference of A.D.V.S. & D.V.S. at 10.33 February Substd. of order to discuss distribution of A.D.V.S. for Limb, and alternation of Duties. Heregoods D.A.D.V.S. to supervise of Divl. Administrator Vety. Officer.	
Houndsley	June 21st 17		General office work. Conference to A.D.V.S. & Webs Inspector of Vety. Duches Food & Letters upon D.D.V.S. about Army & comparison upon various matters & found. Visited horses of 19th & 20th Com. Regts. in station.	
Lisses	June 22nd		Inspected animals of 17th & 18th Battns. for Regtl. Duel. Hy. & Signal Co. office work. Visited sick returns received by Div. Vety. Army Carriage. 6. Destroyed 2. Destroyed 2: Remaining 107: including 6 sligtt wound: sick killed T NM branch medically Unsuitable Run. to Div. sich.	

T2134. Wt. W708-776. 500000. 4/15. Sir J. C. & S.

Army Form C. 2118.

A.D.V.S.,
47th (2.. DON)
DIVISION.

No. ....
Date ....

WAR DIARY
OR
INTELLIGENCE SUMMARY.
(Erase heading not required.)

Instructions regarding War Diaries and Intelligence Summaries are contained in F. S. Regs., Part II. and the Staff Manual respectively. Title pages will be prepared in manuscript.

Place	Date	Hour	Summary of Events and Information	Remarks and references to Appendices
Labassée	June 23rd 17		Visited horses of 20th Ln. Lon. Regt. Dur. Hy. & signal Lm. 3 Cases evacuated sick to 23 Mobile Hosp. DINNER.	
Lindsay	June 24th 17		Inspected horses of French division & 5th Lon. Field Ambce. Their arrangement & case control.	
Montmaux	June 25th 17		Inspected horses. Held Conference. Inspected animals of 2 Coy. new S.A. N.O. Batt. 7th & 8th battalions & 6th Lon. Visited Divisional commander at his request and division authorized to be disabled for entrenchment in condition of animals in low condition: also numbers of R.A.M.D. wants some elevated & unsatisfactory opening. Gave commander to set 7 Div. Mineral wala & to institute inspect & ask casts. No case evacuated to 23 Mob. Hospital OT. MESS.	
Lambresy	June 26th 17		Inspected 6.15th battn & A. Pur Coy. N.O. + Lor. L.G. Dept. of arrangement received from Division for conditions to be D.A. Orson mil in order to stimulate regimental interest & any suggestions rather too.	

WAR DIARY
INTELLIGENCE SUMMARY
(Erase heading not required.)

Army Form C. 2118.

Place	Date	Hour	Summary of Events and Information	Remarks and references to Appendices
Moascar Camp	June 27th 17		Office routine work. Inspection carried of 5th Bn. L. London 19th 120th Rattan London Regt. & Sig. Coy.	
Lumsden Camp	June 28th 17		10th Conference of Voly. Officers at 2nd London M.T. India Convey of Div. Hq. & Signal Coy. Issued extra work.	
Friday	June 29th 17		Forenoon Div. Commanding & A.A. & Q.M.G. will repair to two stages. Inspected transport animals of 10th & 11th Bn. Regt. Weather wet, returned earlier to Div. Coast & Army; afternoon Wisbech 49th Evacuates to Div. No. 6: Dispersed & Reviewing 114 including 3 Slight Head.	
Saturday	June 30th 17		On res somewhat Humid to 23 Polis. Adj. of OYER. Main lecture would be D.A.D.V.S. aust 28: Instructions issued for move of Div. year to 1st July. Inspection Losses of Div. Hq. & Signal Coy. R.E.	

T. Richard Major

D.A.D. H.Q. 47th Div. 1917.

WAR DIARY
or
INTELLIGENCE SUMMARY of D.A.D.V.O. 47th Divn.

Army Form C. 2118.

No 20

Place	Date	Hour	Summary of Events and Information	Remarks and references to Appendices

Sunday July 1st/17 — This office moved with Divl. Hq. from BARRINGTON to WESTOUTRE. M. is a. 5. 9. Cost St. Mr. Vet. Officer. A.D.V.S. X Corps notified.

Monday July 2nd/17 — Dealt with usual office routine. Issued Mobile Section Contribution accounts to 228th and 229th R.F.A. with D.R.'s contribution advisory.

Tuesday July 3rd/17 — Inspection Lines of 142nd Inf. Bde. at form. M. Arrd-a, 3, & Section D.L.C. Issued Mobile Section.
Served this week amendments made for this allowance to be put in tanks of Capt. L. Dunn R.V.C. numbers attached units. Tanks of Capt. L. Dunn R.V.C. submitted for issuance to that remounts on F.P. attached to a Divn? from S. Lion.

Wednesday July 4/17 — Routine office work. Issued of this Section, inspection lines all ten Lossil Horsehides from various unit by request of 2nd Lieutenant. Last inspection of land horses in Lossil Section continuance. Looking questions of opening letter on morning information consider by outgoing Section. Visiting three to 5 Section D.L.C.

Army Form C. 2118.

WAR DIARY
or
INTELLIGENCE SUMMARY of: D.A.D.T.S.
(Erase heading not required.)

Instructions regarding War Diaries and Intelligence Summaries are contained in F.S. Regs., Part II. and the Staff Manual respectively. Title pages will be prepared in manuscript.

Place	Date	Hour	Summary of Events and Information	Remarks and references to Appendices
	Thursday July 5/17		Inspected animals of 6th & 7th (Service) Bn. London Regt. 23rd Bn. and Tilbury Mobile Section. Naval office verbal. 7 O.s of attached Army Corps R.F.A. indented to attend conference on horses.	
	Friday July 6/17		Inspected horses of 52nd Army Bde R.F.A. & supplied or sent to A.D.V.S. Corps. Inspected animals past remedy of 2nd & 3rd Bde. R.F.A. re classification to L.D.	
			In afternoon attended conference of Vety. Officers attached to Divisional Ammunition all matters of veterinary interest, treatment of units under veterinary care of Vety. Officers.	
	Saturday July 7/17		Wet day not going round to Dumps, Depts. Admin. 113. Curve 60. Evacuated to Dump & Deckenge ord. Remaining 53 including 5 slight, mange. Inspected horses of L. and D/277 Army base R.F.A. and Sub Mobile Vety. Sec.	
	Sunday July 8/17		Office routine work. Visited Mobile Section & 4th Line horses of officers in arrears Pte. TILBURY A.V.C. to accordance to instructions on demob.	

WAR DIARY
or
INTELLIGENCE SUMMARY of 2A. D.T.S. 47th Divn

Army Form C. 2118.

Place	Date	Hour	Summary of Events and Information	Remarks and references to Appendices
	Monday July 9th 17		Inspected all lines of Dubl. Town & Companies & visited Mobile Section.	
	Tuesday July 10th 17		Routine office work. Inspected lines at No. 1 Hn Coy and 2 sections of 189th Coy R.E. Visited North Section and 2 coys of Dubl. Sp. Inspn Dubl. Coms and 2 coys D.R. troops.	
	Wednesday July 11th 17		Visited lines of Dubl. Sp. Inspn. to North Section & inspected q.z. Her horses had sent from all units. Mr. D.D.V.S. met our unit veterinary Corp Border A.V.C. with view to command of a North Section.	
	Thursday July 12th 17		Naval office routine: Visited lines of Dubl. Sp. & Sig. of Coy. Inspected animals of 4th, 5th & 6th powers & horses & horses & visited M.V.S.	
	Friday July 13th Jun 17		Held Conference at 10p at office in morning. Troop Lines of Dubl. Sp. & Sig. Cord Regiments Dubl. Sp. & Signal Co.	

Army Form C. 2118.

D.A.D.V.S.,
47TH
(LONDON) DIVISION.

No. ....
Date ....

WAR DIARY
or
INTELLIGENCE SUMMARY.
(Erase heading not required.)

Instructions regarding War Diaries and Intelligence Summaries are contained in F. S. Regs., Part II. and the Staff Manual respectively. Title pages will be prepared in manuscript.

Place	Date	Hour	Summary of Events and Information	Remarks and references to Appendices
	Saturday July 14th 17		Routine office work. Weekly vet. reports rendered to Divn & Corps Director. No: 67. Tournequets and No: Divn 7, Destroyed 4, Remaining 117 including our range. No:68 horses of 40" Mecho No: 3 by ground mobile section. No:69. 22nd Bn & miles no judge as condition of horses. No: Cods. nets. Competitions.	
	Sunday July 15th 17		Interviewed D.A.D.V.S. 4th Aust. Divn regarding annunciation of his Mobile Section at present attached this Divn. Visited M.V.S. Walt, noth office routine.	
	Monday July 16th 17		Inspected animals of 236" Coy R.F.A. & Mobile Section. Visited Horse of Divl. Sig & Signal Coy. D.H.Q., 10th & 11th Aust. Field Amb. reports 35 animals killed & 20 Wounded by low flying from Hostile Aeroplane night of 15th/16" July.	
	Tuesday July 17th 17		Inspected animals of 47th Coy R.F.A. attached found Water and hay articulation rather poor. Reports to A.D.V.S. 1st Corps. Visited Horse of 110th Army Bde R.F.A. and M.V.S.	

Army Form C. 2118.

DADVS
47TH
(LONDON) DIVISION
No........
Date........

WAR DIARY
or
INTELLIGENCE SUMMARY.
(Erase heading not required.)

Instructions regarding War Diaries and Intelligence Summaries are contained in F.S. Regs., Part II. and the Staff Manual respectively. Title pages will be prepared in manuscript.

Place	Date	Hour	Summary of Events and Information	Remarks and references to Appendices
Morcourt	July 15th		Visited North Section. Conference with Div. Commander on putting more horse power into drawing 100BR 6" How & Brigade & Siege ammn. for Div. Completion.	
	Thursday July 19th		Met D.D.S.T. 2nd Army and A.D.N. X Corps at N.T.S. completion also Visited and inspected for obtaining 100BR M.T. of 441 & 440 Coy. Bde. to judge on late batn. completion in Howards etc.	
	Friday July 20th		Held Conference at 10 am. at office re morning, clearing report, near dispersals, all questions & matters of interest concerning heavy carnage. O.C. M.T. detachment to notify matters first to complete of 239; mentioned Div. Coy. having issued ammn. recently from Eng. fund. 100BR ammn. of 4" How & 239; A mm coy.	
	Saturday July 21st		Naval officer visiting Worthy and returns rendered to Dir. Corps. Munitions 65": Lewis 45. Ranges 25 ft 18": Des ki Destroyed 3. Remaining 109 including 12 Slight repair to RE. Trench Mr. P. Ammo of 517 sent to RE.	

Army Form C. 2118.

D.A.D.V.S.
47TH
(LONDON) DIVISION.

WAR DIARY
or
INTELLIGENCE SUMMARY.
(Erase heading not required.)

Instructions regarding War Diaries and Intelligence Summaries are contained in F. S. Regs., Part II. and the Staff Manual respectively. Title pages will be prepared in manuscript.

Place	Date	Hour	Summary of Events and Information	Remarks and references to Appendices
	Sunday July 22nd		Usual office routine. Troops Mobile Section.	
	Monday July 23rd		Inspection made of animals of 104 Bde. R.F.A. to ascertain if any inferior of Observation reported on respect to A.D.V.S. 9th Corps. Visited M.V.S. this unit moving to I.32.A.9.0 abt 28th. Telephoned D.A.D.V.S. 47th Divn. arrangements for taking over of all units attended this Duty for Veterinary administration. Visited M.V.S. in new location. Arranged 5th Lon. Field Ambulance + horses conditions of animals for Dub. Competition.	
	Tuesday July 24th		Visited M.V.S. + A.D.V.S. 1st Corps to discuss various matters. Minor inspection by Mervaro? Cavalry + sick? in matter of D.A.B. Animals 1st Lon. Fd. Ambce. unit went to selection for Brigade Sports.	
	Wednesday July 25th		Inspected horses of Dul. H.Q. Signal Coy. Also all horses of M.O.R.C. Section. Telegraphed Dul. Commanders on proposals of left Volunteers ?? animals sent to horses hospital No office ??? with Dul. H.Q. to BERTHEN	

Army Form C. 2118.

D.A.D.V.S.
47TH
(LONDON) DIVISION.

WAR DIARY
or
INTELLIGENCE SUMMARY.
(Erase heading not required.)

Instructions regarding War Diaries and Intelligence Summaries are contained in F.S. Regs., Part II. and the Staff Manual respectively. Title pages will be prepared in manuscript.

Place	Date	Hour	Summary of Events and Information	Remarks and references to Appendices
Thursday	July 26/17		Visited animals of 8th Bn. Lon. Regt: Attended inspection of Army mules from Egyptian Mails at N.V.S. Also inspected cases in M.V.S. Attended conference of Vety Offrs at North Section.	
Friday	July 27/17		Visited animals of 19th Motor Co. Dvl. Sup. & Lestrad Coy: hence to N.V.S. Dealt with general office routine. Weekly sick return rendered to Dvn.T. LONDON: 90 cases admitted: 27 cured: 11 evacuated: 3 destroyed: 138 remaining including 33 mange.	
Saturday	July 28/17		Inspected horses of 5th Lon. F. Amb. & 47th D.A.C. 15 mules killed & 2 wounded & 2 horses wounded by Bomb dropped night of 28/29th in lines of 4 section D.A.C. Visited N.V.S.	
Sunday	July 29/17		Visited N.V.S. Inspected horses of 23rd Lon. Regt. Office Routine.	
Monday	July 30/17		Inspected animals of 142nd Inf. Coy. Sup & 121st Batn. London N.V.S. 4th Lon. F. Amb.	
Tuesday	July 31/17		Inspected horses of 235 Bde. R.F.A. Travelled Mobile Section. Usual office routine.	

T. Bufford Major. D.A.D.V.S. 47th Divn.

T2134. Wt. W708-776. 500000. 4/15. Str J.C. & 8.

Army Form C. 2118.

Instructions regarding War Diaries and Intelligence Summaries are contained in F.S. Regs., Part II. and the Staff Manual respectively. Title pages will be prepared in manuscript.

D.A.D.V.S.
47TH
(LOND.) DIVISION.

Vol 21

WAR DIARY
or
INTELLIGENCE SUMMARY.
(Erase heading not required.)

Place	Date	Hour	Summary of Events and Information	Remarks and references to Appendices
WARNETON BERTHEN about 2½	Wednesday Aug 1st 17		Inspection animals of 335 Coy. R.E.A. at Interior. Trailer Mobile Section. Called on D.A.D.V.S. 41st Division with him re establishment of Advanced Air Post at KRUISTRAATHOEK. & reported at that dept. Dual Mobile Section. Dealt with general office routing.	
	Thursday Aug 2nd 17.		Advanced G.S. opened 10 above. 24th Lond.m Regt. horses to N.O.H. Section D.M.S. Held Conference of Vety. Officers in afternoon at Mobile Section. Records not upto advance all items of weekly returns.	
	Friday Aug 3rd 18.		Inspection animals of 236th Lon Div R.F.A. + 6th Lon Field Ambce. Trailer Mobile Section. Usual office routine worthy adt. Horses evacuated to Dun. & Corps: 74 cases admitted to Ambce: 13 Evacuated. 15 killed by bombs: 2 Destroyed. 150 remaining including 29 mange.	

T2134. Wt. W708—776. 500000. 4/15. Sir J. C. & S.

Army Form C. 2118.

WAR DIARY
or
INTELLIGENCE SUMMARY.
(Erase heading not required.)

D.A.D.V.S.
47TH
LONDON DIVISION

Place	Date	Hour	Summary of Events and Information	Remarks and references to Appendices
	Saturday Aug 4th/17		Inspection animals of A Section D.A.L. 5th Lon. F. Ambce: Dub. Hq. 1 Canad. Co. R.E. also inspected surplus issue of Dub. Hp. to Inspection of fill Remount Section. Visited Mobile Vety Section.	
	Sunday Aug 5th/17		Inspection animals of 4th Bn. R.W. Fus. & 2 Coy. 15 to Companies Town. Visited Mobile Section. 4th L.D.J.S. Hors & temporarily on exercise worthless.	
	Monday Aug 6/17		Inspected horses of 517-516-1520 F.C.R. Co. F.A. R.E. and 141st M. Gun Coy. Visited Mobile Section. Usual office routine.	
	Tuesday Aug 7/17		Inspection animals of 236 Coy. R.F.A. and 6/15 R.F. A. Visited Mobile Section.	
	Wednesday Aug 8/17		Made inspection of all horse issues at Mobile Section. Held conference of T.Ns Hors: arranged attendance to all units: re different supplies, running of horse lines of Rept. Division: discussed all matters in general.	

T2134. Wt. W708—776. 500000. 4/15. Sir J. C. & S.

Army Form C. 2118.

WAR DIARY
or
INTELLIGENCE SUMMARY.

(Erase heading not required.)

Instructions regarding War Diaries and Intelligence Summaries are contained in F.S. Regs., Part II. and the Staff Manual respectively. Title pages will be prepared in manuscript.

Place	Date	Hour	Summary of Events and Information	Remarks and references to Appendices
	Sunday Aug 9th 17		Two Gas attacks odi: Dnl. Tp. to MIZERNES: was opposed L.T.	
	Tuesday Aug 10th 17		HAZEBROUCK: Irregular arrivals of D.T.B. & Cynists: 4th from 7 Londn. Rgt; Dnl. seen. 18th Sqn Lndn Lon. Regt. all in MIZERNES area. Weekly arpt. returns forwarded to A.D.V.S. Corps – Devn. 43 admd – admitted: 53 Cavr.; 3 Duel; 3 Destroyed. 134 Remaining including 22 mange.	
	Saturday Aug 11th 17		Inspected horses of 3 Coy sectn: Dryal Coy. Dnl. Tp. and Hd Otrs. Dp. Dealt with usual office routine:	
	Sunday Aug 12th 17		Inspection Horses of D.H.B. & Dryal Coy. & attended to office work.	
	Monday Aug 13th 17		Visited & inspected following units in Wizernes area: Depol Co: 17 Ln Regt. 15th, 20th, 23rd Batts. Lon Regt. 141st Machine Gun Co., 2300 & 245 Batting. Lon Regt. 142nd Machine Gun Co. & Loy. Svcs.	

T2134. Wt. W708—776. 500000. 4/15. Sir J. C. & S.

Army Form C. 2118.

D.A.L.V.S.
47TH
(LONDON) DIVISION

WAR DIARY
or
INTELLIGENCE SUMMARY
(Erase heading not required.)

Instructions regarding War Diaries and Intelligence Summaries are contained in F.S. Regs., Part II. and the Staff Manual respectively. Title pages will be prepared in manuscript.

Place	Date	Hour	Summary of Events and Information	Remarks and references to Appendices
	Tuesday Aug 14" 17		Inspected Lewis + rifles of 239 M. Gun Coy. at FERSINGHEM, 4th Bn. ? Inspected HARNES. Normal routine work done.	
	Wednesday Aug 15" 17		Visited Lewis of & Brens: 4th Bn. L. Brigade + again attended lectures Lewis gunners "/2nd London M.F.A. pipers in the area and located at WIZERNES.	
	Thursday Aug 16" 17		Inspected Lewis of following units in WIZERNES area; Bde. 7th; 8th; 9th; 15th. 21st Bgs. 2 Coy. A.D.L. Mobile Veternary	
	Friday Aug 17" 17		Visited 235 + 236 Bges R.F.A. in Forrana area: brought 235. Mes Coyns. nearer to WIZERNES to take change of units in the area. 2nd other units with Ind. Hqs. to RENINGHELST + 28 A.S.I. 221 + 25 ...	

T2134. Wt. W708-776. 500000. 4/15. Sir J.C. & 8.

Army Form C. 2118.

D.A.D.V.S.
47TH
(LONDON) DIVISION.

WAR DIARY
OR
INTELLIGENCE SUMMARY

(Erase heading not required.)

Instructions regarding War Diaries and Intelligence Summaries are contained in F. S. Regs., Part II. and the Staff Manual respectively. Title pages will be prepared in manuscript.

Place	Date	Hour	Summary of Events and Information	Remarks and references to Appendices
	Saturday Aug 18th		Inspected lines of D.T.B. & Signal Coy. R.E.	
	Sunday Aug 19th/17		Duty officer WDG. I.sans administrative inspection received from A.D.V.S. 11no Corps. Letters to all A.D.V.S. to discuss same.	
	Monday Aug 20th		Mobile Sec. animals of 235" & 236" Bns R.F.A. Mount office visited.	
	Tuesday Aug 21st/17		Inspected animals of 504 (action) D.A.C.; 4th & 6th Lon. Field & Dush. by & Signal Co. on return.	
	Wednesday Aug 22nd/17		Visited Dul. Hy. & Signal lines; trans-lo. 22nd, 23rd, 24th London Bde. Regt. & 142" R.F. Coy & Hy. 142nd Inf. Bde. Dealt with office routine.	
	Thursday Aug 23rd/17		Inspected lines of 6" Lon. 7th Lon. D.T.B. Signal Coy. Veterinary Ambulance at 7.0" all officers received such return of Mobilisation of questions of logical enlist.	

A6945 Wt. W14422/M1160 350,000 12/16 D. D. & L. Forms/C/2118/14. 5

Army Form C. 2118.

D.A.D.V.S.
47TH
(LONDON) DIVISION

WAR DIARY
or
INTELLIGENCE SUMMARY.
(Erase heading not required.)

Instructions regarding War Diaries and Intelligence Summaries are contained in F. S. Regs., Part II. and the Staff Manual respectively. Title pages will be prepared in manuscript.

Place	Date	Hour	Summary of Events and Information	Remarks and references to Appendices
Tilloy	Friday Aug 24th		Daily office work. Visited horses of 2nd & 6th Lon. L. Ambce. D.H.Q. & Signal Co. R.E. 2nd Lon M.V.S. arrived in this area & located at A.13.a.9.4. October 28.	
	Saturday Aug 25th		Visited M.V.S: 520 field Coy. R.E. & 4th Lon. Lon. Regt. Weekly vet returns rendered to Divn. & Corps. 56 Animals: 52 horses: 4 animals: 4 Duds: 104 remaining.	
	Sunday Aug 26th		Attended Conference of D.A.D.V.S. at 1st Corps Hq. following matters discussed: Addition of Derby stables: disposal of Derby cases: listing of Mange Cases: progress in evacuating & other minor details.	
	Monday Aug 27th		Visited Divl. Hq. & Signal Co. R.E. Office work.	
	Tuesday Aug 28th		Visited R. H.Q: 140 Machine Gun Coy & Lines of 6th Lon. Lon. Regt.	
	Wednesday Aug 29th		Morn. Office work. Visited horses of Divl. Hq. & Signal Coy.	

Army Form C. 2118.

WAR DIARY
or
INTELLIGENCE SUMMARY.
(Erase heading not required.)

Instructions regarding War Diaries and Intelligence Summaries are contained in F. S. Regs., Part II. and the Staff Manual respectively. Title pages will be prepared in manuscript.

D.A.D.V.S.,
47TH
(LONDON) DIVISION.

Place	Date	Hour	Summary of Events and Information	Remarks and references to Appendices
	Thursday Aug 30/17		Inspected animals of 517 & 518 Field Coy RE. Horses M.T. & inspection went on satisfactorily. In afternoon held Conference of Vety Officers at office.	
	Friday Aug 31/17		Inspected horses of 1 Bry. Town & 2 Durham D.A.C. Tested field stables. Wagon lines & acted as judge of condition of horses for Divl. Competition. Office routine. Weather wet where rendered to Divn. Horses: 92 cases admitted; 40 cures; 23 evacuated; 1 Died; 1 Destroyed; 119 remaining; including 6 Mange.	

C Mayo
D.A.D.V.S. 47th Division

Army Form C. 2118.

WAR DIARY
or
INTELLIGENCE SUMMARY.
(Erase heading not required.)

WO/95/472
Vol 22

Place	Date	Hour	Summary of Events and Information	Remarks and references to Appendices
	Saturday Oct 1st 17 9.25 a.m. about 2.F.		Dealt with routine work at office. Visited Mobile Section. Inspected lines of Corps C.R.E.'s & Div'n Sig. Coy.	
	Sunday Oct 2nd 17		Visited lines of 143rd Machine Gun Coy & North Section.	
	Monday Oct 3rd 17		Inspected lines of the Machine & Coy & patients at Adv. V.L. Post to evacuation. Visited Divnl Dump & lines we found not had much Daily office routine.	
	Tuesday Oct 4th 17		Inspected animals of 2nd, 21st, 22nd & 23rd Divn Emp. Regt and old M.L. Coy. Visited M.V.L. This unit moved to G.22.d.2.4 about 5.	
	Wednesday Oct 5th		Visited M.V.L. Inspected animals of 1, 2 & 6 Corps Sig. Sec's S" Corps of Army Cyc. Bn. & Sig of Reserve C.R.E. Usual office routine.	
	Thursday Oct 6th		Inspected horses of 239 M.I. Co. Received & examined 35 Remounts at WIPPENHOEK station. Attend Board on Pvts at Divnl Train	

Army Form C. 2118.

WAR DIARY
or
INTELLIGENCE SUMMARY.
(Erase heading not required.)

Instructions regarding War Diaries and Intelligence Summaries are contained in F.S. Regs., Part II. and the Staff Manual respectively. Title pages will be prepared in manuscript.

Place	Date	Hour	Summary of Events and Information	Remarks and references to Appendices
Luday	Sept 7th		Gradually normals of 19th Battn. Joined M.D.S. Officer resting: Weather wet where temperature fell. Dur. Essex. 86 Marathon. 7th Essex: 26 Zonnebeke: 3 Durs: 14 Distington: 93 Remaining ordinary 5 Range.	
Saturday	Sept 8th		Attended conference at office of A.D.M.S. 1st Anzac Corps. Sims motor transport of M.D.S. left tonight for STEENVOORDE area.	
Sunday	Sept 9th		Lower M.D.S. & Carried Co. R.E. to act as [illegible] in connection with [illegible].	
Monday	Sept 10th		Main M.D.S. to unsolicited departure of Zonnebeke Contingents receiving movements taken about name to M.D.S. Sabella nose at 4th, 5th & 6th Lov. F. Ambulances. Dul. Hy? 5 th Dul. Lov. R.E. .10 rounds fell on Worries by whole from in line of 235 Fus. R.F.A.	
Tuesday	Sept 11th		Main M.D.S. Loss of Dul. Hy. 8 Signal Co. [illegible] wounded by shell fire whilst up to [illegible] Regt. & 530 4th Co. R.E.	

Army Form C. 2118.

WAR DIARY
or
INTELLIGENCE SUMMARY.

(Erase heading not required.)

D.A.D.V.S.,
47TH
(LONDON) DIVISION.

Instructions regarding War Diaries and Intelligence Summaries are contained in F. S. Regs., Part II. and the Staff Manual respectively. Title pages will be prepared in manuscript.

Place	Date	Hour	Summary of Events and Information	Remarks and references to Appendices
Warloy	Oct. 12th 14		Dealt with usual office routine. Visited M.V.S. Divl. Hy. Supply Coy. & our Fmn.	
Warloy	Tuesday Oct. 13th		Inspected animals of 18th & 20th Battns. Dn. Ranft: & visited M.V.S. In afternoon took conference of Veti. Officers & M.T. Officers recruits weekly vet. return.	
Warloy	Friday Oct. 14th 14		Visited M.V.S. & accompanied Divl. Comdr. in tour of inspection covering 239 Machine Gun Coy: Divl. Hy: In 1st Sup. line & whole of 140th Inf. Bde.	
Warloy	Saturday Oct. 15th 14		Visited A.D.V.S. 1st Anzac to discuss arrangements & disposal of Divisional transport with arrangements in connection with pending movt. Inspected lines of 6th Lon: F.A. Divl. Hy. Supply Coy & M.T.S.	
Warloy	Sunday Oct. 16th 14		Visited M.V.S. superintended evacuations. Usual office routine.	
Warloy	Monday Oct. 17th 14		Inspected animals of 236 M.G. Coy: & one Sec: 4/7 D.H.L.	

Army Form C. 2118.

D.A.D.V.S.
47TH
(LONDON DIVISION)

WAR DIARY
or
INTELLIGENCE SUMMARY
(Erase heading not required.)

Instructions regarding War Diaries and Intelligence Summaries are contained in F. S. Regs., Part II. and the Staff Manual respectively. Title pages will be prepared in manuscript.

Place	Date	Hour	Summary of Events and Information	Remarks and references to Appendices
Tuesday	Sept. 18/17		This office & Mobile Section moved to GODEWAERSVELDE N.3. west HAZEBROUCK 5A.	
Wednesday	Sept. 19/17		Inspected remounts of 2 Coy. 4.2.6. 9th 8th & 19th Battns. Deal. Hrs & N.P.S. all in outstanding state.	
Thursday	Sept. 20/17		Visited M.V.S. D.H.Q. 18th 20th 2nd line Sen Regt. 6th Sqn. 4 Hrsbd. 520. 4Dr. C.R.E. Most horses wet, otherwise remained to Dept & Corps. 42 horses: 22 mules	
		25	Evacuation 15. Div. & 26th Veterinary 34 remaining in charge. One mount (calculations reported to H.Q.) for move of Div. to 21st & 22nd inst.	
Friday	Sept. 21/17		This office moves at 9.a.l. H.Q. to TILLERS-CHATEL M26 approx H.2. 2Lut LENS 11. 13th Corps. First Army.	
Saturday	Sept. 22/17		Mobile Section moved to MARDEUIL: reference J. 3. 2Lut LENS 11.	
Sunday	Sept. 23/17		Visited Mobile Section: also D.A.D.V.S. 63rd. R.D. Division — inspected late arrivals same. Instructions A.D.V.S. 13th Corps received with to mobile light.	

A6945 Wt. W11122/M160 350,000 12/16 D. D. & L. Forms/C./2118/14.

Army Form C. 2118.

WAR DIARY
or
INTELLIGENCE SUMMARY of
(Erase heading not required.)

Instructions regarding War Diaries and Intelligence Summaries are contained in F. S. Regs., Part II. and the Staff Manual respectively. Title pages will be prepared in manuscript.

E.......V.S.
47TH
(LONDON) DIVISION.
No. ....
Date. ....

Place	Date	Hour	Summary of Events and Information	Remarks and references to Appendices
	Monday Oct 25th		Visited Visiting Cards & 2. O. 53 M.W. S. B. to inspect accommodation. Visited the London R.F.C. at ARROEN	
BERLES	Tuesday Oct 26th		Inspection arrivals of 234 M.A. Coy & changes of B.S. and Sup Coy at Duty office routine.	
to ANZIN	Wednesday Oct 27th		This officer went with Col. Eng. to visiting camp L.S.S. 53; M.A.P. Visited M.A.P. & inspected arrivals of it Coy. Sa. Bn.	
	Thursday Oct 28th		Visited areas of Supply Coy, R.E. & M.T.S. Afternoon held conference of D.A.D.S. officers recently sent returned & M. DENTON units for Adj. attendance.	
	Friday Oct 29th		Had great delay of inspection with A.D.V.S. of ferry units - 574.515. 5.20 Held Co-RE and inspection is completed; 2,3,14 Coys Desk. Visited Sup Coy. Weekly Rept which "rendered" to Divn. & Corps: 52 cases handled and transferred to Corps, 6 evacuated. 46 Remaining undischarged and waiting only.	

T2134. Wt. W708—776. 500000. 4/15. Sir J. C. & S.

Army Form C. 2118.

WAR DIARY
or
INTELLIGENCE SUMMARY.
(Erase heading not required.)

D.A.D.V.S.,
47TH
(2ND) DIVISION.

Place	Date	Hour	Summary of Events and Information	Remarks and references to Appendices
Colembert	Sept 29th		Inspected animals to be Q'd for 7th Corps. A.A. Police & a Coy Sect. Local sparse units.	
Querrieu	Sept 30th		Visits to 5th & 6th Divns. of Anzac. acted as guide for Genl. Birkwood to 2nd Austn. Division. Also R.A.M.C. 13th Fld. Amb. & 5th Aus. Inob. veter. animals to be Rd. to R.V.S. 4th Corps R.V.D.	

T. Dillard
Major
D.A.D.V.S. 47th (2nd) London Division.

Army Form C. 2118.

WAR DIARY
or
INTELLIGENCE SUMMARY.
(Erase heading not required.)

D.A.D.V.S.
47TH
(LONDON) DIVISION.
No. ....
Date ....

Place	Date	Hour	Summary of Events and Information	Remarks and references to Appendices
London	Oct 31.17		Inspected animals of 6th, 8th, 15th Battns: also 140 how. Hy., & M. Gun. by. Also Wk. & 18th Battn. London Regt.	
G.H.Q. 2nd Ech.			Dept will round visit relieved & visited Mobile Section	
Lux. Moss	Nov 2. 17		Visited M.V.S. horses of 3rd in field. Co. R.E.	
			Dental visit work.	
Merris by	Nov 3rd		Saw inspection of remounts of Divisional units i.e. 4th, 5/6th & 2nd Lond. Regs. London Regt: 1st & 3rd Corp. Dub. Sigs. & 5th Lond. 2/4 Regt.	
Locality	Nov 4.17		Visited M.V.S. Much sick work	
Locinne	Nov 5th		Attended conference at H.Q. of 142nd Bgde. re move to Louvre via Boise de [illeg]	
			Land Ambulance Inspection horses of 2/2 Lon. F.Amb. & 20th Jon Jen Reg: Mobile U.V.S.	
			H.Q.V.S. sent orders tendering to Direct...	
			...Order of treatment to Garner: 6 horses 2/5, 1 H.U.; 26 remounts arriving...	

Army Form C. 2118.

WAR DIARY
or
INTELLIGENCE SUMMARY
(Erase heading not required.)

D.A.D.V.S.,
47TH
(LONDON) DIVISION.

Instructions regarding War Diaries and Intelligence Summaries are contained in F. S. Regs., Part II. and the Staff Manual respectively. Title pages will be prepared in manuscript.

Place	Date	Hour	Summary of Events and Information	Remarks and references to Appendices
Saturday	Oct 6th	6 P.M	M.O. A.D.V.S. M.R.V. inspected lines sick horses & at Energetic attempts to exterminate fur & lice. Inspected records of A.V.Cp's batteries 235 Bd. R.F.A. condition of horses improved. Dusty after wet weather of last week. Completion of shelters for horses before winter hastening.	
Sunday	Oct 7th		Major M.V. inspected animals of Sp. 1 & 2 Sections D.A.C. through guards made by any other unusual attempts of catching of horses for exercise. Daily exercise routine maintained to the extent with regards to selection of Remounts + invalids with about 950.	
Monday	Oct 8th		Inspected lines of 220 1/8 Coy horses. Troubles amongst animals rest grow. Revaccination + other sick parades. Isabella	
Tuesday	Oct 9th		Major D.A.C. + annexes to Ambulation of affected Section; Isabella D.A.O. + lines of B.E. & D. batteries 236 How. R.F.A. Horses fired wounds	

Army Form C. 2118.

WAR DIARY
or
INTELLIGENCE SUMMARY.
(Erase heading not required.)

Instructions regarding War Diaries and Intelligence Summaries are contained in F. S. Regs., Part II. and the Staff Manual respectively. Title pages will be prepared in manuscript.

Place	Date	Hour	Summary of Events and Information	Remarks and references to Appendices
[illegible]	Oct 10th		Mr D.D.V.S. 1st Army & M.R.V.S. 26 Corps. 3 inoculated with [illegible]	
			inoculation of D.A.C. H.Q. & 1st R Can Coy	
			Dealt with Daily office returns	
[illegible]	Oct 11th		by motors A1/138. remounts at A/236, D & B/235 Relands R. R.	
			Witnessed the performance of Lt. [illegible] at Officers Records work by	
			sick returns - discussed the questions of weekly reports.	
[illegible]	Oct 12th		Lt Colonel M.D. [illegible] Down office routine matters with out visitors returns to	
			Divn & Corps. 114 cases Admitted to 5 conv: 11 evacuated. 1 Died: 2 D10 Corps 24	
			21. Remounts reaching on arrival. increased in numbers, due to Bull Arty	
			Long march.	
[illegible]	Oct 13th		Visited Horses of 517, 315 & 520 Tri M Coo R.E. 5th Lon Lbro. Divns	
			#6 for R.W. Eng. M.L.G. & Mont Pollian. Nothing new in progress	
			vaccination generally good	
			[illegible] at 12 a [illegible] 1 to Decl[illegible] D.A.C.T. March Section	
[illegible]	Oct 14			

WAR DIARY or INTELLIGENCE SUMMARY

Army Form C. 2118.

D.A.D.V.S. 47TH (LONDON DIVISION)

Instructions regarding War Diaries and Intelligence Summaries are contained in F.S. Regs, Part II. and the Staff Manual respectively. Title pages will be prepared in manuscript.

(Erase heading not required.)

Place	Date	Hour	Summary of Events and Information	Remarks and references to Appendices
Mbray	Oct 15th		Complete details of mobilization to No 1 Section A.V.C. went under horses & of remounts handed to for London. Lt. Col. B. & 25th A.Y. & Co. R.E. & 19th Bn. Lon. Regt.	
Lillers	Oct 16th		During office routine. Visits D.A.D.C. with D.A.D.M.S. to approve & arrange for sanitary arrangements, water troughs etc. Mobilin transport animals of 20th Bn Lon Regt. & M.T.S.	
Wednesday Oct 17th			Visited H.Q. 18th Bn Lon. Regt & 6th Bn Lon. & Bombay. During office routine. Cmdt HQ. S. towards A.V.C. sections down Lieut T.	
Thursday Oct 18th			In morning visited horses of 4th & 7th Y.B. 10th & 20th troops Lon. Regt. Afternoon D.A.M. conference of H.Q. officers at office & discussing meetings etc. Returns & appointing water troughs watering orders.	
Friday Oct 19th			Visited with A.D.V.S. Mobile section 1/st Lon F.A. 25th A.V.C. R.E. and 1st London Sanit. Ft. Afternoon saw 2nd & 18th Bn Lon Regt.	

Admitted 2 chevals. 5 evacuated: 1 Dead: 2 D.S.T.A. 110 Remaining. Nil Mange
Visit office routine: Weekly vet return rendered to D.V. & 10790 & 42 cases.

Army Form C. 2118.

D.A.D.V.S.
47TH
(LONDON DIVISION).
No. ......
Date ......

WAR DIARY
or
INTELLIGENCE SUMMARY.
(Erase heading not required.)

Place	Date	Hour	Summary of Events and Information	Remarks and references to Appendices
Lillers	Oct 20th		Inspected Horses of 520 [?] F. Co. R.E. Also Glenoco Garages & 10 Motorised Lorries to 141st Inf. Bde. Harold Eva to Stable management in both units. Usual H.Q.S. Daily Office Routine. Capt R. BRYDEN A.V.C. proceeded on leave.	
Lundry	Oct 21st	Cuedo	Usual examination on horses at 2 new Lower M.V.A. and A.D.V.S. 3rd Office routine.	
Monday	Oct 22nd		Inspected animals of Nos. 1, 2, 3 J.H. two Dub. Sup. Columns AAA. Clothing harnessing etc. very clean. Notice Mobile Section.	
Tuesday	Oct 23rd		Inspected transport animals of 140th Inf. Bde. & Dub. H.q. Notes MDS. General office routine.	
Wednesday	Oct 24th		Inspected animals of 2nd Lon. Fd. Amb. 518 Yorks & P.S. 577, 522 Do. & 210th Lon. Fd. Rest. & Mobile Section.	
Thursday	Oct 25th		Inspected Horses of A/235 by. at TREVENT-CAPELLE (not AAA. In afternoon left Lillers at 2pm. Officer to act as Lieut over all outposts of [?] interior	

WAR DIARY or INTELLIGENCE SUMMARY

Army Form C. 2118.

Place	Date	Hour	Summary of Events and Information	Remarks and references to Appendices
Fosseux	Oct 26/17		Visited & inspected Hd Qr. Bttn H.Q. of 17th & 18th Battns. & 7 Mobile Section. Daily office routine. Weekly pack returns forwarded to Divn. Topo. 66 Munitions to be issued as accessories: 3 Drums to Divisional H.Q. & Remainder.	
Rebreuviette	Oct 27/17		Inspected horses of A/235 & B/236 Battery: Visited Mobile Section. Two officers moved to St Catherine.	
Barneville	Oct 28/17		Visited horses of 518 Yuks to Rd. marks P.M. exam. Inspected Regnal lines. Horses & M.T.s.	
Monchy	Oct 29/17		Rept. Movements Exam Erskin in connection of 14/07 Fort full 19th & 20th Corps for for Horsemastership. Inspected animals of A/235 & B/236. the Brigade. - graph Completion.	
Yvrench	Oct 30/17		Completed exam of Divl. 3rd D.: A.E & D Batteries R.F.A. with J.O.C. Fired M.T. Found opice working.	
Monchy	Oct 31/17		Inspected units & animals at 14.00. Long talk in connection of all my satisfactory in Drivers & Horsemaster work. Informed M.O. & arrangements for him to officials opinion on board on Leave from 1.11.17.	

Signed
D.A.D.V. 47th Division

Army Form C. 2118.

D.A.D.V.S.,
47TH
(LONDON DIVISION).

No. 24

WAR DIARY
or
INTELLIGENCE SUMMARY

(Erase heading not required.)

Instructions regarding War Diaries and Intelligence Summaries are contained in F.S. Regs., Part II. and the Staff Manual respectively. Title pages will be prepared in manuscript.

Original

Place	Date	Hour	Summary of Events and Information	Remarks and references to Appendices
ST. CATHERINE. G.9 CENTRAL SHEET 51B	Thursday Nov 1st 17		Met A.D.V.S. B^n Corps & inspected with him 517, 518, 520 Lon. Fd. Amb. R.E. & 4th Lon. R.M.Y.A. In afternoon attended Monthly Parade of animals for inspection with D.D.R. Received weekly vet. return from V.Os. of Units. Horse duties at Mobile Section.	
	Friday Nov 2nd 17		Inspected horses of C/236 & A/235 Batteries in Roa H.A. Dual Tp. Ingrola on return. Dealt with Army Office routine. Vent. vet. statistics returned to Divn. & Corps: 45 Admitted; 42 Evacuated; 1 D.O.R.; 1 Destroyed. 85 Remaining; no mange. Horse duties at Mobile Section.	
	Saturday Nov 3rd 17		Inspected horses of C/236 & A/235 Batteries. Visited 25th A.J. Co. R.E. - 236 Bde. R.H.A.; Daily office work & vet. duties at Mobile Section.	
	Sunday Nov 4th 17		Inspected horses of 518 Fd. Amb. Co. R.E. Office - Mobile Section duties.	
	Monday Nov 5th 17		Inspected horses of 1st N. Lan. Coy. - 20th Lon. Lab. Regt. Pr. Pontoon Pant. R.E. Daily Office routine & vent. Mobile Section duties.	
	Tuesday Nov 6th 17		Met A.D.V.S. B^n Corps - inspected with him detail of animals of 235th Bde. R.H.A. Office routine & vet. work at Mobile Section.	

D.A.D.V.S.
47TH
(LONDON DIVISION).

Memoranda of

Wednesday Nov 7th 1917. Inspection wagon of A/236 & A/235. 2 Coy. Divl. Train. Mobile Section duty. Office routine.

Thursday Nov 8th 1917. Visited animals of DAH Signal Coy. Divl. Commander visited Section. In reference to Conference of T.O.s at office. Recorded stamp received all entries of monthly report.

Friday Nov 9th 1917. Inspected animals of 19th Lon. Lon. Regt. 35 + 7th Lo.R.I. 1st section Pk. R.F.a. Weekly act returns rendered to Divn + Corps. 65 Admitted 35 evac. to Base & 2 Evacuated Ba. 1 Destroyed. 1 Died = 94 Remaining. Daily office work + Inspn. at Mobile Section.

Saturday Nov 10th 1917. Inspected animals of A/235 + A/236 Batteries R.F.A. in Rest Area: 19th Lon. Regt. Mobile Section work.

Sunday Nov 11th 1917. Visited horses of D.A.H. & Signal Coy. R.E. Office routine + Mobile Section work.

Monday Nov 12th 1917. Attended inspection of Mares branded for breeding by Committee from War Office. Daily office routine + Mobile Section work.

D.A.D.V.S.
47TH
(LONDON DIVISION).

Tuesday Nov 13th) No A.V.D. Inspected horses at 517K 518K 452K Hd.Qrs Co.
R.E. Duties at M.V.D and Office routine

Wednesday " 14th) Inspecting animals of 142 Brigade A.C.
Duties at the V.D. and Office routine

Thursday 15th") Superintending evacuation of sick animals to Base Vety Hospital
Held weekly Conference of V.Os at Office received returns and
discussed answers of weekly inspn. Duties at M.V.D & Office routine

Friday " 16th.. Inspected horses at 141 Hb. S. Co. 2016 London Bath 1st Rodn. Cole
R.E. Duties at M.V.D & Office routine.
19. A.V.D returned from leave and resumed duties.
Weekly sick return to Suri. + Corps 74 Admitted 39 Cured 12 Evacuated
- Destroyed - Died in Remaining

Saturday " 17th. Visited and inspected 516 London Field Amb. 140 142 Brehom
D.A.C. Office routine

D.A.D.V.S.,
47TH
(LONDON) DIVISION.

Sunday Mar 18th 17 Visited and Inspected 19th Bath and 131 Paxton Park RE.
                    Usual Office routine

Monday 19th Visited and inspected horses of APM, 4th R.W.F. Portion of
              140 Bde HQ, 21st Bath. Inspected 255 MGCo on arrival in
              this area. Daily Office routine

Tuesday 20th Visited and inspected 6th London Field Amb. 518 Coy, 517th Coy
              520th Coy RE. Also visited Divisional HQ Artillery Inspected
              horses. Office routine

Wednesday 21. Visited MLO inspecting horses for evacuation. Market & conferred
               with ADVS XIII Corps. Usual Office routine

Thursday 22. Office moved to Armanville 17th Corps area.
              Office routine

D.A.D.V.S.
47TH
(LONDON) DIVISION.

Hermanville Nov 23/17 Office transferred to Fosseux - Mule belonging to 141 Brigade HQ
 died on road Office routine. A/2000 returned 43 Admitted 34 Evac'd
Fosseux }   31 Evac'd 1, Destroyed 1/7 Remaining 7

" " 24/17 Office transferred to Achiet le Petit & Corps Area - treated 6th
 London Field Ambulance Horse Lines. Noted Office routine A36Admits

Achiet le Petit
 Nov 25th } Visited Mobile Veterinary Section. Office routine

" 26 " Visited Div HQ horse lines. Office routine

" 27 " Office removed to Hoplincourt J.34.a.2.7 (Sheet 57C) 4th Corps
 Area. Visited AVC K/O dis-reported to him.   Office routine

" 28 " Inspected 236 Bde R+A. At V/O went K N.4 t-cent Sheet 57C
 Office routine

D.A.D.V.S.,
47TH
(LONDON DIVISION).

Hoplincourt
29/1. Nov. 17 Office transferred to Provisional H.Q. Neuville Bourjonval

Neuville Bourjonval
30 " 17 Battle took place - Several killed and wounded horses
Weekly return of Pack Injured animals sent to A.R.4 5th Corps.
53 Admitted 26 Cured 23 Evacuated 3 Killed 11 Destroyed 70 Remaining

[signature]
Major
D.A.D.V.S. 47th Division.

Army Form C. 2118.

VA 25

D.A.D.V.S.
47TH
(LONDON) DIVISION.

WAR DIARY
or
INTELLIGENCE SUMMARY
(Erase heading not required.)

Place	Date	Hour	Summary of Events and Information	Remarks and references to Appendices
NEUVILLE-BOURJONVAL G.22. CENTRAL 51.C	Saturday Dec 1st		Interviewed A.D.V.S. & Capts. on four details of administration in his area. Rode over by 5th Corps. Stated M.F.S. + horse of D.A.D. Ougnal Co. R.T. Daily office routine.	
	Sunday Dec 2nd		Taken on A.D.V.S. 5th Corps interview with Comm. the horses I with M.F.S. Arranged for flat cart to move to move forward to station. 10h 23b am R.V.A reports 2 mure horses Ormatitis.	
	Monday Dec 3rd		East Corps M.F.S. moved to d. NEUVILLE with Advanced Secl. at HERNIES. Usual office routine. Veterinary arrangements during present operations considered to Ass. Dir. Vet. Services.	
	Tuesday Dec 4th		D.R.C. horses + inspected horses of whole of 140th Infantry Bde + L.A.A. Dockers D.R.C. 3 more Ormatitis reported in 47 D.A.C. - Cats reported. T.O.V. + examined Ion as to preventive + curative action. 11h 2 more reported in 236 Bde R.V.A.	
	Wednesday Dec 5th		Inspected horses of 20th + 22nd Lon Regt. 517, 518, 520 Lon + 20 L.R.F. Daily office work of 4th Vet Dir. until 14h to VTRES.	

WAR DIARY or INTELLIGENCE SUMMARY

Army Form C. 2118.

D.A.D.V.S.
47TH
(LONDON DIVISION)

Place	Date	Hour	Summary of Events and Information	Remarks and references to Appendices
Thursday	Dec 6		London Lodge of 400 Labour Coy 6th Lon Y Bakr. Signal to R.E. In afternoon embusments 14y officers at other Nation area of Dimitriis reported. Manure to to form Screen.	
Friday	Dec 7		Toilet M.Y.S. Inspection Rdays arrivals from 974 R.Y.R. les may his men on arrival known. Report of live made to Deuxme Own D.A.O.V.S. 1st A.O.V.S. 5th Corps with him inspected Dimatitis cases at 1/7F. then to 336 Hyan. Weekly aft returns rendered to Dir V Corps. 116 cases admitted including 56 Dimatit rounds: 45 Evacuees: 17 Died: 3 Destroyed 26. Workings including 17 Dimatitis.	
Saturday	Dec 8		235th Bow R.Y.R. + Harnessment Work out Parles to 2nd 236 Hev R.Y.R. Not 70E. 235th Bow R.Y.R. + discussed outbreak of Dimatitis. Daily office work.	
Sunday	Dec 9		Toilet 236 Hev R.Y.R. at 76 a.b. Inspect 4 arrange for mot divergent Execution to Latrin to melt Dimatitis outbreak. Called upon D.A.O.V.S. 61st Divnis in Country to Istallam Item of prevalence his Drvand. Report made to A.D.V.S. Corps in return	

Army Form C. 2118.

WAR DIARY
or
INTELLIGENCE SUMMARY of

(Erase heading not required.)

D.A.D.V.S.
47TH
(LONDON) DIVISION

Instructions regarding War Diaries and Intelligence Summaries are contained in F. S. Regs., Part II. and the Staff Manual respectively. Title pages will be prepared in manuscript.

Place	Date	Hour	Summary of Events and Information	Remarks and references to Appendices
	Monday Dec 10th		Visited BAPAUME Station & inspected 4th Remounts. Visits Mobile Section. Daily office routine.	
	Tuesday Dec 11th		Inspected horses of 4th, 5th & 6th Divs. Full strength: 400th Lab Coy & 27th D.A.C. Interviewed D.A.D.V.S. & Stomatitis cases & advised hem of M.V.S. to isolate all stomatitis. Visits Mobile Section.	
	Wednesday Dec 12th		Inspected animals of D.A.A.S. Signal Coy R.E. Have to visit Inf. Bde at ROYAUX COURT & Mobile Section NEUVILLE. Head office work on return.	
	Thursday Dec 13th		Visits lines of D.A.D. Signals & Mobile Section. In afternoon interviewed Vety. Officers at office discussing chiefly prevalence of Stomatitis and Spotsmina & all means to suppress this disease. Weekly act return visaed.	
	Friday Dec 14th		Conferred with D.A.D.V.S. 59th Div. concerning his line to take over at Rivachim & list radio, left in car for selection by Division. Weekly act return visaed: Own Trops: 20 sick, 46 Lamed: 25 Evacuees (10 sick, 6 gunshot) (15 Jan-Jul) (63 Remaining from Sick)+24 Returned +24 Returned.	

Army Form C. 2118.

WAR DIARY
or
INTELLIGENCE SUMMARY.
(Erase heading not required.)

D.A.D.V.S.
47TH
(LONDON) DIVISION.

Place	Date	Hour	Summary of Events and Information	Remarks and references to Appendices
Saturday	Dec. 15th		Horses over until to 59th Divn. including Mobile Section to function as Divisional for Dismobile case only. M. Vety Officer & A.D.V.S. Corps worked up arrangements. Visit M.O. & 5th Corps, & received general situation as regards units being left behind. Inspected horses of 3rd London Bart. R.E. at BERTINCOURT. Capt. R BRYDEN A.V.C. to proceed with Divn to new area.	
Sunday	Dec.16th		Div office moved to HERMY. Duck. Hq. to BAZEAU. Arrival reported to M.D.V.S. 3rd Corps.	
Monday	Dec.17th		Interviewed Capt. BRYDEN A.V.C. & arranged for him to take charge units in the area. Horsey full of sick & worn out horses.	
Tuesday	Dec. 18th		Wire sent only. Unable to visit units as roads impassable owing to continued frost.	
Wednesday	Dec. 19th		Visited animals of Divl. Sig. Seginel Cov. R.E. also M.M.P. Daily office routine	
Thursday	Dec. 20th		Inspected horses of 21st Bn Lon. Regt. & Sig. Trans. & 142 M.Gun Bn. DAP & Signals. Usual office work.	

Army Form C. 2118.

WAR DIARY
or
INTELLIGENCE SUMMARY.
(Erase heading not required.)

Instructions regarding War Diaries and Intelligence Summaries are contained in F. S. Regs., Part II. and the Staff Manual respectively. Title pages will be prepared in manuscript.

D.A.D.V.S.
47TH
LONDON DIVISION

Place	Date	Hour	Summary of Events and Information	Remarks and references to Appendices
	Friday Dec. 21st		Visited animals of Divl. Sig. Sigmal Coy. & 255 Machine Gun Coy. Naval officer visited Worthy and obtained references to Divn. & Corps. 22 mules. Visited 6 reservists. 1 Div. 22 remaining.	
	Saturday Dec. 22nd		Inspected horses of 6th Lon. & 8th Lon. Ambul. & 22nd Hon. Lon. Regt. Daily office work.	
	Sunday Dec. 23rd		Inspected horses of 140th Machine Gun Coy. Visits to make usual Wells mung to condition of roads.	
	Monday Dec. 24th		Visited horses of Divl. Sig. Signal Coy. & M.M.P. 255 Machine Gun Coy. 5 horses in Lutteris, very poor condition & two suspects of Mange. Daily office routine.	
	Tuesday Dec. 25th		Inspected animals of 140th Lond. Sty.	
	Wednesday Dec. 26th		Inspected animals of 6 & 7th Lon. Lon. Regt. & visit with office routine.	
	Thursday Dec. 27th		Inspected animals of 8 & 15 Lon. Regt. Continued Capt. BRYDEN A.V.C. at office, Ricard not returned & anomay of attendant of mules in the Lutt.	

WAR DIARY or INTELLIGENCE SUMMARY

Army Form C. 2118.

(Erase heading not required.)

Place	Date	Hour	Summary of Events and Information	Remarks and references to Appendices
Friday	Dec 28th		Hospital trains London M.T.S. in 4yr D.W.R. sent to rail transport of Divisionelle cadre; journal demands of hedged now collected & sent on services; (full 35 animals of 2nd D.R.C. also on par will." Weekly rent return forwarded to D.W. Corps; 14 cabs as noted 11 drivers: 6 travelled; 35 remaining.	
Wednesday	Dec 29th		Office work; only coming to investigation.	
Thursday	Dec 30th		Inspected animals of 520 Lon. F.O. Coy. R.E. 6th Lon. F. Amber. 4th Lon. R.W. Fus. 22nd & 24th Servis. Lon. Regt. Capt. Mac BRIDE M.T.C. arrived in this area & posted to Divl. Train temporarily.	
Monday	Dec 31st		Inspected horses of 4th Lon. F.B. Amber. & 140th M. Lion Bay. Usual office work.	

T. Mann
D.A.D.V.S. 47th London Div.

Army Form C. 2118.

D.A.D.V.S.,
47TH
LONDON DIVISION.

WAR DIARY
or
INTELLIGENCE SUMMARY.
(Erase heading not required.)

Vol 26

Instructions regarding War Diaries and Intelligence
Summaries are contained in F. S. Regs. Part II.
and the Staff Manual respectively. Title pages
will be prepared in manuscript.

Place	Date	Hour	Summary of Events and Information	Remarks and references to Appendices
HERLY WOOD AMIENS	Jan 1st 15	G.L.	Inspected animals of 5th Lond. F. Ambce & No 3 Coy. Train. Daily office work.	
	Jan 2nd 15		Visited horses of Dub. Hy. T. Regnl. Co R.F. in morning. In afternoon met Capt. Mac BRIDE R.F.C. & arranged with him to take charge of various units.	
	Jan 3rd 15		Office work only, unable to visit owing to condition of roads; no Car available.	
	Jan 4th 15		Inspected animals of 208 Machine Gun Coy, 4th & 13th Brigades R.F.A. 140 mgs. M.G. Coy & 2 Coy. Train. Worked being rapidly proceeded with. Usual office work.	
	Jan 6th 15		Instructions received to move to Quin, saw 140 Inf. Left troops in 6 mots. delivered to Capt. Mac BRIDE at office & directed him to remain with 140 Bgd. troops in sector being vacated.	
ETRICOURT N.T.C.IL.	Jan 6th 15		This office moved with Dub. Hy. to ETRICOURT A.D & 5 Cord outlays Administration of whole Devl. units already in area resumed.	
	Jan 7th 15		Visited 236th Bde. R.F.A. & 7th Bgd. London M.T. Car Bus: inspected horses & cases of Ulcerated Lymph. Glands to be temporarily segregated. Called upon D.A.D.V.S 47th Quin: & discussed general condition of animals of Divn. unsatisfactorily admonished in Divn. Visited a few units on return.	
	Jan 8th 15		Visited horses of D.H.Q. & Signal Coy. 320 Fluid L.C.R.T. Office routine	
	Jan 9th 15		Inspected animals of 21st Lon. Regt. & noted Mobile Section.	
	Jan 10th 15		Entrained this office at once. received Mobile Section returning at Drevings all animals of both units. 140th Inf. Lod. troops moved in this area.	

WAR DIARY or INTELLIGENCE SUMMARY

Army Form C. 2118.

D.A.D.V.S.
47TH
LONDON DIVISION.

Instructions regarding War Diaries and Intelligence Summaries are contained in F. S. Regs., Part II. and the Staff Manual respectively. Title pages will be prepared in manuscript.

(Erase heading not required)

Place	Date	Hour	Summary of Events and Information	Remarks and references to Appendices
	Jan 11th 15		Inspected animals of 520 Fwd Co. R.E., 1/4th Bn R.W. Fus. Watched act returns rendered to Divn. & Corps: 63 Animals: 31 Evact: 14 Casualty: 5 Out & 2 Diseases: 148 Remaining including 77 Debilities. Most of latter now fit for duty but still under isolation owing to Mange in contacts.	
	Jan 12th 15		Inspected animals of 7th, 19th & 22nd Bn Regts: 141 Machine Gun Coy. and M.T. Section. Duty & office routine.	
	Jan 13th 15		Visited horses of 515 Bn, 1/6 R.L, 3rd Bn, 7 Bns, Instructions with reference to accommodation by 1st Labour Companies issued to Divn. Duty & office routine.	
	Jan 14th 15		Visited horses of M.V.L. Signals to 236th Coy. R.E. M.T. Mobile Section. Distances generally satisfactory.	
	Jan 15th 15		Proceeded to BAPAUME Station to inspect the Remounts on arrival. Num. Inspected animals of 18th Bn. Rct. on return. 15 good standard.	
	Jan 16th 15		Capt. J. Martin R.E. visited on leave for ... R.E.A.: 1147/148 Labour Coys & 520 Fwd Co. R.E. Horse est: 232 Army Bct.	
	Jan 17th 15		Rev horses of D.H.B. Signals Visits. M.V.O. In afternoon conferred with ... Officers of Corps, in all matters pertaining to their charges. Dealt with duty & office routine.	
	Jan 18th 15		Inspected animals of 1/12 Lnc. Reserve 167 Labour Coy. Mobile Section. Watched art returns rendered to Divn. & Corps: 70 Animals Arrived: 33 Evact: 15 Casualty: 2 Out & 2 Diseases: 169 Remaining including 76 Debilities. Most of these now awaiting discharge.	
	Jan 19th 15		Visited horses of Div. all Coys 6th Bn & 520 Fwd Amb. & R.L. Usual office routine.	

Army Form C. 2118.

WAR DIARY or INTELLIGENCE SUMMARY

Army Form C. 2118.

D.A.D.V.S.
47TH
(LONDON DIVISION)

Place	Date	Hour	Summary of Events and Information	Remarks and references to Appendices
	Jan 20th 18		Visit 17 Fd. Ambce. Co R.E. Ophthalmia cases there to L. Anglo Treatment. Extinguished at Transfusion MDS & arranged for return to duty of Convalescent patients.	
	Jan 21st 18		Inspected Horses No 4 Coy M.G.C. 2.3.7ºd +24th Bns Lon. Regt. & M.T.Y.	
	Jan 22nd 18		Visit principal of M.T.O. about Lairage + attached 12 mules & certain horses to duty. Duty officer inspected M.T.Q. 10 inspect mules & horses also to return to duty. Transfered to MDS.	
	Jan 23rd 18		Ophthalmic case sent to 4th Fd Amb. R.W. Fm. Sd Duk Ruty. 255 Machine gun Coy. Gun Regt. twice daily Fd. Amb. By. Condition of all animals good but standings of 2nd Fm. bad.	
	Jan 24th 18		This office moves with DHQ to G Hb. t. 2.3. about 51.C. An Application centered with this office at once, received them with reports. Mount office routine.	
	Jan 25th 18		Visited horses of the 5th Lon. Regt. 140 O.H. Gun Long + 140 Bat. Hy. Mortar act. strength 72 Gun + Trains. 68 cobs admits. 132 mules 22 Transpt. 2 Discharged 117 Remaining including 9 animals only	
	Jan 26th 18		Visited Horses MDS + horses of DHQ + Royal Lon. R. Normal office routine.	
	Jan 27th 18		Visit MTS t 2 Coy. Duk. Trans.	
	Jan 28th 18		Inspected horses of M.Ch & D.H.Q. Symnola planking good but approaches to Lon Regt 9 1st 4th & 6th Bns. Lon. Coy. Game that flies made unsafe as 119th & 14th Labour Coys. 6th Lon Regt. 21st Bn.	

Army Form C. 2118.

D.A.D.V.S.
47TH
(LONDON) DIVISION.

WAR DIARY
OR
INTELLIGENCE SUMMARY.
(Erase heading not required.)

Instructions regarding War Diaries and Intelligence Summaries are contained in F. S. Regs., Part II. and the Staff Manual respectively. Title pages will be prepared in manuscript.

Place	Date	Hour	Summary of Events and Information	Remarks and references to Appendices
	Jan 29th/16		Inspected Horses of Divnl. Sup. Col. R.E. Light establishments also those of 5th Lon. F. Amb: & 5th Fuld. Amb: R.E. 2/4.o. 5.18 & 5.20 5.15 & 5.20 R.E.	
	Jan 30th/16		Inspected animals of 17, 18, 19, 20, 22, 23, 24 & 25th Bn. Lon. Regt. Also 11th Btn. & 1.701 Remounts at their units their morning. Duty officer visits.	
	Jan 31st/16		Inspected animals of H.Q. 236 Bat. R.F.A. C.236 Bat. R.F.A. and O.A.U. section R.A.M.C. Reinforcements from Base units of Divisional shortages in Bat. Ration strength previous week. Reports came in 6.0.0 p.m. No Veterinary interviews with officers at 11.0.a.m. Requires with reports.	

T. Richard
Major
D.A.D.V.S. 47 London Division.

Army Form C. 2118.

D.A.D.V.S.,
47TH
(LONDON) DIVISION.

WAR DIARY
or
INTELLIGENCE SUMMARY.
(Erase heading not required.)

Place	Date	Hour	Summary of Events and Information	Remarks and references to Appendices
LITTLEWOOD	Jan. 26 central		Inspected Lines of Comm. Signal Corps. Tested M.T.Q. & 110th Labour Co.	
	Jan 27 to Jan 1st 1915		and 5th Lon. F. Amb. 3 Horses. Daily office routine. Wrath set Course Finished	
			to Div. F. Lange. 59 horses admitted: 36 Evacd: 28 Evacuated: 1 Discharged: 57 Remaining	
			including 3 admitted sick.	
	Feb. 2nd 15		Inspected animals of L.T.Dx36 R.G.A. & Ammo Section. Attempted to pay adjustment	
			with D.P.Y. 2 lines army at 11.30 am but no appearance made by him. up to 12.30m.	
			Daily office work on return.	
	Feb. 3rd 15		M.T.Q. & office routine only.	
	Feb. 4th 15		Inspected animals of A.S.C. 9x35. R.G.A. & no. A.T.C. found animals well supplied	
			with 7 animals dig. nails to be personally exd. R.T.Q. on 5th to receive of general disease.	
			Legacy animals made to re-open M.T.Q. on 5th for reception of general disease.	
	Feb. 5th 15		By appointment of D.P.V. D.D.V.S. and Dr. M.T.Q. 5 cases accompanied by the	
			American officers & conducted them round M.T.Q. + Lines. Both same D.V.O. explained	
			himself entirely with arrival with management and organisation & general discipline places arrangements	
			Daily office work on village. M.C. animals & general veterinary places on arrivalho	
			worked by Com. Villa. Case assembly. M.T.Q. arrivals in rear of horses for return base. Capt. M.R.S.	
			EDWARDS. Attached to Officials during this period.	
	Feb. 6th 15		Inspected horses of 5th Lon. Div. 15 steep Batty. inferior quality of horses noted to	
			bought to my notice. Futures.	
			Visited M.T.Q. & examined car of Capt. Le R.A.M.C.	
	Feb. 7th 15		Inspd. M.T.Q. & 4.370 F.H.Q. Labour Coys. two horses. In afternoon interviewed Lt.	
			Officers at office discussed with fellow veterinary to amend their charge.	
	Feb. 8th 15		Examined 77 Remounts at M.T.Q. army arrived for Divn. Rec. Dury. One case of	
			Strangles, 3 sterile 4 filling Rehoumt. This enables to own efforts & general to typification of all Remounts + pneumonia Stalien	

Army Form C. 2118.

WAR DIARY
or
INTELLIGENCE SUMMARY.
(Erase heading not required.)

D.A.D.V.S.,
47TH
LONDON DIVISION.

Place	Date	Hour	Summary of Events and Information	Remarks and references to Appendices
	Feb. 9th 15		Visited 1st Corps & conferred with A.D.V.S. re Mobile Veterinary outbreak. Usual office routine & Mobile Section.	
	Feb. 10th 15		Inspected animals of 23rd & 24th Bns. Lon. Regt. 1st & 2nd M.G. Coys. & 2nd & 79th Tr. Coys. R.F.A. Condition of all good. Also inspected Remounts at Mablé.	
	Feb. 11th 15		Inspected animals of 517-518 & 520 Field Coys. R.E. Condition from satisfactory to good. 4th Bn. R.W. 260, 255 M. Gun Coy, 7, 141st Siege Bty &c. Mobile Section, usual office routine.	
	Feb. 12th 15		Inspected with A.D.V.S. horses of 517, 518 & 520 F.Coys R.E., 4th Bn. R.W. 3rd Daily office routine.	
	Feb. 13th 15		Visited horses of D. 24 & Regt Lo R.F.A. & Bn. & Ambce. 141st M.A.Bry 17, 18 & 7 19th Bns & Army Corps.	
	Feb. 14th 15		Inspected animals of 4 & 7th D.F.C. at PONT-NOYELLE.	
	Feb. 16th 15		Inspected animals of 140th M.Gun Bde & M.T.M. Usual office work. Weekly ret. returns received for Divn. 4 Londs: 61 equine unsuitable, 62 issues, 20 evacuated & Ret. 90 remounts including sub Mobile Veterinary Sec.	
	Feb. 16th 15		Inspected horses of Nos 1 & 2 Coys. Divnl. Train. Horses Mobile Section.	
	Feb. 17th 15		Visited 142nd, 166th & 179th Londs Horse Coys. One A.O. killed & one wounded by shrapnel, in on visit night & 16th & 17th inst. Horses rapid settlement. Usual office routine.	
	Feb. 18th 15		Inspected animals of 15th, 19th, 21st & 22nd Lon. Regts. Inspec R.T.S.	
	Feb. 19th 15		Inspected animals of 16th & 5th Bns Lon. Regt.	

WAR DIARY
or
INTELLIGENCE SUMMARY.
(Erase heading not required.)

Army Form C. 2118.

Instructions regarding War Diaries and Intelligence Summaries are contained in F. S. Regs., Part II. and the Staff Manual respectively. Title pages will be prepared in manuscript.

D.A.D.V.S.,
47TH
LONDON DIVISION.

Place	Date	Hour	Summary of Events and Information	Remarks and references to Appendices
	Feb. 20.15		Inspected horses of Divl. Hq. M.M.P. & Dep. Tn. Co. R.E. Horses to A.V.S. 236 Batt. R.F.A. Myself sickish & attended to usual office work.	
	21	20th	Spentish. Horses of London Scottish. 119th & 140th Fd. Ambs. In afternoon inspected horses of artillery office at H.Q. 1 Coming to B.S. reported for duty one slight [?] case of [?] to take charge of [?] to [?] 5th [?] but [?] still remounts under degrees of M.T.D. [?] to take the remounts was retained for treatment	
	22	22nd	Inspected horses of Dvl 235 Bde Div. R.F.A. & 520th M.T.D. Capt. Shoe Smith A.V.C. applied to A.D.V.S. that [?] mules [?] return [?] R. Knight reported to our Remb. St. routine. Myself with [?] [?] 1 Dec. 22: 94 Remounts arrived at [?]. 37 mules to succeed? 1 Dec. 23: 94 Remounts	
	23rd		148th M. Ac. & horses of & for 2 Batteries. Usual office work in absence.	
	24th		Also office work with Capt. Hy. to YPRES. Conferring with A.D.V.S. Corps in absence of Surrey [?] Horse Show Ruth for Prevention of [?] and [?] Public	
	25th		Inspected horses of Signal Co. R.E. D.A.C. Mobile Section & 4" x 5" for 2 Batteries French office [?] Inspected horses of L.B.C.(233) R.G.A. condition of all good. Jewels M.H.	
	26th			
	24th 15		Inspected animals of [?] officials appro. & compones of Survey [?] R.G.A. & Signal Co. R.E. In afternoon	
	25th		Inspected horses of the 3rd 5th 520 3rd Div R.G. & Signal Co R.E. + Cable Section + 2 Ambs. Inst. Sam Cap 1 Cap of [?] A.V.C. Middle Section horses arrived this morning. Horses of animals good & all passed fit for duty.	

T. Dipper. Major
Capt. A.D.V.S. London Divn.

WAR DIARY or INTELLIGENCE SUMMARY

Army Form C. 2118.

Place	Date	Hour	Summary of Events and Information	Remarks and references to Appendices
YTRES	21	3 15	Records previous to this date have been destroyed. Enemy apparent anxious, distinctive permit to us Ally. Reports for support of casualties in event of retirement	
	22	3 15	G.7. Shells are employed to entrance shelling depot. 2 CRAIG A.T.P. slightly wounded and shewing at duty	
	23	3 15	Louis wounds of F.M.B.P. turned to R.T. also Lt under M.T.P. Lant heirinthed to A.T.O.	
			Moved with F.D.V. to SEMBLES. East of SOUTHERL 276 from from	
	24	3 15	Moved to LONGUEVAL from to LONTERMAISON, thence to ALBERT	
	25	3 15	Remained at ALBERT	
	26	3 15	Moved to JENKIS thence to LOUVINCOURT	
	27	3 15	4 H.T.F. Regiment at LOUVINCOURT. Capt 2.Gray 107 plunder Infantry command	
	28	3 15	Moved to PUBEMPRE. Joined M.T.F. at PUCHEVILLERS	
	29	3 15	Proceed loss of D.H.B.I. Lapach.	

Army Form C. 2118.

WAR DIARY
or
INTELLIGENCE SUMMARY. of 2%% 47th Divn
(Erase heading not required.)

Instructions regarding War Diaries and Intelligence
Summaries are contained in F. S. Regs., Part II.
and the Staff Manual respectively. Title pages
will be prepared in manuscript.

Place	Date	Hour	Summary of Events and Information	Remarks and references to Appendices
	31	3.15.	(report (?) arrived at D.H.Q. at 6"x6" from Field Ambce 7 7x15) Medical Section	
	31	3.15	Casualty Return for week 7:23 4th Corps Mtd. Troops 1st & 6th Infantry Bde. With casualties in w/s : 34 Killed, D.W. & Missing & 144 Wounded and 15 Sick. 11 evacuated.	

R. Stevens
Lt Col G.S. 47th London Divn

Army Form C. 2118.

WAR DIARY
or
INTELLIGENCE SUMMARY. of 7. D.A. DHS 4th DIV?
(Erase heading not required.)

Instructions regarding War Diaries and Intelligence Summaries are contained in F. S. Regs., Part II. and the Staff Manual respectively. Title pages will be prepared in manuscript.

Place	Date	Hour	Summary of Events and Information	Remarks and references to Appendices
RUBEMPRÉ MAR 4th E.6. Lat LENS II.	1st Nov 1915		Inspected arrivals of 614, 515 & 520 Field Coys. R.E. & 4th Pon R.W. Reo. Today the whole section & Ca. 3 Coy. Dull Drain. Daily office routine in reference	
	2nd Nov 1915		Inspected Remounts; inspected arrivals of 141st Inf. Bde. & 6th Lon 9. Amb.	
	3rd Nov 1915		Received Remounts at Barracks at PUCHEVILLERS. Return of WDR & T.L. & Losses of 12nd & 6th Lon Bttn & 4th Lon Bttn Sutton.	
	4th Nov 1915		Inspected...many office work only on intelligence	
	5th Nov 1915		Capt ? CRAIG R.E. inspected to ... ... Issued WDR NT & Casu? as to Post Issued at WDR & OV. 105 Lewis Wanted & 21 With ... returning ... to Butr Parks. 2B Remounting ? Lines of Communities pass to LON fort.	
	6th Nov 1915		Issued losses of D.Z.B Kingrah to R.E. M.T.S and Iry. Dull Drain.	
	7th Nov 1915		Issued Advances? D.Z.B summary of 4th & 5th Pon. BN Ankers. Office routine on deliny.	
	8th Nov 1915		Inspected Lines of 141st Inf. Coll. and 3 Field Coys. R.E.	
	9th Nov 1915		Div office more unit D.M.O to PUCHEVILLERS.	
	10th Nov 1915		Inspected Remounts & 15th 19th & 20th Bns. Lon Regt. 46 Labour Corps 2B. D.O. Call. Section R.E. Fire Corps Sydnets. Pm 2 Mules in 19th Bn showing ... petting of bits reviewing.	

(A7091) Wt. W12539/M1293. 75,000. 1/17. D. D. & L. Ltd. Forms/C.2118/4

Army Form C. 2118.

WAR DIARY
or
INTELLIGENCE SUMMARY of 35075
(Erase heading not required.) 1/1 London Div.

Instructions regarding War Diaries and Intelligence Summaries are contained in F. S. Regs., Part II. and the Staff Manual respectively. Title pages will be prepared in manuscript.

Place	Date	Hour	Summary of Events and Information	Remarks and references to Appendices
	11th Apl 1915		Move to DOMART-EN-PONTHIEU Map ref B.6. Left LENS 11 Div & 4th Divs arrived at AMIENS 4.5 was at ZOUAVE 10 arrived 13 Remained 14 Div & 3 Division. 33 Remaining	
	12th Apl 1915		Visited remnants of RFA Signed by Office work	
	13th Apl 1915		Move to CANCHY. Div HQ at Div HQ Met N. BEETHUKE arrived & posted to HQRE	
CANCHY	14th Apl 1915		Br. CENSOR arrived at Div. H.Q. Div H.Q. opens remain	
	15th Apl 1915		Visited troops of 20th Lon Lm. Regt, 6th Bull Fukes & 2nd B's Lime C.E. McCUREA and 7th Worcs? RE IG's Coy Lant Govenment DT. vacated RE Dn. 3.15 with Derham E. Gy Duct Staff.	
	16th Apl 1915		Inspected wth 2nd/8th Lons of Reg at Ing RE Recent made to 20. very Reg. Reconnaissance, Stening Dr 18th Lon Lon Rest. 20h 00 + 17h 20 Br O Apbr at at 2 Lon. Bull amba	
	17th Apl 1915		Visited horse of 19th Lon Lm Regt. OBA Section 275 577 518 & 520 Field Coo R.E. Horses where made in Ration arrives	
	18th Apl 1915		Inspected remnants of 8th London Regt: I.M.H.G. In afternoon interviewed offer to speak, & wounded with adv. horses.	
			Divl Service. Visited	

WAR DIARY
or
INTELLIGENCE SUMMARY.

(Erase heading not required.)

Army Form C. 2118.

Place	Date	Hour	Summary of Events and Information	Remarks and references to Appendices
	19th April 1915		Inspected animals of 23rd & 24th London Regt. Inspected 6 R.E. & 7 R.W.F. Duty officer visited Wulverghem with Veterinary sergeant to Divn. & Corps. 33 cases admitted & found 13 exchanged & discharged. 21 Remaining. Punk Children were attached to another formation.	
	20th April 1915		Visited horses of 21st London Regt. & 2 Coy. Divnl Train also M.T.E.	
	21st April 1915		Met R.H.T. & Corpo. A.D.V.S. to discuss organisation of slaughter yard and collection of a 7th Corps enquiry & infection and for transfer of A.V.C.	
	22nd April 1915		Inspected horses 4th Squad. Hry R.E. 4th & 1st R.W.Fus. & purchases at completion L.O.B. Coy. 3rd Lon. Staff.	
	23rd April 1915		Visited M.T.R. 3 Coy. Dress & 21st St. Lon. Regt. Went off on return.	
	24th April 1915		Inspected horses of 6 Loss. & 2 Monts. 15th, 17th & 20th Lon. Regts. & Divnl Ammn. in act of mobilization.	
	25th April 1915		M.O.W.W. ordered of Demolition at LANLEY. Inspected on taking over long R.E. and Dud Dud. Ammn. Coln. Same location of self.	
	26th April 1915		Day devoted in rest & 2 Veterinary Hospl. MEZERILLE for dental inspection.	
	27th April 1915		Inspected what still further cattle in DOMVAST and report result to Dtr. Cand L.O.R. Cand LOB & tramp on afternoon return in afternoon inspection of army horses by L.W.R. at M.T.E.	

Army Form C. 2118.

D.A.D.V.
47th
LONDON DIVISION

WAR DIARY
or
INTELLIGENCE SUMMARY.

(Erase heading not required.)

Instructions regarding War Diaries and Intelligence Summaries are contained in F. S. Regs., Part II. and the Staff Manual respectively. Title pages will be prepared in manuscript.

Place	Date	Hour	Summary of Events and Information	Remarks and references to Appendices
	5th Feb 1918		Graziolii Dism'y of Multi section. Draft of 4 sections	
	17 Feb 1918		Holly Databasto Lieutt to ALBERTVILLE on leave personal. Drovers Domuscules sent to Rustichio Wago sale.	
	20 Feb 1918		Graziolii trends BHQ trsport to R.E. Graziolii Hosp of SVD Draught of SVD troops remits for hosp of BEAULIEU and Horses. There were plenty on hay coming	

[signature]
[signature]
D.A.D.V. 47th London Division

Army Form C. 2118.

WAR DIARY
or
INTELLIGENCE SUMMARY.
(Erase heading not required.)

Vol 30

DADVS
47TH
LONDON DIVISION

Place	Date	Hour	Summary of Events and Information	Remarks and references to Appendices
C.I.C (vicinity) Beaut 6/D	1st May 1918		Arrived at Iberts Farm with D.A.D.V.S. utilizing the Australian Corps Anvil returned to A.D.V.S.	
	2nd May 1918		Interviewed the officers in charge of distribution of units for attendance. Passed all veterinary reports of animal interest.	
	3rd May 1918		English animals of 5.L.M., near 4th Lon. Field Ambulance. Twelve horses debilitated. 5 Evacuated: 5 Remaining. Starving 10mil Artillery Station.	
	4th May 1918		Inspected D. Branch ammunition in the field at 4th Bn Lon Regt. at Low Farm. Made inspection of animals of Q.A.C. (Wilson sect.) 7th & West Surrey, 4th Lon Regt. Disney area rented 7 mules M 7.6.	
	5th May 1918		Horse artillery rejoined. Village of Beaucourt. Field X Trench Mortar lanced Mtd. to foundation	
	6th May 1918		Inspected horses of Q.A.C., R.R., 20 Bn "B" Co, 4th Lon Bn. April Co. F.L.L Lin. Gave further advice on administration. At 3rd London Instruction reminder of 517, 518. 4th 520 7th Corps R.E. Back to 5th Lin. Field Ambulance.	
	7th May 1918		Inspected horses at 15th 17th 18th 19th 20th & 22nd Bns. Lon Rwrs. M.T. & officers horses.	
	8th May 1918		Inspected animals of "D" Coy 4th Lon Bn in Lon Field Ambce. T.M.B Afternoon called on A.D.V.S. 3rd Corps re papers re admin.	
	10th May 1918		To Ville ABBEVILLE for field medical & HORSE: 17 arrived. Dentistry refitting resident & turned in wounded: 3 evacuated: 13 Remaining	

WAR DIARY
or
INTELLIGENCE SUMMARY

(Erase heading not required.)

Army Form C. 2118.

Place	Date	Hour	Summary of Events and Information	Remarks and references to Appendices
	11th May 1915		Inspected A.C. & 2nd Battalions at 2nd Battery Posts. R.F.A. 180 + 253. A.D. Coy R.E. Visits M.T.E. Daily office routine.	
	12th May 1915		Inspected returns at M.T.G. Divn. Ammunition Column fort B.A.C. 724. Visit M.T.E. Office routine.	
	13th May 1915		Inspected animals of B.A.C. & Div. Ammn. Col. R.F.A. Divn. Train 46th Divn. 25th Hussars.	
	14th May 1915		Inspected lines at A.D.S. R.A. Hospital R.A. Hy. Brigade. Carts at M.T.G.S. for evacuation.	
	15th May 1915		Visit A.D.S. Inspection of animals at 557, 518 & 520 2nd Co R.E. Inspected Field Ambulances & Officers of Brigade 25th Officers met returned & arrival of wounded in motor transport.	
	16th May 1915		Visited Motor Section & inspected the lines of the R.M. Bns. Arranged with Divn records to have for sentral treatment Lt wounded: 12 hands; 19 knees admitted. 15 Runaways.	
	17th May 1915		Inspected lines at M.T.G. for evacuation. Visited Signed to R.F.A & 3 Coys. Divnl Office routine.	
	18th May 1915		Visits Lines at 4th Dn. G. Mortar. Inspected returns at M.T.G. before evacuation. Daily office work.	
	19th May 1915		Inspected animals of A.C.D. & H.Q. 34th Machine Gun Bn. & 3 Coys. Evacn.	
	20th May 1915		Day occupied in visit to Hospital for initial treatment.	

WAR DIARY or INTELLIGENCE SUMMARY

Army Form C. 2118.

D.A.D.V.S.
47TH
LONDON DIVISION

Instructions regarding War Diaries and Intelligence Summaries are contained in F. S. Regs., Part II. and the Staff Manual respectively. Title pages will be prepared in manuscript.

(Erase heading not required.)

Place	Date	Hour	Summary of Events and Information	Remarks and references to Appendices
	21st May 1918		Inspected lines of 6th Jor. Field Ambce: A.D: "A" & "D" Companies 47 Bn. M. Gun Corps: Also inspected Mobile Section horse evacuation.	
	22nd May 1918		Daily office routine: Visited M.G. transport waggons at MHQ to arrange with transport employees to firewash transport in absence of Company Officers at "Gillespie Huts" at office. 47th Divl Artillery where Reviewed Today.	
	23rd May 1918		Inspected animals of 15th & 17th & 21st Bns. Jon. Regt: 253 H.Co. R.E. & attended Presentation of M.M.R. Routine visit to paid to Dun. & Corps. to consult with their office agents Strengths & funds: 6 evacuations: Deaf of Wounds & 2 Sickness. Inspected animals of 3 Coy.	
	24th May 1918		Daily M.G. Inspected cases for evacuation. Rest of day office routine.	
	25th May 1918		Inspected animals of 6.7.8.23rd Bn. R.I.R. & Mobile Section.	
	26th May 1918		Inspected Lines of 140 C.O. to R.E. Owl. V.O.: Owl. Insp. 20 Owl. duty. & R.P. Design &c. Rufus with usual office routine.	
	27th May 1918		Day spent in completing total treatment.	
	28th May 1918		Inspected animals of Bn. 2 Bn. 150 Bn. R.I.R. 400. 1 & 2 Section & Remount evacuation sent at HQ.	
	29th May 1918		Inspected animals of 21st A.B.D.3. Wens; 577 A.C.O. 4th Lon. Owl. V. & N.G. in absence of Director Vet. Services of HQ. Office routine.	
	30th May 1918		Inspected M.T. Signal Co.R.E. Owl. 2.O. 4th Lon. Owl. Inty. 2.O. 18 Sig. Bde. Regt.	

Army Form C. 2118.

D.A.D.V.S.,
47TH
LONDON DIVISION.
No............
Date............

WAR DIARY
or
~~INTELLIGENCE SUMMARY.~~
(Erase heading not required.)

Instructions regarding War Diaries and Intelligence Summaries are contained in F. S. Regs., Part II. and the Staff Manual respectively. Title pages will be prepared in manuscript.

Place	Date	Hour	Summary of Events and Information	Remarks and references to Appendices
	31st May 1915		Inspection remounts of 180 A.D.Co R.E, 7 Coy, 47 Ldn Div. & M.T. Duty officer reporting	
			[signature] Major D.A.D.V.S. 47" Divn	

Army Form C. 2118.

Vol 31

D.A.D.V.S.,
47TH
LONDON DIVISION.

WAR DIARY
or
INTELLIGENCE SUMMARY
(Erase heading not required.)

Instructions regarding War Diaries and Intelligence Summaries are contained in F. S. Regs., Part II. and the Staff Manual respectively. Title pages will be prepared in manuscript.

Place	Date	Hour	Summary of Events and Information	Remarks and references to Appendices
	1st June 1915		Inspected animals of 517, 518, & 520 Lon. Field Cos. R.E. also 7th 8th 9th Bns. 1st 4th Lon: 34th Bn. M. Gun Corps: 3olts Mobile Section & examined patients for evacuation. General office routine.	
	2nd June 1915		Tested horses & mules of 2 Bde R.F.A. & Corps: 47 Bn. M Gun Corps. Inspected horses of RA HQ & Mobile Section.	
	3rd June 1915		Inspected animals of Divl. H.Q. Signal Co R.E. 4th & 6th Lon: Field Ambces. and M.T.S. Daily office routine.	
	4th June 1915		Tested animals at M.T.S. Signal Co R.E. H.Q. 47 Divl. Engrs: Tested charger of O.C. 1 Mort investigation of cases Epizootic Lymphangitis alleged to have occurred in which 23. 5. 15 at 211 Base evacuated by 1/235 Bde R.F.A. 1. 22. 4. 15 & discovered as such.	
	5th June 1915		Inspected & examined horses of 1/235 Bde R.F.A. & 1/236 R. FA.: Reported result to A.D.V.S. 3rd Corps. Mobile Section: Lept: DERAIG A.V.C. proceeded on leave.	
	6th June 1915		Inspected animals of 1/236 Bde R.F.A. M.T.S. Divl. Q. Signal Co R.E. Daily office routine.	
	7th June 1915		Tested office of A.D.V.S. 3rd Corps re. Increase Epizootic Lymphangitis and furnished list of horses up to date of evacuation; also list not returned to Duty of Corps: 32 cases admitted: 32 Cures. 16 evacuated: 2 Died & 2 Destroyed 50 Remaining.	

Army Form C. 2118.

D.A.D.V.S.
47TH
LONDON DIVISION.

No ....
Date ....

WAR DIARY
or
INTELLIGENCE SUMMARY.
(Erase heading not required.)

Instructions regarding War Diaries and Intelligence Summaries are contained in F. S. Regs., Part II. and the Staff Manual respectively. Title pages will be prepared in manuscript.

Place	Date	Hour	Summary of Events and Information	Remarks and references to Appendices
	8th June 1918		Visited M.V.S. inspected animals of 1/235 Bde R.F.A. No further outbreak of strangles. Lymphangitis. Daily office routine.	
	9th June 1918		Visited M.V.S. D.D.V.S. 1st A.A. D.A. Return D.M.C. 253 A.D.C. R.E. D.R.S. 377 A.E.D.C. RTC. 150 A.D.C. R.E. & D.D. Dud. duty.	
	10th June 1918		Mor A.D.V.S. 3rd Corps & with him inspected Lines of 1/235 Bde R.F.A. Visited M.T.S. of 235 R.F.A. & No. 3 Coy. A.S.C.	
	11th June 1918		Examined evacuation cases at M.V.S. Visited D.H.Q. Usual office work	
	12th June 1918		Inspected Lines & M.Os of 22nd & 23rd 7 24th Bns Lon Regt & D.D. M.S. and S.F. B.G.C. In afternoon held Conference of this officers at officers B.G.C.	
13th	"		Office routine only owing to illness of A.D.V.O.	
14th	"			
15th	"			
16th	"			
	17th June 1918	11am	Inspected Lines of D.H.Q. Signal Co. R.E. 377 A.E.D.C. Co. A.S.C. & No 4 Coy Dul. Visited D.M.C. Return.	
	18th June 1918		Inspected Lines of 253 A.D.C. R.E. L.N. Return D.M.C. D.D. M.V.C. C/235 Bde R.F.A. & No. 2 Coy, A.S.C. Mor M.V.S.	
	19th June 1918		Visited 6th Lon Field Ambce & M.V.S. Daily office work	
	20th June 1918		This office moves with D.H.Q. D to CAVILLON B.1 south AMIENS.	
CAVILLON	21st June 1918		Inspected animals of 5 Lon F.Ab. Ambce & M.V.S. this unit arriving at BREILLY	
	22nd June 1918		Visited M.V.S. R. duty. Hy at ARGOEUVES & arranged for inspection by A.D.V.S. on following day. Daily office work on return.	

Army Form C. 2118.

D.A.D.V.S.
47TH
LONDON DIVISION.
No. ....
Date. ....

WAR DIARY
or
INTELLIGENCE SUMMARY.
(Erase heading not required.)

Instructions regarding War Diaries and Intelligence Summaries are contained in F. S. Regs., Part II. and the Staff Manual respectively. Title pages will be prepared in manuscript.

Place	Date	Hour	Summary of Events and Information	Remarks and references to Appendices
	23rd June 1915		Visited Lines of Sgnl. Co. R.E. & D.H.Q. Batteries of 22nd & Bde R.F.A. Inspected mules of ADMS 3rd Corps all in R.A. Rest Unit.	
	24th June 1915		Inspected animals of 22nd T.M. Bde Lon. Regts. 3 Cav. men & evacuated patients at M.V.S. for evacuation. Office routine as return.	
	25th June 1915		Inspected horses at 518 Lon. Fld. Co. R.E. a.c. & 235th Bde R.F.A. 6 cas of Mange reported in Cruchan Lines at LONGPRÉ area occupied by 17 DAC. 18th Bgd. instructed to deal with case and put all precautionary measures.	
	26th June 1915		Inspected animals of 15th & 19th Bns Lon. Regt. In afternoon Lab conference of 7th Officers at office.	
	27th June 1915		Inspected horses of 20th Bn Lon. Regt. Visited 4th 5th 7th Lon. Fld. Amb completion Transport. Inspected to Div. Corps 33 cases admitted, 20 cases acted to Quartz for Dud. Worthy Sick Debris removed: Own destroyed: 1 Destroyed: 32 Remaining:	
	28th June 1915		Inspected No.s 1 & 2 Sections D.T.C at LONGPRÉ & visited M.V.S.	
	29th June 1915		Investigated reported case of Contagious Stomatitis at AMNY-SUR-SOMME horse belonging to French Army. Visited M.V.S. Daily office routine.	
	30th June 1915		Visited M.V.S. Also above mentioned case to take course for Microscopical Daily examination & office routine.	

(signatures)

WAR DIARY or INTELLIGENCE SUMMARY

Army Form C. 2118.

Place	Date	Hour	Summary of Events and Information	Remarks and references to Appendices
CAVILLON B.1.S. or AMIENS	1st July 1918		Inspected animals of 517, 518, 520 Coy. R.E. & 4th Bn. R.W. Regt. & allied no. Coys. in Horsemanship Competition. Visited Mobile Section. Daily office routine on return.	
	2nd June 1918		(Capt. M.S. BRIDE AVC. specialist with QMG) Forwarded to Remounts at PICQUIGNY Field Remount Section. Horses proceeded to LONGPRÉ R.E. at LONGPRÉ to investigate case of Zoogloeic Lymphangitis.	
	3rd June 1918		Visited horses of Divl R.O. & Signal Co. R.E. In afternoon held conference of Vet. Officers of area. Visiting work & also whims increasing all questions of weekly employm.t	
	4th June 1918		Made inspection of horses & mules of Divl. M. Gun Bn. 15th 17th & 21st Bn. on Regt. Area. Q.B. & 40th Sqd. Corpo. Leave granted me to proceed on 5th inst.	
	5th June 1918		Returned to 6th inst. Weekly cart returns received to Divn. Corpo. etc. 48 cases admitted 22 cured, 31 evacuated, Died 2, Destroyed 39 Remounts 3 Remount, D.A.O. & Arrid Co R.E. Section cow belonging to Twolit Mobile Section attendant at CAVILLON.	
	6th June 1918		Proceeded on 14 days leave of absence. Capt. CRAIG AVC operating during that period.	
	7th June 1918		Examined Remounts for Divn at Field Remount Section PICQUIGNY. Office routine & own duties at Mobile Section.	
	8th June 1918		Usual office routine work & own duties at Mobile Section.	

Army Form C. 2118.

D.A.D.V.S.
47TH
LONDON DIVISION.

WAR DIARY
or
INTELLIGENCE SUMMARY.
(Erase heading not required.)

Instructions regarding War Diaries and Intelligence Summaries are contained in F.S. Regs., Part II. and the Staff Manual respectively. Title pages will be prepared in manuscript.

Place	Date	Hour	Summary of Events and Information	Remarks and references to Appendices
	9th June 1917		Daily office work. Town duties at Mobile Section	
	10th		Do	
	11th		Do. Weekly sick returns to Div. Corps. 74 cases admitted. 24 evac: 2S Dev. & Destroyers: 41 Remounts: Officers in meetings Sub to Bomb & Coll. Wounds in Div. Amb. units with Australian Corps	
	12th		Evac: 25 Evacuated. 3 own duties at M.T.S.	
	13th		Horse office work & own duties at M.T.S. Do. Office work with P.Z.O. to CONTAY U 27 Sept 57.D	
	14th		Daily office routine & duties at M.T.S.	
	15th		Do	
	16th		Do	
	17th		Do	
	18th		Do	
	19th		Do. Weekly sick returns to Div. & Corps 49 cases admitted. 114 Evacuated: 17 Evacuated: 1	
	20th		Dev. Sic. Remounts	
	21st		Daily office work & M.T.S. duties	
	22nd		Do	
	23rd		Returned from leave of absence: Signal Co R.E. & D.A.Q. Trailer M.T.F. Inspection Parades of 6th Lon. Fd. Amb. Duty office visited.	
	24th		Ordered to Rest Camp by Medical Authorities. Duties taken over by Capt CRAIG O.C. M.V.S.	
			New Conference of 7th Officers issued sick reports & discussed all matters of Weekly import.	
	25th		Own duties at Mobile Section & office routine only. Weekly sick returns endorsed to Div. & Corps. 54 cases admitted. 19 Evac: 22 Evacuated. 1 Dest. 60 Remaining	

Army Form C. 2118.

WAR DIARY
or
INTELLIGENCE SUMMARY.
(Erase heading not required.)

Instructions regarding War Diaries and Intelligence Summaries are contained in F. S. Regs., Part II. and the Staff Manual respectively. Title pages will be prepared in manuscript.

Place	Date	Hour	Summary of Events and Information	Remarks and references to Appendices
	26 June 1918		Office work and Mobile Section Duties only	
	27"		Do.	
	28"		Do.	
	29"		Do.	
	30"		Do.	
	30"		Do. ADVS Conference of Tchy Officers at office.	

H Craig Captain A.V.C.
DADVS. 47 London Div.

Army Form C. 2118.

23

WAR DIARY
or
INTELLIGENCE SUMMARY.
(Erase heading not required.)

VA 33

Place	Date	Hour	Summary of Events and Information	Remarks and references to Appendices
CONTAY U.27. b.2.0.5	57D Aug 1st 1918		Daily Office routine + town duties at Mobile Section. Weekly ret. Offices rendered to D.ADVS + Corps. 54 Cases admitted. 28 Cases 22 Evacuated. 2 Ould + 65 Remaining	
	Aug 2nd 1918		Major J.E. McCREA A.V.C. proceeds on Special Leave to U.K. Lieut. J.E. HIBBARD returns to duty. Lieut. W.E. WINE receives Photographs of Personnel, Horses & Equipment of D.V.O. + Signal Company on loan at Daylight permits to making the necessary studies which from loan as daylight permits to making the required confirmatory Studies.	
	Aug 3rd 1918		A/horse Cases destroyed at Mobile Section. 1 mule tetanus taken. Condition loss of all + V.S + NOS of LAWH pull met, usual days' routine. Condition loss of all for 5 mm. yet Amber for treatment, out having fully recovered.	
	Aug 4th 1918		M.V.S. Office work + 5th yet Amber to again resume treatment.	
	Aug 5th 1918		W/SJt M.V.S. Horses of Signal Co. R.E. at No. 76. Spr. yet Amber. 1 Daily office work	
	Aug 6th 1918		Office routine only. Remainder of day received in preparing to visit Units for Inspect. 5 horses killed by shell on Rd No 140 nr Pont Noyelles.	
	Aug 7th 1918		Conducted inspects to 4th Bn. R.W. Bns. 8/A 6th Suffolks 7 K.Y.C. Weekly ret. not receiving nothings to DADVS + Corps. 96 Cases admitted. 33 Cases 15 Evacuated. 76 Ould Remaining.	
	Aug 8th 1918		Visited Horses by D.V.A. + Signal Co. R.E. M.V.S. + Daily office routine.	
	Aug 10th 1918		Visit the M.V. Horses to 5th Suffolks for treatment. 20 remounts drilled for 27 Aux Mt. by London Scottish. No 1 Section in Reg Ambulance.	
	Aug 11th 1918		Office routine M.V.S. + G. normal movement only.	
	Aug 12th 1918		Ref. Office moves to HENENCOURT. No 16 GRATTEN	

Army Form C. 2118.

D.A.D.V.S.
47TH
LONDON DIVISION.

WAR DIARY
or
INTELLIGENCE SUMMARY.

(Erase heading not required.)

Instructions regarding War Diaries and Intelligence Summaries are contained in F. S. Regs., Part II. and the Staff Manual respectively. Title pages will be prepared in manuscript.

Place	Date	Hour	Summary of Events and Information	Remarks and references to Appendices
HEILLY Sht. 62.D	August 13/15		Visited A.D.V.S. 3rd Corps to discuss general matters of administration. Visited M.V.S. & Hospital for mules in the BONNAY following day. Daily office routine.	
	August 14/15		Visited M.V.S. & horses of D.H.Q. & Signal Co. and to HAY 106. Inf Bde. Usual office routine.	
	August 15/15		Evacuated sick of 30th Divl. Stn. at SAILLY-LAURETTE. 11 animals killed & 15 wounded by enemy bombs on 15th. 2nd 721st Bn. Lon. Regt.	
	August 16/15		Inspected animals of 1/6 L.T.D. Engrs., Machine Gun Bn. 23rd & 24th Bns. Lon. Regt. & M.V.S. D Coy. office work. Sick returns received to Divn. & Corps. 58 cases admitted. 43 Evacd. 25 wounded. 20 Died. 10 destroyed. 72 Remaining	
	August 17/15		Visited horses at Divl. H.Q. M.M.P. & Mobile Section. Interviewed A.D.V.S. 3rd Corps. Usual office routine	
	August 18/15		Inspected transport horses of 15th 19th & 20th Bns. Lon. Regt. & Nos. 2, 3, & 4 Coys. Train	
	August 19/15		Visited horses of 9. L.A.M. & T.S. & An.T. & Vet. Conv. Station.	
	August 20/15		Inspected animals of Pioneer unit, 15th Brigton Regt. 6th Bn 4th Ambce. at Pm. R.M.R.M. Corps. 517.M.G.B. yet Divn. R.E. & Large M. Lean in. Daily routine work.	
	August 21/15		Inspected horses of 256th Travelling to & visited Mobile Section. In afternoon left Conference at Vety. Offer at office	
	August 22/15		Inspected animals of 15th Army Batt. R.G.A. reported in Debilitated condition to Deputy required 7 Remounts for exercise. Visited Gun Section 115th Northumberland Horsers & admitted to hospital cases ne to attacks of [illegible] this [illegible] Weekly sick return rendered to DDVS Corps: 72 cases admitted 35 evacuated: 6 Divl. 6 Stationary: 72 Remaining: 32 [illegible] of Cavalletos [illegible] de humor: 4 Brit. Womens:	

Army Form C. 2118.

WAR DIARY
or
INTELLIGENCE SUMMARY.
(Erase heading not required.)

Instructions regarding War Diaries and Intelligence Summaries are contained in F. S. Regs., Part II. and the Staff Manual respectively. Title pages will be prepared in manuscript.

Place	Date	Hour	Summary of Events and Information	Remarks and references to Appendices
	August 23rd 1918		Made inspection of Horses at L.O.A.B. the Batteries 175 Brigade R.F.A. no serious discrepancy at any Unit. Tested M.V.S. & Horses of B.T.B.G.T. Mobarak's Coln. Brigade unit: Daily office routine.	
	Aug. 24th 1918		This office moved with D.H.Q. to GUERRIEU. Tested Advanced M.V.S. Post	
	Aug. 25th 1918		Tested Horses of Signal Co. R.E. & 1/4th Lon. Fld. Ambl. Usual office routine.	
	August 26th 1918		This office moved with D.H.Q. to J.24.b.7.5. Sheet 62D. Tested M.V.S. BONNAY.	
	August 27th 1918		Inspected animals of 17th, 22nd & 24th Bns. Lon. Regt. Tested M.V.S. & saw Patients. Here awaiting evacuation. M.V.S. moves to MERICOURT.	
	August 28th 1918		Daily office work. Tested M.V.S. 18th, 19th & 20th Bns. Lon. Regts. "B" Coy. 49th M. Gun Bn. held Conference of Vety. Officers at Office in afternoon.	
	August 29th 1918		Tested M.V.S. & carried out move to MEAULTE. Eighty officers requiring Weekly return during the 10 wks. ending 30 Aug. admits 36 evtd as Evacuation cases during 78 cases admitted: 30 of these consisted due to Bomb & Gun Shell wounds: 69 Remaining 14 undet.	
	August 30th 1918		This office moves with Rear D.H.Q. to M.S.6. Sheet. 62d. Tested M.V.S. & inspected patients for evacuation.	
	August 31st 1918		Tested M.V.S. this unit moves to MAMETZ. Inspected Horses of 4 Coy 2nd D.A.W.I.F. 47 London Div.	

Silford
D.A.D.V.S. 47, London Div.

WAR DIARY or INTELLIGENCE SUMMARY

Army Form C. 2118.

D.A.D.V.S.
47TH LONDON DIVISION

Place	Date	Hour	Summary of Events and Information	Remarks and references to Appendices
A.D.C. near H.Q. Sept 62c	Oct 1st 1915	9 M.V.S.	Graduated horses of 47 Bde M. Guns signal to R.E. Dual A.D. No.1 Coy. train. Usual office routine.	
	Oct 2nd 1915		Visited arrivals of 3 Coy. Train M.V.S. & 142nd Inf. Bde A.D. – Makes 3 Corps for arrival of Remounts & M.V.S.	
	Oct 3rd 1915		Inspected arrivals to D.V.H.Q. & Coy. Train & several details at M.V.S. on demarcation.	
	Oct 4th 1915		Duties move to 47 M. Gun Bde. 317 & 318 Fields Cos R.E. One afternoon spent. Conference of officers at office for discussion of all questions relating to animals under their charge.	
	Oct 5th 1915		Inspected horses with Bvt. O. & B. 13 CENTRAL Cook. 62c M.D. O.C. I.C. V.S. & note how selected sets for slight work. D.R.A. 9 ack gun animals. 20 sick [ill] 112 Destroyed; 70 Remaining: 33 Immovable; 31 Inf Those evacuation due to Wounded & Bomb Wounds.	
	Oct 6th 1915		Carried on 110th & 112 Field R.Q.A. but failed to locate. Visited M.V.S. & 4th Bn. R.E. 10 Guns.	
	Oct 7th 1915		Interviewed Staff's 58th Divn & arranged with him takeover of two new trains M.V.S. & 4 Coy. Train also arrival of D.H.Q.	
	Sept 8th 1915		Our office moved with D.H.Q. to CORBY. Itinerary arrangements re same.	
	Oct 9th 1915		Entrained for LAPONNE RIQUART. 2ith Army Area.	
	Oct 10th 1915		Arrival at LAPONNE RICQUART. Proceeded home to LABEUVRIERE. reported arrival to A.D.V.S. 13th Corps.	

Army Form C. 2118.

WAR DIARY
or
INTELLIGENCE SUMMARY.
(Erase heading not required.)

Instructions regarding War Diaries and Intelligence Summaries are contained in F.S. Regs., Part II. and the Staff Manual respectively. Title pages will be prepared in manuscript.

DADVS 47th DIVISION B.E.F.

Place	Date	Hour	Summary of Events and Information	Remarks and references to Appendices
	Sept 11th 1915		Left H.Q. V.S. 13th Corps & with him inspection of 517, 518 & 520 Field Coy R.E. Visited M.V.S.T. Wait with Daily Expect visiting.	
	Sept 12th 1915		Inspected Horses of 4th Jam. Field Ambce. In afternoon was confirmed of Telg officers at office. Distribution of units garages & general arrangements discussed.	
	Sept 13th 1915		R.W. Jus. Units set at: LAPUGNOY for M.T.S. Office & units animals of 4 Bn Ryffl out returns received. Owners Corpl 31 evacuated 18 Dust. 12 Dysty 20 : 36 remaining. 24 of these remaining one to wounds.	
	Sept 14th 1915		Inspected horses of 21st Bn Lon Regt. also 120 Remounts at M.T.S. Condition & quality of these not up to usual standard.	
	Sept 15th 1915		Inspected animals of D.H.Q. Signal Co R.E. 23rd and 22nd Lon Regt. & 4th Bn. A & H Bn of Loyal North Lancs Regt. No 2 Coy Divnl Train Coy animals generally good although signs of hard of field work.	
	Sept 16th 1915		Inspected horses of H.Q. 140 Inf. Bde. 7 Ports Lon Regt. 1st & 5th Jam. Regt. Anbre.	
	Sept 17th 1915		Inspected with H.D.V.S. animals of B/235th Bde. R.F.A. & A.B. & D/236th Bde. Visited M.V.S. evacuated patients then for discussion.	
	Sept 18th 1915		Inspected animals of 4th Bn M.N. Corps M.T.S. & Suln. Office routine: Left Our Arrangements for Treatments No 12 recovd. Reference move of 47th Lytton from FRANCE. Veterinary arrangements in connection therewith made to all concerned.	
	Sept 19th 1915		Visited forces of 4th Jam Ambce & 4 Coy Train. In afternoon met H.D.V.S. 13th Corps & D.D.V.S. 3rd army at Ruitz. Setback & conducted them round the units. Held conference of Vetry officers at office & discussed all questions of weekly interest.	

Army Form C. 2118.

WAR DIARY
or
INTELLIGENCE SUMMARY
(Erase heading not required.)

D.A.D.V.S.
47TH
LONDON DIVISION

Instructions regarding War Diaries and Intelligence Summaries are contained in F.S. Regs., Part II. and the Staff Manual respectively. Title pages will be prepared in manuscript.

Place	Date	Hour	Summary of Events and Information	Remarks and references to Appendices
	Sept 20th 1915		Visited lines of D.A.D.V.S. Signal to R.E. Daily office routine. Weekly returns rendered to 1st Army Corps. 64 cows admitted 30 Emd: 33 evacuated, 1 died. 3 Destroyed 5-3 Remaining	
	Sept 21st 1915		Visited M.V.S. lines of 5th Lon. Fld. Amb. & 140th Inf. Bde. Usual office routine.	
	Sept 22nd 1915		Inspected lines of 4th Lon. Fld. Amb. M.V.S. Nos 1 & 2 Evac. Tram	
	Sept 23rd 1915		Visited M.V.S. & lines of D.A.D.V.S. Signal Co. Capt. J. MacBrine R.V.C. arrived on no days leave.	
	Sept 24th 1915		Visited M.V.S. Investigated outbreak of Foot & Mouth disease at a farm in RUCHEL, also some turn at same place. Reported to all concerned. Took necessary precautions until the later	
	Sept 25th 1915		Inspected lines of 19th Bn Lon Regt L.R.D. Daily office routine	
	Sept 26th 1915		This office moves with D.H.Q. to HOUTKERQUE via ST. POL. M.V.S. to HERNICOURT. Reported arrival to D.D.V.S. 3rd Army	
	Sept 27th 1915		Visited M.V.S. Remainder of day occupied in office routine.	
	Sept 28th 1915		Inspected lines of 22nd Bn. Lon. Regt & D.H.Q.	
	Sept 29th 1915		Inspected lines of 4th Coy Divisional. Train Regt. & signal to R.E.	
	Sept 30th 1915		Visited animals of 1st, 2nd Lon. Fld. Ambs. & D.H.Q. returned inspection of Infantry Bdes. and with matters. Daily office routine.	

A. Leijth Lyon
D.A.D.V.S. 47 Lon. Div.

WAR DIARY
or
INTELLIGENCE SUMMARY.

Army Form C. 2118.

Place	Date	Hour	Summary of Events and Information	Remarks and references to Appendices
LAUTECLOQUE	Oct 1st 1918		Visited lines of M.O. & Signal to R.T. Daily office routine	
	Oct 2nd 1918		This office moves with D.H.Q. to MENSECQ XIth Corps area	
	Oct 3rd 1918		Interviewed DMYS 59th Divn at LESTREM & arranged taking over in relief of Ours	
	Oct 4th 1918		This office moves with D.H.Q. to RIEZ-BAILLEUL. Also relieve M.7 & embus Loct 36	
	Oct 5th 1918		Visited M.V.S. & conferred with A.D.V.S. 11th Corps upon matters of administration in area.	
	Oct 6th 1918		Inspected animals of 1/1 Lon M Gun Bn, A/235 Bde RFA. M.V.S. 1, 2 & 3 Corps Mtd. Resv & Divl. Signal horses at advanced H.Q.	
	Oct 7th 1918		Inspected horses of D.H.Q. & treated several sore eyes. Visited M.V.S & remount cars. Daily office routine	
	Oct 8th 1918		Inspected animals of 18th 19th & 20th Bns Lon Regt, H.Q 142nd Inf Bde & M.V.S	
	Oct 9th 1918		Inspected horses & mules of A.B.C. & D. Coys 47th Machine Gun Bn & M.V.S	
	Oct 10th 1918		Held conference of Vety Officers at office: Capt J. MacBRIDE R.V.C. returned from leave & attend. Daily office routine.	
	Oct 11th 1918		Inspected animals of B.E.F 1/255 Bde 9 & 10 Bns R.W. Fus. Weekly Lab returns rend. Qual of Avds Animals 22 Event; 7th Corps, 7th Corps 22 Event 22 Evacuated: 5 Both 3 Disolvpt;	

Army Form C. 2118.

D.A.D.V.S.
47TH
LONDON DIVISION.

WAR DIARY
or
INTELLIGENCE SUMMARY.
(Erase heading not required.)

Instructions regarding War Diaries and Intelligence Summaries are contained in F. S. Regs., Part II. and the Staff Manual respectively. Title pages will be prepared in manuscript.

Place	Date	Hour	Summary of Events and Information	Remarks and references to Appendices
	Oct 12th 1915		Inspected animals of 236th Bde. R.F.A. & N.S. 3rd London Field Ambce. Daily office routine.	
	Oct 13th 1915		M.P.S Edwards took over D.A.D. Signal to R.E. & 6th Lon. Field Ambce. Explain to the Officers on the duty & hours of Marches	
	Oct 14th 1915		Arriving N.V.S. & to Emg. Train; also L'EPINETTE to arrange taking over on return by 37th Division.	
	Oct 15th 1915		Inspected horses of A.S.C. Supply Section: 5th & 9th Ambce. Forward Depot to R.E. & N.V.S. Usual office routine.	
	Oct 16th 1915		Inspected horses of H.Q. "A" & "D" Coys. & Train Bn. & 2nd H.Q.	
	Oct 17th 1915		Inspected animals of "B" Coy & Train Bn. & 23rd Bn. Lon. Regt. In afternoon conference of V.O.s Officers at Divnl.	
	Oct 18th 1915		This office moves with Div. H.Q. to NORRENT-FONTES: N.35 central sheet 36A. Whilst passing through Div. Troops: 39 cases arrived : 26 cured : 23 evacuated : one death : 3 destroyed : 72 remaining	
	Oct 19th 1915		Usual office routine. Inspected horses of 13th, 17th, 21st Bn. Lon. Regt. & 140th Inf. Bde. H.Q. & return.	
	Oct 20th 1915		Inspected horses of 15th Bn. Lon. Regt. & M.V.S.	
	Oct 21st 1915		Visited animals of 2T&S Cav. Train. M.V.S.; 15th Bn. Lon. Regt. & 5th Lon. Bde.	
	Oct 22nd 1915	Ambce.	Inspected horses of 142nd Inf. Bde. H.Q. & 6th Lon. 9th Ambce. & N.V.S. Animals Remounts now arrived loved to await to arrival	

WAR DIARY or INTELLIGENCE SUMMARY

Army Form C. 2118.

Place	Date	Hour	Summary of Events and Information	Remarks and references to Appendices
	Oct 23rd 1915		Inspected lines of M.M.R., 22nd & 24th Bns Lon Regt, No 4 Coy Sanit Coy & office work.	
	Oct 24th 1915		Inspected animals of 517 2/6 Co R.E.; M.T.S & usual office work.	
	Oct 25th 1915		Visited horses of 18th Bn Lon Regt & M.T.S.	
	Oct 26th 1915		Div office demo with D.A.D to LAMBERSART near LILLE.	
	Oct 27th 1915		Visited Artillery units & inspected animals submitted for Remount Casting. Went to M.T.S.	
	Oct 28th 1915		Div office work with D.A.D. to MONS-EN-BAROEUL and at K.35 & J.5 sheet Sanit office work. Visited Horses into LILLE.	
	Oct 29th 1915		Inspected horses of 143 & 141 Bn F.A. & 22nd Bn Lon Regt. Let out on trial horses & 57th Cav. Bde unable to proceed on breakdown of Car. Usual office work.	
	Oct 30th 1915		Inspected with M.T.S. 11th cobs animals of A B C D & 226 R.F.A. Interment & arranged above with an 8.1st and 57th Div.	
	Oct 31st 1915		Visited M.T. Sick & Bglsh & Lon 47th Ambce. Verbal Conference of Vety Officers. Daily office routine & Tele-trunk.	

T Richard
Major Q.V.C.
D.A.D.V.S. 47th London Division.

WAR DIARY or INTELLIGENCE SUMMARY

Army Form C. 2118.

Place	Date	Hour	Summary of Events and Information	Remarks and references to Appendices
WILLEMS M.T.D.	Nov 1st/18	11.15 R.M. 3.15	This office now with F.A. 6 to Willems. Inspected sanitary arrangements of L.R. Bn. Bury, atrocious wiring. Wounded sick Wilmot marched to Bavin & Corps. 41 Evacuations 426 Remain, 12 Evacuated, 2 Died, 3 History of Sick Remained well.	
	Nov 2nd/18		Talk to Wor. Gdn. Amb: Inspected Horses & Interment arrangements at Unit from 11 a.m. to 1 p.m.	
	Nov 3rd/18		Inspected Horse Transport of 4.th to tom Bn. Scots G.R. Calling. L. Chagnon A.V.C. arrived. Their duty was Capt. Wm. D. S. Edwards attached to hospital under Beuvry.	
	Nov 4th/18		Inspected horses of L.A.R.G., M.R. P. 517 Gld. Co R.E., S.R.A. Section. D. + E. 5 of 19th Regt. 10th D.S. Edwards A.V.C. returned to duty. Instructions asked for as to disposal of Capt. Chagnon.	
	Nov 6th/18		Travel horses of 11th to 11th Bn. Glos. Ambers Signal Co R.E. Conferred with A.D.V.S. 11th Corps to detail Burgo Horse Signal Carrying Co arrive + many other Units of D.H.Q. and 1st M.V.S. Malbery.	
	Nov 6th/18		Inspected Forwards of 23rd Bn. Lon. Regt. 515 + 520 Gld. Co. R.E. Duties on return & duties M.V.S. from 1 p.m.	
	Nov 7th/18		Moves to 6 + 8 Lon. Bt. Ambers. Capt. H. Chagnon A.V.C. Evacuated to Vet. Hosp. In afternoon Conferred with the officers at office.	
	Nov 8th/18		Inspected animals of 1 Sy 3rd Portuguese Battery R.F.A. Usual office routine. 112 Sick religions to Oren & 5 Gds. 77 cases admitted: 16 Cured: 5 ½ Evacuated, 3 Died. 6 Destroyed. 42 Remaining.	

Army Form C. 2118.

D.A.D.V.S.
47TH
LONDON DIVISION.

WAR DIARY
or
INTELLIGENCE SUMMARY
(Erase heading not required.)

Instructions regarding War Diaries and Intelligence Summaries are contained in F. S. Regs., Part II. and the Staff Manual respectively. Title pages will be prepared in manuscript.

Place	Date	Hour	Summary of Events and Information	Remarks and references to Appendices
	DEC. 25th		Usual office work & own duties at Mobile Section.	
	DEC. 26th		Do. Held Conference of VOs at Office in afternoon.	
	DEC. 27th		Do. Weekly Sick return to Divn. T. Lorks: 47 cases admitted : 23 cured. 21 evacuated, 1 Died: 51 Remaining.	
	DEC. 28th		Daily office routine: own duties at M.V.S. 9 Jumpers in 2oth Ambce. Transport Competition.	
	DEC. 29th		Office work & Mobile Section.	
	DEC. 30th		Do. — 9 Jumpers in Ambce. from Transport Competition.	
	DEC. 31st.		Do. —	

J Craig, Captain R.A.V.C.
A/DADVS 47 Lon Divn

WAR DIARY or INTELLIGENCE SUMMARY

Army Form C. 2118.

D.A.D.V.S. 47TH LONDON DIVISION
1-2-16

Date	Hour	Summary of Events and Information	Remarks
Nov 9/16	9.1900	Inspected animals of 23rd & 24th Bns Lon Regt. Visited M.T.S. & D.H.Q. Daily office work & visit with.	
Nov 10/15		The office moved with Divl. H.Q. to FROYENNES. O.14 Sheet 37. Observed M.T.S. Established at this place.	
Nov 11/15		The office moved with D.H.Q. to LA TOMBE. O.11 Sheet 37. 36. day o. Brussels commenced from 1100 hours.	
Nov 12/15		Inspected animals of 2, 3, & 4 Coys Train. M.T.S. H.Q. & 4th M. Cun Divl. P.O. & Signal Co R.E.	
Nov 13/15		Inspected stables of C.R.E. M.M. P. & 4th Field Amb. to certify fee from Contagious diseases. Spotted horses of 17th Bn Lon Regt. Visited M.G.S. & D.H.Q.	
Nov 14/15		Inspected horses of 1 Coy Train & M.T.S. In afternoon Conference of V.Os. Officers at office.	
Nov 15/15		Visit M.T.S. & inspected patients here for inoculation. Daily Office routine. Weekly Lick Veterinary returned to Landon & Corps. 35 cases. Received 22 & with 14 ? wounded. 1 Killed. 2 Destroyed 21. 35 Remaining.	

Army Form C. 2118.

D.A.D.V.S.
47TH
LONDON DIVISION
1-12-18

WAR DIARY
or
INTELLIGENCE SUMMARY.
(Erase heading not required.)

Place	Date	Hour	Summary of Events and Information	Remarks and references to Appendices
	Nov 16th 18		This office moves with D.H.Q. to CHERENG. M.T.S. sect 37 finished M.T.S. Daily office routine.	
	Nov 17th 18		Visited M.T.S. & lines of Divl. T.B. Attended Thanksgiving Service. Usual office work.	
	Nov 18th 18		D.H.Q.	
	Nov 19th 18		Inspected two Batteries of 236th Bde R.F.A. Usual M.T.S. Daily office work.	
	Nov 19th 18		Interviewed Brig. Commander with regard to inspection of Jumping horse occupation. Visited M.T.S.	
	Nov 20th 18		Inspected animals of two Batteries of 236th Bde R.F.A. Visited M.T.S. also 577 Cy R.E.	
	Nov 21st		Visited and inspected animals of 22nd, 23rd & 24th Battn Lon Regt. also all 142 Infantry Bde. held conference of VOs.	
	Nov 22nd		Inspected the animals of HQ 142 Infantry Bde, 17 & 2/F. Batteries & No 4 Coy Train	
	Nov 23rd		Visited & inspected animals of 578 Cy R.E. 1/256 Bde R.F.A.	

Army Form C. 2118.

WAR DIARY
or
INTELLIGENCE SUMMARY.
(Erase heading not required.)

D.A.D.V.S.
47TH
LONDON DIVISION.

No. 1/12/16

Place	Date	Hour	Summary of Events and Information	Remarks and references to Appendices
	Nov 25th		Visited & inspected animals of 15th London Battn.	
	Nov 26th		Visited LOZINGHEM, AUCHEL, FERFAY, for the purpose of inspecting horse lines, stables & office work	
	Nov 26th / 27th		Division moved to LOZINGHEM. — Capt Craig proceeded on leave to England	
	Nov 28th		Inspected animals of 6th Field Amb, 2/4 Battn, 4/142 T.M.B.	
	Nov 29th		Visited & inspected animals of "B", "C" & "D" Coys 2nd 2/B, Sigs, 4th D. Amm., 21st Batt & 1/02 Coy Train & M.M. M.G.B.	
	Nov 30th		Visited M.V.S. at FERFAY. 5th D. Amm. & Engineers reported British horse died at M.J.B. SEILLIUTS in killer 32 AMETTES on Sept 15/18	

Arthur Wright Capt
D.A.D.V.S. 47

WAR DIARY or INTELLIGENCE SUMMARY

Army Form C. 2118.

Place	Date	Hour	Summary of Events and Information	Remarks and references to Appendices
LOZINGHEM & C. 17 CENTRAL SHEET 44A	1st Dec. 1915		Inspected animals of 520 Field Coy. R.E. Signal Co. R.E. & mobile BETHUNE to indent at present station for Fd. Artillery. Visited Mobile Section. Daily office routine.	
	2nd Dec. 1915		Inspected horses of U.B.C. & D/235 Bde R.F.A. Visited Mobile Section.	
	3rd Dec. 1915		Inspected animals of 4th Bn. R.W. Fus. 517 & 518 Field Cos R.E. Daily office work.	
	4th Dec. 1915		Inspected horses of + Coy. Train, 6th Lon. Fld. Ambulance & examined patients at M.V.S. for Evacuation.	
	5th Dec. 1915		Inspected horses & mules of 47th M. Sen. Bn. A,B & D Coys. In afternoon Lt. Conference at HQ Officers at HQ.	
	6th Dec. 1915		Inspected animals of 17th Bn. Lon. Regt & visited Mobile Section.	
	7th Dec. 1915		Inspected animals of 18 & 3 Lon. & Train & 23rd Bn. Lon. Regt. Daily office work. Welsh sick return rendered Sick & Casualties. 333 cas't. Admitted 13. Evacd. 113. Remaining transferred sick: 3. Destroyed 1. Ref used: 1. H.Q.	
	8th Dec. 1915		Inspected horses of A.D., & L/236th Bde R.F.A. Visited M.V.S.	
	9th Dec. 1915		Inspecting animals of C.B.C. of M. Lon. Bde. & Lon. Fld. Amb & 2nd Br. Lincoln Regt. Visited Mobile Section.	
	10th Dec. 1915		Inspected horses of No. 1 Section & F.G.A. Section D.A.C. also Mobile Section.	
	11th Dec. 1915		Inspected animals of 2nd Lon. Divl. Train & M.V.S.	

Army Form C. 2118.

WAR DIARY
or
INTELLIGENCE SUMMARY
(Erase heading not required.)

Instructions regarding War Diaries and Intelligence Summaries are contained in F. S. Regs., Part II. and the Staff Manual respectively. Title pages will be prepared in manuscript.

Place	Date	Hour	Summary of Events and Information	Remarks and references to Appendices
	DEC. 12th 1915 afternoon		Mobile Mobile Section & Cars at D.H.Q. Signal Co R.E. Sn afternoon. D.H. conferred at Jet. Officers at Mess.	
	DEC. 13th 1915		Attended Conference at Gnl. Commandant re issue transport completing establishment. Signed Locomotion Regts. & 520 Gulla. Co R.E. 24th Bn Lon.	
	DEC. 14th 1915		Attended Inspection of Brod. trans at AUCHEL. Inspected animals of Divl. Train.	
	DEC. 15th 1915		Inspected horses of 18th & 20th Bro. Lon. Regt. & mobile mobile Section. Daily office routine.	
	DEC. 16th 1915		Inspected animals of 19th Bn. Lon. Regt. D.H.Q. & mobile M.V.S. Usual office work.	
	DEC. 17th 1915		Unable to carry out duties owing to illness. Daily office routine only.	
	DEC. 18th 1915		Do	
	DEC. 20th 1915		Do	
	DEC. 21st 1915		O.C. 1/2nd London M.V.S. Proceed to ENGLAND on 14 days ordinary leave. Capt. T. CRAIG R.A.V.C. deputed to act during his absence.	
	DEC. 22nd 1915		Attended to office routine & ran duties at Mobile Section.	
	DEC. 23rd 1915		Do	
	DEC. 24th 1915		Do	

Army Form C.2117.

WAR DIARY
OR
INTELLIGENCE SUMMARY.
(Erase heading not required.)

Wd 39

Place	Date	Hour	Summary of Events and Information	Remarks and references to Appendices
LOZINGHEM C.15 CENTRAL SHEET 44B	Jan 1st 1919		Daily office routine at Mobile Section.	
	"	2nd	Do	
	"	3rd	Do	
	"	4th	Veterinary Board assembled for examination & classification of animals at preliminary Veterinary hospital to Investigation. Present: Majors Hurry, Brands of unit, undergoing grouping. Animals of Sec. 9 O/236 & 9.L. Boarded.	Printer O: Z.O. 236
	"	5th	Animals of B/2 st R.F.A. Boarded. Major O. HIBBARD returned from leave.	
	"	6th	0/236 n Bee. R.F.A. & M.V.S. written off Winning Board.	
	"	7th	2/236 R.F.A. & R.E. Divl. Arty.	Do
	"	8th	R.E. M.L. & N°2. Section.	Do
	"	9th	N°1 Section M.L.	Do
	"	10th	S.A.A. Section M.L.	Do
	"	11th	Z.O. 235 n Bee R.7.0 & 8/235 n R.F.A.	Do

Army Form C. 2118.

D.A.D.V.S.
47TH
LONDON DIVISION.

WAR DIARY
or
INTELLIGENCE SUMMARY.
(Erase heading not required.)

Instructions regarding War Diaries and Intelligence Summaries are contained in F. S. Regs., Part II. and the Staff Manual respectively. Title pages will be prepared in manuscript.

Place	Date	Hour	Summary of Events and Information	Remarks and references to Appendices
	Jan. 12th 1919		2/235 Bde. R.F.A. visited by Veterinary Board	
	13th	13h.o.	C & D/235th Bde. R.F.A. D.O.	
		14h	Visits to V.S. L.O. 47th Divl. Arty & 236th Bde. R.F.A.: Head offices parties on return. 9 horses transferred to 11 V.E.S.
	15th	15h	189th Army Bde. R.F.A. visited by Veterinary Board.	
		16h	Do	
		17h	Do	
	18th	18h	517: 518 & 520 Field Coys. R.E. visited by Vety. Board.	
		19h	No work by Vety. Board as bar not available. Daily office routine.
	20th	20h	47th Machine Gun. Bn. visited by Vety. Board.	
		21.st	1+2 W. Inf. Bde. Do	
	22nd	22nd	1+1 St. Inf. Bde. Do	
	23rd	23.rd	4 ; 5th & 6th London Field Ambces. Do	
	24th	24h	140th Inf. Bde. Do	

WAR DIARY or INTELLIGENCE SUMMARY

Army Form C. 2118.

D.A.D.V.S.
47TH
LONDON DIVISION.

Place	Date	Hour	Summary of Events and Information	Remarks and references to Appendices
	Jan. 25/1919		Visited H.Q. Signal Co. R.E. & 4th Bn. R.W. Fus. visited by Vety. Board.	
	26th		No work by Board as horses not available. Daily office routine only.	
	27th		Visited Divn. Train visited by Vety. Board; thus completing the whole Divn. Grouped as follows:— GROUP: A B C D D- HORSES 225 599 1153 897 76 39 TOTAL 2956 MULES 30 3 274 251 239 20 18 11.45	
	28th		Daily office routine only owing to sickness.	
	29th		Inspected horses of D.H.Q. & Signal Co. R.E. to assist any signs of re-action to mallein test.	
	30th		Visited M.H. & 159th Army Bde. R.F.A. In afternoon held conference of Vety. Officers at office.	
	31st		Attended D.V.H. Board on following units; 23rd Bn. Lon. Regt. 5th Febr. Ambu; Stand'g Vety. office returns: weekly wk returning to Divn. Troops; 61 cases admitted. 27 cures; 19 remained: 2: V.W.: 13 Hstrong ac: 132 Remaining.	

Richard
Major
DADVS 47 London Divn

26

WA/175 Diary 47 Div   HQ 40

Army Form C. 2118.

WAR DIARY
or
INTELLIGENCE SUMMARY.
(Erase heading not required.)

Place	Date	Hour	Summary of Events and Information	Remarks and references to Appendices
	Feb 1st		Visited 6th London Field Ambce and usual Office routine	
	" 2nd		Usual Office routine.	
	" 3rd		Visited 4th Bn R.W.Fus. D Battery and H.Q. 236 Bde R.F.A. also D.A.D.G.	
	" 4th		Visited with D.A.D.R. 189 Bde Army Field Arty and 19 & 20 Bn Lon Regt	
	" 5th		Visited M.V.S. and usual office routine	
	" 6th		Visited Signal Co R.E. and D 235th Bde R.F.A. and held conference in afternoon at Office with V.O.s	
	" 7th		Visited with D.A.D.R. A, B & C Batteries 236th Bde R.F.A. also M.Gun Bn and usual office routine.	
	" 8th		Visited 1st/2nd London M.V.S. and usual office routine.	
	" 9th		Visited 6th London Field Amb. and usual office routine	
	" 10th		Visited 1st/2nd London M.V.S. and usual office routine.	
	" 11th		Visited 3rd Battery 189 Bde Army Field Arty in connection with Epizootic Lymphangitis discovered 39 T.C. crowds, and 2 in contact, ordered all necessary precautions to be taken.	

Army Form C. 2118.

WAR DIARY
or
INTELLIGENCE SUMMARY.
(Erase heading not required.)

Instructions regarding War Diaries and Intelligence Summaries are contained in F. S. Regs., Part II. and the Staff Manual respectively. Title pages will be prepared in manuscript.

Place	Date	Hour	Summary of Events and Information	Remarks and references to Appendices
	12th		Visited 4th & 6th London Field Ambces, also proceeded with Mallening	
	13th		Visited and Inspected 4, 596th London Field Ambce, also 34th Battery 189 Bde R.F.A. and met D.D.V.S. together with A.D.V.S.	
	14th		Visited B&D Batteries 235th Bde R.F.A. for Inspection with D.A.D.R.	
	"15		Visited with A.D.R. 140th & 142nd Inf Bdes also M.R.P.	
	"16		Attended the Major General's horses, also A.D.S.'s horses and usual Offices routine.	
	"17"		Visited 6th London Field Ambce with D.A.D.R. and usual offices routine.	
	"18"		Visited Divisional Train H.Qs. No 2 & 3 Coys R.W.Fus. 4 & 5th London Field Ambces also No 1 & 2 Coys Divisional Train.	
	"19		Instructed Captain T. Craig. as to Sale of Animals, Attended D.H.Qs Stables, and proceeded with grooming and Mallening of Animals. Also held conference of officers with V.O.s	
	"20		Visited D.H.Q. Stables, 518 & 520 Field Co R.E., 6th London Field Ambce, 23rd Bn London Regt, and No 1 Coy Divisional Train.	
	"21st		Visited D.H.Q. Stables, 518 & 520 Field Co R.E., 6th London Field Ambce, 9 23 Bn Lon Regt. also No 1 Coy Divisional Train for the purpose of Inspecting Mallened Animals	

Army Form C. 2118.

WAR DIARY
or
INTELLIGENCE SUMMARY.
(Erase heading not required.)

Instructions regarding War Diaries and Intelligence Summaries are contained in F.S. Regs., Part II. and the Staff Manual respectively. Title pages will be prepared in manuscript.

Place	Date	Hour	Summary of Events and Information	Remarks and references to Appendices
			Results of Sale is as follows. Average price all round over Francs 709.70. Average for Corps H.D. Francs 688.50. Divisional L.D. Francs 808.50. Mules Francs 554. 50 animals were sold in all. 20 L.D. horses and 10 Mules for Divisional and 20 H.D. for 11th Corps.	
	"22nd		Visited M.V.S. and usual Office routine.	
	"23rd		Proceeded with and completed Mallenning of animals	
	"24th		Inspected Mallened animals and usual Office routine	
	"25th		Visited 517, 518, & 520 Field Co R.E. and selected animals for sale, also visited No 4 Coy Divisional Train. Captain Craig came to Division.	
	"26th		Usual Office routine.	
	"27th		Inspected and purchased 200 tins of petrol no collected at Beachine and Huncourille.	
	"28th		Usual Office routine.	

D.A.D.V.S.
47th
LONDON DIVISION.

D.A.D.V.S. 47th Divn

WAR DIARY
or
INTELLIGENCE SUMMARY.

(Erase heading not required.)

Army Form C. 2118.

Place	Date	Hour	Summary of Events and Information	Remarks and references to Appendices
Lozinghem	March 1st		Sale of 200 Animals at Lillers. Total Amount received 146,275 Francs. Average price for Horses 800½ Francs. Mules 639½.	
	" 2		Office Routine	
	" 3		Received report from Captain W.P.G. Edwards of suspected Rabies at Lahoussoie, visited and confirmed suspicion. Also attended Board of Enumeration for Divise Mark of 5th Lon Field Ambulance for Showing Smith Spavins	
	" 4		Office Routine	
	" 5		Visited and examined Horses for Sale or Maad 8th and held conference with VOs at Office.	
	" 6		Office Routine	
	" 7		Attended Horse at D.H.Qrs Flathers. Visited XIth Corps and assumed duties of Acting A.D.V.S.	
	" 8		Sale of 200 Animals at Lillers. Total Amount received 125,900 Francs. Average price for Horses 794 Francs. Mules 638 Francs. Visited XIth Corps and office routine	
	" 9		Inspected Animals for Repatriation and completed at £s C.1640	
	" 10		Visited XIst Corps, 189 thing Bde R.F.A & 1/2nd London M.V.S.	

Army Form C. 2118.

WAR DIARY
or
INTELLIGENCE SUMMARY.
(Erase heading not required.)

Instructions regarding War Diaries and Intelligence Summaries are contained in F. S. Regs., Part II. and the Staff Manual respectively. Title pages will be prepared in manuscript.

Place	Date	Hour	Summary of Events and Information	Remarks and references to Appendices
	"11		Sale of 200 Animals of 59th Division at Bruay. Total Amount realised 155,275 Francs. Average price for Mules 634.5 Francs. Horses 918.25 Francs.	
	"12		Interviewed D.D.S. at Bethune. Visited R.W. Sec. and No 4 Coy Div. Train.	
	"13		Started at Bethune, and arrived Captain Craig in selection of Animals for sale at Lillers on 15th.	
	"14		Attended Office at XI Corps. Visited Mobile Veterinary Section Signal Co R.E. and D.H.Q.	
	"15		Sale at Lillers of 200 Animals. One returned sick. Total amount realised 143,153 Francs. Average price for Horses 740 Francs Mules 666 Francs.	
	"16		Attended Office at XI Corps, 189 Army Bde R.F.A. and 3rd Lord Field Ambce.	
	"17		Visited X Siege Bn. No 3 Coy Train, and several office routine.	
	"18		Usual Office routine	
	"19		Visited and inspected animals at Pernes.	
	"20		Started Bethune and inspected Animals for sale at Lillers 22nd also visited No 518 Field Co. R.E. and attended 3 sick horses.	
	"21		Completed inspection of animals at Bethune for Sale at Lillers and office routine.	

Army Form C. 2118.

WAR DIARY
or
INTELLIGENCE SUMMARY.
(Erase heading not required.)

D.A.D.V.S.
47TH
LONDON DIVISION.

Place	Date	Hour	Summary of Events and Information	Remarks and references to Appendices
	"22		Sale at Lillers. Total amount realised 257,975 francs. Average price for Horses 887 Francs. Average price for Mules 819 Francs.	
	"23		Visited office at XI Corps. and usual office routine at Divn Office	
	24		Visited Fields used in specific districts for sale at Bruay on the 25.	
	"25		Sale at Bruay of 214 Divisional animals and 7 to XI Corps. Total amount realised 180,850 francs. Average for animal 853½ francs. Average for Divisional Animals. Horses 781 Francs. Average for Horses 819 Francs. Mules 732 Francs	
	26"		Visited XI Corps. and 165 Co. Divisional Train and office routine	
	27"		General office Routine	
	28"		Visited XI Corps. and usual office routine at Divn Office	
	29"		General office Routine	
	30"		Interview with D.D.V.S. at Bethune and office routine	
	31"		General office routine	

Arthur ?
Major
D.A.D.V.S. 47th Divn

D.A.D.V.S.
47TH
LONDON DIVISION.

www.ingramcontent.com/pod-product-compliance
Lightning Source LLC
Chambersburg PA
CBHW080835010526
44114CB00017B/2315